T0163235

'This book is an inspiring testament to the belief that age is no barrier to enjoying life to the utmost, as Hilary and Liz explore the world gobbling up every adventure they can find and living and learning along the way.' SANDRA LEVY

'It's the ideal time of life to travel: the uninhibited years. Having relished the saucy stories and unique observations, you too will be inspired to grab a friendly granny, decimate the super fund, stockpile the meds and let your gut prevail . . . A sensuous book tingling with the romance and adventure of an old Girls' Own Annual.' SUSIE CARLETON

Growing Old Outrageously

A memoir of travel, food and friendship

HILARY LINSTEAD AND ELISABETH DAVIES

ALLEN&UNWIN
SYDNEY • MELBOURNE • AUCKLAND • LONDON

Allen & Unwin
83 Alexander Street
Crows Nest NSW 2065
Australia
Phone: (61 2) 8425 0100
Email: info@allenandunwin.com
Web:www.allenandunwin.com

Cataloguing-in-Publication details are available
from the National Library of Australia
www.trove.nla.gov.au

ISBN 978 1 74331 469 2

Set in Adobe Caslon Pro by Midland Typesetters, Australia

For my son, Duncan, with my love,
and to the memory of Frances McDonald,
whose spirit was an inspiration to me—*HL*

In loving memory of two great friends and travellers,
Selma and Nuha—*LD*

Contents

Prologue

Undaunted, the dream team steps out

Had I been wise to answer an unexpected telephone call from Miranda?

Miranda and I had shared a flat in London when we left school and had been best friends from around the age of ten, all of forty years ago. Over the years our lives went in different directions, even though we both ended up living in Sydney. But I was curious to know what had provoked her call.

'Liz would like to see you,' she said.

'Who's she?' I replied.

'Come on, Hilary, you went to school together at Cheltenham Ladies College.'

My mind trawled back over the years.

'Oh, you mean LIZZIE, with the buck teeth!'

'How cruel!' said Miranda, laughing. 'Fancy not remembering Liz. You introduced us in London.'

'Fair enough. But you stayed in England and the two of you kept up over the years. By the time you came to live in Sydney I'd gone into film production as well as running the agency. My private and professional lives overlapped totally for thirty years.'

'Yes, you were always busy,' said Miranda.

'Too busy. I didn't see my family or friends nearly enough. And I haven't seen Liz since I was seventeen—not even in London on work trips. But I'm really glad you rang. I liked her a lot; she was splendidly eccentric and funny as a circus. Why don't you both come round for a meal tomorrow evening?'

On the dot of 6.30 pm the next day the two of them arrived on my doorstep. Liz hadn't changed, even though her hair was now long and grey and worn loosely below her shoulders, giving her a wild, 'bag lady' look. But she still had her youthful energy and the inquisitive eyes that I remembered. While she and I tucked into roast chook and potato wedges with garlic and rosemary, followed by apple and hazelnut crumble, tiny reed-thin Miranda picked at peas and a tiny portion of breast. Tongues loosened over a bottle of red and Liz regaled me with stories of her minimalist existence in the civil service in England—'a sheltered workshop for the inadequate', she called it. She had taken early retirement at fifty-five.

'I left my farewell party and caught the first plane to Sydney to stay with Miranda and Tom. I knew they would be the perfect couple to teach me how to retire. Nothing like the tranquillity of leafy Wahroonga.' Liz beamed in Miranda's direction.

We had a riotous evening and I felt Liz's call to freedom, like the dreams of a schoolgirl about to leave school. By the end of the night we had vowed to go on 'holliers' (as Liz called them) together at the earliest opportunity.

'We'll get up early every day and take a healthy one hour's walk before breakfast,' Liz had said.

'You have to be joking,' I replied. 'I'm a late starter. Exercise was never my strong suit. Do you like good food?'

'Not remotely interested,' said Liz. 'If it's a choice between a good meal and another museum, I'll choose the museum.'

'I can see I'll be eating alone!'

We embraced each other delightedly when she left. The evening had been a resounding success.

'Remember, you've only got one life,' Liz called out as she wove her way down my garden path.

Six months later I was stressed at work and knew I needed a break. Normally I would have taken off for Bali or some other island, but I thought of Liz. I needed to start practising for retirement and wanted fun with a capital F. Who better to have fun with than Liz? I sent her an email:

> How would you like to go to any of the following: Split, Morocco, Havana or Prague? Let me know pronto.
> Hil xxx-x

She emailed back straight away.

> Prague and Morocco—fine. Any time you like. I've been staying in Ireland with friends who will be delighted if I move on. Lliizzzz

And from that exchange of emails arose the story of two unlikely individuals who reconnected late in life and for fifteen years travelled the world together having fun.

Our decision to travel together could have been a recipe for disaster. We hardly knew each other; our childhoods, life trajectories and our personalities could hardly have been more different.

Holidays are difficult things at the best of times, yet we voluntarily took ourselves away from the familiar and plunged into the excitement and challenges of the unknown. Any sensible person would go with a trusted friend or partner, but we threw caution to the winds.

This is the story of what happened on our travels: how we coped with each other; how we changed; how we discovered other worlds out there; and, above all, how we behaved outrageously and had a ball—almost all the time.

I had been born into an academic family, but didn't want the strain of going down the university path and failing to meet my father's expectations—so at twenty-one I packed my bags and followed Leon, a man I had met in London, to Australia. After three years based in Sydney working as an actor, I married Leon, had a baby and built a successful career in the arts. As an agent I was known for being a tough negotiator who fought hard for my clients. It wasn't long before I decided that I had very little experience of life and was far too immature to sustain a married relationship. I needed to spread my wings and gave little thought to the difficulties of bringing up a child on my own. Duncan, my son, saw Leon regularly, but it was hard having a job and looking after a little boy—in those days there were few childcare centres.

Liz says I have a gargantuan appetite for life and she's probably right.

'Hilary is one huge orifice,' she says, 'always shovelling more and more experiences into her cavernous depths.'

Liz, on the other hand, was brought up in a small town in rural Wales. Her intellectual abilities and the advent of meritocracy in post-war Britain saw her win a scholarship to Cambridge University. After leaving there she idled away thirty years in an anonymous government bureaucracy. She says, 'My emotional life has been equally arid, lacking any sort of commitment even of the shortest duration to anything, let alone a person or a pet.'

She insists that her appetites are restrained and minimal. But I maintain she is irrepressible in her pursuit of knowledge and a veritable cornucopia of brains, wit and humour.

As I planned our holiday in Morocco and Prague, I cast my mind back to our school days. Even then I was practising the art of manipulating people to bring about the result I wanted. When I needed to avoid a bad school report I made an appointment to see the headmistress to point out my failings. She fell for this ploy, hook, line and sinker: 'Hilary works diligently,' she wrote, 'and is aware of her shortcomings. This augurs well for her future.' Winner!—my father was completely taken in and trouble averted. I realised that manipulation was a winning card if cleverly used.

Liz meanwhile was into Defiance and Fun. She pinched the human skeleton from the zoology laboratory and hung it on the school fire escape for the whole town to see; she sewed up the gym mistress's shorts and changed the hymn numbers so that 900 girls in assembly remained silent as the organ played a different tune. And that was in a single week.

Escapades like these were repeated at Cambridge. Judy, Liz's sister, told me that Liz would climb out the window of her ground floor room in college after 'lights out' and go to all-night parties, returning via the window in the early hours. On one occasion it snowed overnight and, climbing in, she realised that the footprints led to her room. So she climbed out of the window again and stepped up to the windows of all the rooms on the ground floor, leaving a trail of footprints so as to incriminate everybody.

As I sent Liz the final arrangements for our first holiday I remembered another holiday we had been on together in our last year at school: in sodden tents in the rain on the Norfolk Broads with three Cambridge undergraduates. Liz had a dalliance with the amusing intellectual, I scored the doe-eyed romantic with beautiful eyelashes and the poor girl who had organised the holiday was left with her brother. She wasn't amused.

On the third day of that holiday Liz woke at daybreak and suggested that we dump the boys and sneak out for an early morning sail on our own. We'd show those boring macho males who the real sailors were. We ran down to the mooring still in our nighties, pushed the boat out and climbed aboard. We easily got the sails up, but in our simple-minded determination, failed to notice that the wind was freshening and we were gathering speed fast. By the time we reached mid 'Broad' we had lost control of the rudder, the sail was flapping wildly and we couldn't 'come about'. One minute the boat was upright, the next it was upside-down and we were clinging to it frantically, weighed down by our nighties. After what felt like an eternity, and exhausted by fruitless efforts to right the boat, I was scared and convinced that we were going to drown. I was desperate to call out to the boys for help.

'Don't be silly, Hilly. They wouldn't hear us. And we're fine.'

With her own brand of logic Liz had decided that we could not be in any danger.

'We're not sinking, I'm sure of that.'

'Not yet,' I squawked.

It turned out she was right—we were merely stuck in mud five feet below. Once Liz had convinced me that I wasn't going to die we both began to laugh hysterically, our teeth chattering.

'Now all we need is a suitably lurid story for the boys,' I said.

'Abducted by rogue fishermen,' said Liz.

'Perfect,' I replied.

As I continued making plans, Liz emailed me:

> I wonder what happened to those four others who were
> with us on the Norfolk Bs? Any chance of meeting
> them in Morocco do you think? L

I doubted it, but it sounded like a cheery omen, I thought: both of us remembering the Broads story dating back thirty-five years and with us now living 40,000 kilometres apart.

*

We wrote this book as a celebration. A celebration of a schoolgirl friendship renewed later in life. A celebration of the excitement of travelling, of the quirky incidents and fun we shared with hundreds of people we met along the way. But above all, a celebration of the fact that two outrageous women of advanced years can still get out and have a bloody good time. We hope our book will inspire others to live their dreams and fantasies, whatever their age.

1

Off to Morocco and Prague

'What wouldn't I give for an icy pole!' I called out to Liz as I wandered around our hotel room in the nude, fanning myself with the laundry list.

We had arrived in Marrakech the night before. The temperature was 45 degrees, the air thick with insects and the cloying perfume of jasmine, gardenia and lemon. We could hear Arabic voices chattering in the gardens below.

Liz had just wandered in from the swimming pool. Her expression froze in horror as she sighted my Buddha-like stomach.

'Put something on,' she said as she disappeared into the bathroom. A few minutes later she emerged covered from head to foot in a hand-woven caftan.

'I'm going for a walk,' she said, and made a dash for the door, carefully averting her eyes.

Charitably, I supposed this theatrical response was aimed at setting me a good example. I put on a flimsy cotton nightie—not quite the thing for a would-be nudist. Having had an English upbringing in which nudity was frowned upon (a sign of 'whore-ish' behaviour), I spent most of my life trying to overcome shyness about naked bodies and was proud that I had largely overcome my problem. *Oh well*, I thought, *I'll have to confine nudity to times when Liz is out on her early morning walk. Just as well she's an early riser and is gone before I've even thought about getting dressed.*

I never thought I would have to compromise over nudity in the bedroom! I felt liberated and was damned if I was going to give in to Liz's hidebound approach to the naked body.

By the time she returned from her walk she had put the 'nude' episode behind her and was keen to give me the 'good oil' on Marrakech. Meanwhile, I had secured an upgrade to our room by insisting to management that I had originally booked a room facing the garden. Liz was delighted when she walked into a larger room on the third floor. We now overlooked a tiny court-yard with ornamental tiling and the gentle splash of a fairytale fountain.

'Brillio. What a gorgeous view,' she said.

Despite her change of mood I still had a lingering worry that Liz was going to weigh me down with 'rules and regs'. What would she say in the evening about late-night CNN and BBC World, to which I was addicted? I would soon see.

*

I had arrived at Heathrow after twenty-two hours of flying. I stared out of the plane window at the drizzling day and thanked my lucky stars that forty years ago, throwing off parental shackles, I had escaped those interminable grey skies and sailed away to Australia, romantically following a man and a dream of becoming an actor. Even though neither of those dreams had proved long-lasting, it had been a good move.

Liz was there to meet me.

'Hurry up, Hilly, the next Heathrow Express to Paddington leaves in five minutes—we'll just make it.'

'Hang on. I've got to wait for my luggage.' I pointed behind me to a porter who was bent double pushing a low loader with my multiple suitcases.

'Good heavens, Hilly, you're only staying four weeks. It's a holiday, not a lifetime.'

Liz started calling out to anyone who would listen, pointing to my luggage.

'She's brought all this stuff—will someone please take it away?'

'Sure, I'll take it—and you too,' said one aspiring wit, peering lasciviously at Liz.

When we finally got into a taxi, Liz said, 'When we go to Marrakech you must take only what you can carry on and off the plane, because I won't be helping you.'

'Charming! I'll remember that when you're groaning with Marrakech belly and incapable of carrying even a knapsack,' I replied.

'We don't want to be held up at Heathrow by baggage handlers with their endless stop-work meetings. It's bad enough enduring the body search at security.'

*

Liz had a tiny two-storey house in Vauxhall, a working-class area just across the Thames from Westminster.

'In among the monuments,' she pointed out. She hardly spent any time there now that she had retired.

'Sixty-four days last year,' she said proudly.

Comfort was not her bag. 'I don't have a bedroom, I don't care where I sleep. You can have the big bed in the front room. You sleep all the time anyway, I've heard, and you'll need to get over your jet lag.' I was touched by her offer and recovered from the flight lulled to sleep by the swish of trains rolling into Waterloo Station.

Her house was very cosy: books and pictures lined every wall. Jars of nuts and fresh ginger mingled happily with strange little sculpted figures on the kitchen bench while the dining table was covered in articles of interest cut out from the daily papers. When I remarked that she was a hoarder, she countered, 'They're not mine. Guests leave things behind when they go. Every time I come back to VW (Vauxhall Walk—she called it vee double-u) I find eggcups, jars of pickled herrings and pot scourers. They assume I cook, when nothing could be further from the truth.'

It was exhilarating to be in London, so after a cup of tea I bussed it into the West End and made for my favourite clothes shop for fatties. Liz was horrified by the number of bags I brought back.

'Not more stuff, Hilly. You don't need it, and there's no room.'

My luggage was to become a constant irritation for her during our travels. For me, shopping is an addiction. I travel overseas with one large and heavy case (which has inside it a large, soft bag that returns to Australia containing presents and the detritus of travel), an overnight bag, a handbag and a haversack (if I can get away with it).

'You can't leave all this here,' she said. 'The Paks are coming while we're away.' (She was referring to her Pakistani friends.)

'Sorry, Liz,' I said. 'This is my luggage. Half of it is pills anyway.'

'You can't be serious, Hilly.'

Well, I was, and I suffered the dressing-down. I am a disgracefully obvious traveller and Liz said that we would not be able to visit what she called RIZs—Robber Infested Zones—with me standing out like a neon sign. Liz travelled light, either with a backpack or carrying a red sail bag held together with a piece of yellow rope.

The bag contained multiple pairs of knickers, notebooks, assorted socks, thick handmade cotton nightshirts and brightly coloured ribbon-covered skirts made to measure in Karachi. And then there were her T-shirts. With messages such as 'Recycle now' or 'Aged for maturity and taste' blazoned across the front of them, I thought Liz, too, might be a magnet in RIZs.

I noticed after a day or two in London that washing did not appear to be high on her list of priorities.

'Unnecessary,' said Liz, 'a waste of water. Why do you wash so often?'

'Once a day is not excessive,' I replied.

'I've been doing my research,' Liz continued. 'You only need an occasional brief shower, none of these vast baths you go in for.'

'Well, I'm not sure that I'm prepared to wait until someone points out that I smell.'

But Liz was unstoppable.

'And what are you going to do about your food? It's all processed, genetically modified and full of poisons,' she cautioned, wagging her finger. 'AND the quantity you eat. Coupled with no exercise and diabetes, you're a recipe for heart attack or stroke.'

'What you fail to grasp, Liz, is that haranguing me is the worst way to get me to change my behaviour. So lay off.'

Liz was quick to discover the topics that got a rise out of me and she quite enjoyed needling me about them. (Over the years I would learn to silence her patronising put-downs with 'Be careful not to fall off your plinth, Liz' or if she started to bang on about my unfortunate food habits, I'd say, 'It's just as well, isn't it, that you will make such excellent compost.' The needling has abated with time—or maybe we have become more accommodating because we are exhausted with arguing.)

Two days later we were off on our first holiday together. As we flew out of London, Liz commented that she had never been on a planned holiday with a proper itinerary before.

'When I was young I would leave the office at five o'clock on a Friday evening in high heels and a suit and be cycling in Ireland the next morning in the same high heels and suit.'

'Really! Didn't the heels get caught in the spokes?'

'There wasn't any leisure wear in those days,' said Liz, quick as a flash. 'Or I might catch the night train to Paris and see some Goyas in the Louvre and then move on to Madrid to see some more. If I spent a long weekend in New York I would fly back overnight to arrive at Heathrow at eight o'clock in the morning and be at my desk in the office by nine o'clock. My holidays were tough, none of that dotty "chilling out". I'd be up at dawn and still trucking at midnight. And I'd travel alone.'

'Why?' I asked her.

'I haven't a clue. Maybe I wanted to get away from everything and everybody. Get off people's map. It was the heyday of hippiedom, so perhaps I was trying to find myself, plumb my potential, gain wider horizons. Who knows?'

'And did you find yourself?'

'I lost interest as I grew older. After a while I ceased to care. That in itself was relaxing. And anyway, who wants to relax? We'll be dead soon, so we're better off trucking!'

Liz's holidays sounded heady with promise, dangerous and quite rarified to me, and I felt a bit envious. I wish I'd been as bold as she had been, but really I'd had so little time for holidays. I'd just tack on a few days to the end of a business trip—like the time I went to Hong Kong with my cabaret group, Pardon Me Boys, and to Edinburgh for the international launch of *Tap Dogs*.

It was incredibly exciting to be part of the whirlwind of openings in London and Los Angeles and then New York and Paris, but for me it was always bound up with the stress of looking after 'the Dogs', which meant picking up the pieces if something went wrong. On the way home I'd stop off at a resort and recline in a bubble bath, with a masseuse at the ready. Or I'd book into a health farm for yet another attempt at weight loss.

When I told her this, Liz looked at me in wonderment. 'Golly,' she said. 'What an adult life you lived.' I, by contrast, saw Liz as a free-spirited, brightly coloured gypsy bird flying on wind currents all over the world, dropping in on friends, stirring the pot, delivering her famous one-liners and catching up on gossip, then taking off again before she could outstay her welcome.

*

The flight I'd booked us arrived at Marrakech airport at midnight, where Liz was quick to draw attention to my lack of travel experience.

'Not a good idea to arrive anywhere later than teatime,' she muttered as we staggered out into the hot, starlit night, the last passengers to emerge.

There were a few taxis waiting at the kerb. I had asked the flight attendant the cost of the fare into town and was appalled when the first driver I approached mentioned a figure three times higher than the sum she had suggested. I tried to bargain but he was tough and wouldn't budge an inch. Neither would the second driver; they were in cahoots, I was sure. I joined Liz, who was tapping her foot.

'I refuse to let them get away with it,' I said.

'We'll be here all night,' she replied, 'and the airport's closing.'

'Airports don't close.'

The story had an almost happy ending. One driver, older and more kindly than the others, had been watching us arguing and took pity, agreeing to take us into town for double instead of triple the fare.

We sank back in the taxi as we drove through the velvet night, stars studded brightly above. Ahead, Marrakech beckoned to us with twinkling lights: there was no orange neon glow hovering over it like most cities.

When we finally reached the hotel it was a delight, an oriental fantasy dreamed up by an American architect who had fallen in love with Marrakech and poured his heart into the building. Even the gardens had been lovingly designed as a series of courtyards, each decorated with exquisite tiles and featuring an ornamental fountain. Modern craftsmen had refashioned tiles with ancient designs for every surface of the building. The result was colourful and inviting. We were far too excited to go to bed, so sat on our balcony and ordered Moroccan cocktails. They arrived—vodka and pomegranate juice with the liberal addition of mint and ginger and a splash of ginger ale and apple juice. Delicious. We soon felt at peace with the world.

The next day Liz bounded off for her walk while I eased myself into the day and consumed a leisurely breakfast. She joined me for coffee and outlined her suggested activities for the day. She was agitating to get going, so I picked up my pace and we took off for the Grand Bazaar. I had seen nothing to equal it. Dark alleyways seething with merchants, beggars, tourists, locals bargaining, thieves, little kids, carts, even the odd donkey. Stalls were piled high with merchandise, tantalisingly laid out. I could hardly restrain myself at the food stalls: huge pyramidal piles of spices, nuts, rice, currants and dates poured out of sacks while shopkeepers sat cross-legged above them, their eyes seeking out potential customers, cajoling them to sit down for a glass of mint tea before selling them a vast quantity of spices, later to be confiscated at customs! I was desperate to buy a large quantity of saffron at a fraction of the price I would pay in Sydney, but Liz restrained me.

It was the carpet part of the bazaar that provided the ultimate lure. We drifted towards the shops, the owners positively salivating at the sight of two innocents. White teeth flashing, they invited us inside the back rooms behind their carpet-draped stalls to sit and savour small cups of coffee flavoured with cardamom. Meanwhile, small boys unfurled rolled-up carpets and held them up expectantly while the suave shop owner pointed out their provenance and urged us to feel the softness of the pile. Eventually common sense and Liz prevailed ('How on earth are you going to carry a six-foot carpet back to London, Hilly?') and we left the bazaar empty-handed. Believe it or not, it was the first time I had ever been shopping and not bought anything.

By this time we were hot and thirsty so retired to the fabled La Mamounia Palace hotel. It had been closed for renovation for three years and had only just reopened. The renovation had been faithful to its original Moorish and Art Deco style, while achieving the ultimate in modern fixtures and fittings. Winston Churchill had visited Morocco on many painting holidays, and the hotel had a bar named after him.

'I played pat-the-balloon with Winston Churchill once when I was eight,' I told Liz, hoping she'd be impressed.

'Oh yes, where?'

I was taken aback that Liz didn't seem to believe me. At that stage I had no idea what a consummate liar she is. She's probably in the same league as Lillian Hellman—someone said of her that 'every word she says is a lie, including *and* and *the*'. And like all liars, Liz assumes nobody else tells the truth either. I was so surprised by her disbelief that I elaborated my story in some detail.

'My best friend at that time was Edwina Sandys and she was Churchill's granddaughter. It was her birthday and her grandparents gave her a party at Hyde Park Gate. I was the only friend she was allowed to invite. I remember that I was given *Pigeon Post* by Arthur Ransome, and my nanny was late to pick me up. So to pass the time I patted a balloon to Mr Churchill, who was sitting in a high-backed chair, smoking a cigar. And he patted it back.'

'Fantastic story, Hil.' It was impossible to discern whether Liz believed me or not.

We reached the lounge and sank into huge, comfortable sofas. It was as different from the teeming bazaar as you could imagine. Impeccably dressed waiters moved soundlessly around serving coffee and iced water.

Maria, a smart young travel consultant, came up to talk to us.

'Where do you come from?' she asked.

'Sydney and London,' I replied.

'How are you enjoying Marrakech?'

'It's brilliant,' we chorused.

Responding to our enthusiasm, Maria sat down and started to tell us about the history of Marrakech. 'If you are interested, I would be happy to introduce you to my father, who is custodian of one of the most ancient mosques. I will first speak to him and if he is free I will take you to meet him this afternoon. I am sure he would be happy to show you treasures in the mosque he looks after.'

I thought this was a wonderful opportunity to delve more deeply into the history of Marrakech and meet new people. Liz left the table abruptly and called me over, out of earshot.

'Hilly, I can't believe you're being so naïve. Maria isn't an "official Mamounia travel consultant", she's on her own touting for business. There is no way I am coming back this afternoon. We wouldn't be meeting her non-existent father—we'd be deposited in a jewellery shop and expected to give her a large tip.'

'You're so cynical. I believe her.'

'Well, you're on your own.' Liz flatly refused to go, and rather than make waves I reluctantly declined Maria's offer. We will never know who was right.

We had been told not to miss the famous Djemaa el Fna Square at dusk. The square was suffused in a soft pink haze, the smell of incense and spicy food mingling in the air, and steam rose from the food stalls where tourists and locals sat on wooden benches consuming mouth-watering *bisteeya*, a triple-layered pastry of chicken covered with egg and a lemony onion sauce; couscous with dates and currants; *harira*, a Berber soup traditionally served during Ramadan; sweet and sour tagines; kebabs; chickpeas and *mechoui*, a slow-roasted lamb dish.

From the moment I savoured my first mouthful of *mechoui*, falling apart on my fork, the flavour of cumin and paprika, garlic, cloves, ginger and coriander all perfectly blended into a ravishing dish, I was determined to remember the flavours and to experiment when I returned home until I had recreated the recipe. It was right at the start of our travels that I decided to gather dishes together in the hope that I would be able to share them at some time, somewhere, so when Liz and I decided to write this book it seemed like a good idea to include a smattering of the recipes I had gathered. After all, good food is one of the delights of life.

* * * * *

Lamb Mechoui

Makes 6 generous helpings

Ingredients

2.2 kg leg or shoulder of lamb

1 cup fresh crushed pomegranate seeds

8 boiled potatoes, mashed

flat-leaf parsley, finely chopped

olive oil

4 hot green chillies, grilled

cumin salt (blend of 1 tbs ground cumin with 3 tbs sea salt)

Smen paste

5 garlic cloves, chopped

50 g fresh ginger, peeled and chopped

1 red chilli, deseeded and chopped

1½ cups coriander, chopped

1½ cups flat-leaf parsley, chopped

2 tsp ground cumin

2 tsp ground coriander

2 tsp sweet paprika

100 g butter, softened

½ tsp saffron threads, crushed

1 tbs olive oil

¼ tsp turmeric

sea salt and freshly ground black pepper, to taste

Salad

4 tomatoes, diced

4 Lebanese cucumbers, deseeded and diced

1 white onion, finely diced

1 bunch rocket

juice of 1 lemon

½ cup extra-virgin olive oil

1 tbs dried mint

Preparation

1. For the *smen* paste, place all ingredients in a food processor. Season with sea salt and freshly ground black pepper and blend to a fine paste. Transfer to a bowl.
2. Cut small incisions in the lamb with a sharp knife and rub with the *smen* paste, especially into the incisions.
3. Place in a roasting tray, cover and refrigerate for at least 2 hours.
4. Remove the lamb from the refrigerator and allow to return to room temperature.
5. Pour 3 cups cold water around the lamb and roast in a preheated oven at 220°C for 20 minutes.
6. Reduce the heat to 160°C and continue to roast for 2–3 hours, basting occasionally with the juices in the pan, or until the meat is tender and has a crisp, brown crust that can be removed easily.
7. Sprinkle with pomegranate seeds and serve with mashed potatoes dressed with the flat-leaf parsley and olive oil; grilled green chillies and chopped salad.
8. Serve cumin salt in a bowl as an accompaniment.

* * * * *

Apart from the pleasure of cooking for family and friends, unfortunately for my avoirdupois, I enjoy eating—the anticipation of food, the flavours, the smells; dinner 'outings' at newly discovered restaurants; noisy arguments round my dining table while consuming a roast; tucking into pasta—shoes off, ugg boots on—in front of the television; growing my own herbs and vegetables; and pursuing recipes and ingredients on our travels. It all amounts to great joy for me. And I find I can turn my mind off and relax when I cook.

Liz used to laugh at what she said was the way I drooled over food. She said it was all an elaborate ploy to prevent people discovering the huge amount of food I was actually eating. She said I derived the same enjoyment from blister-packed ham of dubious provenance, bought from a gas station shop, as I did from a meal cooked by a famous chef in a five-star restaurant. I was outraged when she first made these comments; I didn't think they were funny. I fired back a rude reply and as a result rarely heard from Liz on the subject of me and food again.

Liz maintains she has little interest in food unless it is one hundred per cent organic. But here in Djemaa el Fna Square it was a different story; she was more than happy to sample the mind-blowing variety of food and I could not stop tucking into the myriad dishes laid out on the tables and, as usual, ate until I could eat no more. We watched a kid, hanging round the stalls hoping for a titbit, dragging a baby Barbary ape behind him on a lead. But the boy hadn't a hope; the last thing the chefs wanted was an ape and a street urchin anywhere near their food or the tourists, and angrily chased them away.

After capturing a particularly fetching snake charmer on camera I got a second wind and started sampling the tagines. The pans were none too clean but I imagined they bore traces of scrumptious meals cooked by countless family chefs, all contributing to the flavour, while Liz worried that we would both contract bubonic plague.

As the night progressed the square grew more crowded, and, after savouring a last mouthful, I moved away from the food stalls to watch dancing boys, jugglers and acrobats perform. They were Shilha, the indigenous people of the central Moroccan coast. Story-tellers told competing tales in Berber or Arabic to rapt groups of locals, magicians made birds disappear and pedlars offered us dirty bottles of evil-smelling liquid medicine. Everything imaginable was for sale, from piles of false teeth to heaps of eyeglasses and mounds of every conceivable spice. We drank in the scene, our senses on overload. Liz was bubbling with information, even taking notes as we sat in the square. I kept happily snapping away with my camera, returning to capture scenes that Liz pointed out I had missed.

When we got back to the hotel, the trouble started. I had flung off my clothes and lay naked on the bed (forgetting the episode of that morning), trying to tune in to BBC World, anxious to catch up on what was happening in the world.

'You can't want to watch television,' Liz exclaimed, 'after all the amazing things we've just seen?'

It would be a constant refrain on our travels. Unfortunately we have completely different approaches to getting off to sleep. Liz likes solitude and silence in which to savour the day, while I need to tune out and relax with the familiar—television or a good read. We never really resolved these differences. We never had a flaming row about them, either—there were just small simmering resentments which erupted now and again. I tried various ploys to deal with the situation: a towel over the bedside lamp (invariably singeing the towel) or just putting the lamp on the floor and squinting as I attempted to read the print. I even bought a torch with which to read under the bedclothes. Liz had her ploys too. She would keep us out late enjoying ourselves so that when we finally got back

I was so tired I could hardly press the TV switch on. Another of her ploys was to suggest I had an early night while she amused herself in the hotel bar. By the time she came up I was invariably asleep with the lights blazing and the TV blaring. Separate rooms would have been the obvious, if expensive, answer, but except for those times late at night, we enjoyed each other's company too much to resort to that.

*

The seaside town of Essaouira was a two-and-a-half hour drive from Marrakech and had been recommended by English friends as essential viewing. I bargained with a taxi man to take us there for a quarter of what he had originally demanded.

'I couldn't possibly haggle like that,' said Liz, impressed.

In 1949, Orson Welles had used the old Portuguese fortress as a setting for his film *Othello*, which helped to put Essaouira on the map. The brooding ramparts provided a backdrop for the action and set the scene for jealousy and betrayal on a grand scale. We walked along the battlements and watched the sea heave and crash onto the rocks below us only to be sucked into an unforgiving and relentless whirlpool. We imagined Desdemona's lifeless body lying still before us while Othello buried his head in her bosom and howled in despair.

We stayed at a hotel in Essaouira overnight while our driver slept in his car. In the morning we went down to the port, where Liz perched on a lobster pot with the fishermen's wives as they mended their nets. She offered to help them using a laboriously mimed sequence. Producing an imaginary needle and a long piece of twine, she squinted and held the needle up to the sun, trying to thread the twine through the eye of the needle without success. The women were transfixed by this routine, then pointed in amazement at her feet and doubled up with laughter. She was wearing polka-dotted socks and odd shoes, one red and one yellow. Liz followed their gaze and stared at her shoes in mock horror. Then, gesticulating wildly, she burst into a stream of gibberish. The women were captivated by her antics. '*Está loca*,' I threw in by way of explanation—she's mad. They beamed their agreement and I beamed back.

Before we left Marrakech for Fez we looked at the Koutoubia Mosque, which dated back to the twelfth century. Being non-Muslims, we could not enter the mosque but hotfooted it to the Pizzeria Venezia on the opposite side of the road and mounted the stairs to their rooftop terrace, from which you had an ace view of the mosque and its gardens. Next we had a look at the Bahia Palace. Built in the nineteenth century, the palace was once home to a harem and had been richly decorated with painted wood, ceramics and formal gardens. As we wandered around I told Liz how much I was enjoying travelling with her. 'I could take to this in a big way,' I said.

'Well, I'm in heaven,' replied Liz. 'There is nothing I would rather do than wander around surrounded by beautiful things.'

'Wouldn't you rather be here with a lover?' I asked.

Liz hesitated. 'Not really,' she said. 'The best way to see things is to have an easygoing person like you around. So often people, even lovers, complain and argue the toss about what to do, where to go and how much time to spend anywhere. But you seem quite equable. Are you really like that?'

She sounded suspicious, so I left the question dangling. Equability was hardly a characteristic most people would associate with me. Perhaps Liz had mistaken my eagerness to plunge into new excitements and experiences as proof of an easygoing nature. Let's hope so.

*

My introduction to Liz's vertigo started as we climbed the Atlas Mountains in a taxi I had hired to take us to Fez. We started up the winding, precipitous road, pot-holed and with barely room enough for two cars, and a sheer drop on one side—Liz's side of the taxi, as it turned out. When she suddenly lowered her head and curled up on the floor of the cab wailing and shrieking, I was irritated. I had no previous knowledge of vertigo and in my ignorance thought Liz was playing up and that her howls of distress were exaggerated. After all, she was prone to extravagant reactions, so I was unsympathetic.

'What's the matter?' I asked, terrified that the driver was going to grab our money and put us out of the car.

She was crying now. 'Pleeeeease, let me out.'

'Don't be dotty, I'm not going to leave you alone in the middle of nowhere. Tell me what's wrong.'

Finally I gleaned the word 'vertigo'.

'Lizzie, you must try to calm down. We can't go back, we've come too far, but we'll stop in a moment and you can sit on my side of the car.'

Such a simple solution was no solution as far as Liz was concerned. As we swung round the next hairpin bend she let out bloodcurdling yells, followed by moans, followed by even louder bellows. The driver, seemingly oblivious, drove doggedly on, ignoring my taps on his shoulder until I had to shake him with both hands and demand that he stop. Liz tottered out of the car and teetered towards a roadside stall selling fossilised stones. I quickly grabbed her.

'Please don't wander off,' I implored. 'We've still got to get to Fez.'

It took another nailbiting two hours, but we finally got there, with a shaken Liz staring fixedly at the side of the road away from the sheer drop, missing the spectacular views that spread out before us as we descended. Once on ground level, she recovered quickly.

'You've never told me that you suffered from vertigo,' I began. 'I'm afraid I wasn't very sympathetic—I thought to begin with that you were having me on.'

'It hasn't come up before,' replied Liz.

'Have you ever tried hypnosis? I've heard it can help.'

Liz dismissed this idea with a withering look, so I didn't pursue it.

Our hotel in Fez was perched on the hillside overlooking the Medina. It was large and old-fashioned, but had been recently renovated for the moneyed, undiscerning tourist.

We came down to breakfast late the next day and sat down at a window table facing the city below. The faux Louis Quinze chairs were upholstered with equally faux ancient scrolls. Four hovering waiters placed napkins in our laps and brandished important-looking parchment menus. We were the only people in the dining room and I started giggling as Liz tried it on with the waiter.

'*Fatuur ... tarwiqa?*'

'What on earth are you saying?' I asked.

'It's breakfast in Arabic,' said Liz proudly.

The waiter stood on one foot looking confused and anxious. He conferred with his colleagues, then disappeared and returned minutes later with bacon and eggs. As I spluttered with laughter into my double damask I realised with horror that stress incontinence had come upon me. I froze.

'Hil, what's happened?' asked Liz anxiously.

'I've wee'd on the seat,' I replied.

The waiters were still hovering, hoping that we would eat quickly so that they could set the tables for lunch. How was I going to get out? I grimaced at the thought of the dark, wet stain beneath my bottom spreading further onto the upholstered seat.

'You'll have to produce a diversionary tactic,' I said. For one ghastly moment I thought she was going to show me up.

'*Aiuta!*' she cried as she rose shakily to her feet, grabbing the nearest waiter before affecting a stumble. The remaining waiters raced forward to prevent her from falling and supported her out of the restaurant, depositing her in an armchair in the lobby. I grabbed the opportunity, leapt to my feet, flung my napkin over the large damp patch and raced for the lift.

Back in our room, as I changed my clothes, I blurted out my thanks.

'You were magnificent—a veritable Sarah Bernhardt, dear girl—you saved my bacon. What a nightmare! I suppose they'll be looking at us askance when next we enter the dining room—'Who is that disgusting scrubber?' they'll be whispering to each other.

'Well, at least you didn't vomit,' commented Liz.

'Oh lord,' I eyed my watch. 'Now we're running late. Asif will be waiting.'

'Who's Asif?'

'He's our guide.'

'Why do we need him? It's a waste of money.'

'I'm not going to argue with you and change the arrangement. It's very easy to get lost in the Medina.'

We found Asif in the foyer and introduced ourselves. Asif was a professional guide and took his responsibilities very seriously, particularly as we were his only clients that morning. 'You lead the way,' I suggested. We descended the hill and soon reached the entrance to the Medina. Liz had pounced on a fresh topic as we walked. 'Fez,' she announced to Asif, 'unlike Marrakech, makes few concessions to tourists. It's still medieval. It doesn't seem to have noticed that the world outside has abandoned guilds, feudalism and community and galloped off into High Capitalism with its destructive competitive individualism.'

I wondered what Asif was making of Liz's outburst but only half listened to it myself. Asif brought Liz's rave to a full stop by saying firmly, 'Please, stay close to me, ladies, and look after your bags.' We wandered into the chaos of the Medina. It was intoxicating— the alien sickly-sweet aromas, the ancient tiled courtyards behind half-open wooden doors, the covert stares and whispers and the scurrying crowds of people preoccupied with the daily business of survival. We walked down alleyways, trying to avoid being pushed, jostled and occasionally pinched by beggars following us. Liz soon detached herself and to no one's surprise, got lost in the swirling whirlpool of people and had to be wrested from the hands of a few persistent beggars by Asif, who then frogmarched us both down a narrow alley towards a huge wooden door festooned with brass bolts, knockers and studs and ushered us upstairs and onto a rickety balcony. Below us in the backyard were thirty or forty vats of bubbling, coloured liquids. The colours were extraordinarily vivid: reds, oranges, blues and greens.

'Those colours would be wonderful in an abstract painting,' said Liz.

'You're so right—I'd love one on my wall at home—it would be a lasting reminder of Fez.' A few sinewy men climbed ladders to stir the brews with large ladles.

In an adjacent yard we saw bales of cloth skilfully lowered and trawled around in great baths of dye. Finally the dyed cloth was dried on strings slung across the open space. No factory conveyor belt here; no hired hands working by the clock. Liz and I marvelled at a millennium-old cottage industry still surviving in the twentieth century.

I had wondered why Liz was taking copious notes on our travels and was such a fund of knowledge about Morocco. She told me that when she was staying in Karachi a few years ago she had met the editor of the *Karachi Evening Star*. He had asked her to send him a 1200-word article on every place she visited. Liz waxed lyrical about how much fun she had writing the articles. Down the track, when she realised that I was a reasonably competent photographer, she briefed me about specific photographs she needed. But we soon took to arguing about what should appear in the shots. Liz rarely wanted people in the photographs. One time when we discussed it, a dejected note entered her voice.

'You know, Hilly,' she said sadly, 'my editor asked me to make the articles more personal. He said that the readers would like to know more about me and my reactions to the places I visit. He is always asking me, "What about the people you meet? Tell us about them."'

'Why don't you?' I said.

'I can't do it. I'm not interested in people. Anyway, I don't think my readership is interested. They want history and the facts. They like my impersonal style.'

'I think it's bollocks that you're not interested in people. You're the one who wanders up to strangers and starts up conversations with the weirdos we meet. And,' I added, 'for someone who doesn't like people you have an extraordinarily large number of friends.'

Liz shrugged dismissively. 'My relationships are strictly formal.'

*

On the flight to Prague Liz befriended an American called Bill who offered us a lift from the airport into the city. We accepted with alacrity; we had been warned to avoid taxidrivers freed from communist constraints. They reputedly charged huge fares and, according to one story Liz heard, were electrocuting the bottoms of passengers who failed to pay up handsomely. I was secretly thinking an electrocuted bottom would make an interesting change from incontinence on the faux Louis Quinze.

'Thank you. See you around the traps maybe,' we called out to Bill the American, as he dropped us off at our hotel.

'What sweeties they can be,' said Liz. Americans scored a brownie point that day.

The Prague Music Festival was on and, as Liz reminded me, the Czech Republic was not only the home to Semtex and the Škoda car, but also to the four composers known as the Prague Quartet: Smetana, Dvořák, Janáček and Martinů.

'We must hear music by each of them,' she said, and so we did. We raced around town looking at the boards outside all the churches and palaces announcing the concert programs that would be on that day. By a miracle we managed to hear the Smetana Trio in the very grand Lobkowicz Palace, a Martinů quartet in the equally grand Lichtenstein Palace and, later that day, a number of Dvořák's Slavonic dances in the Chapel of Mirrors, where angels joined in, cavorting with ribbons against a thoroughly baroque pink and gilt altar piece. With the Sinfonietta by Janáček we rounded off the fourth, goodness knows where! For me it was all about the sound of the music and the beauty of the surroundings. I rarely remembered the name of the church. But I always tried to buy a postcard to remind me where I'd been.

We lucked out by catching up with the young pianists' competition while we were looking over the ornate Prague Town Hall. Ignoring a 'no entry' sign announcing that the building was not open to the public that day, we breezed in, revelling in our daring, discovered that the semifinals were in progress, followed the sound of the piano to a large hall and sat down to listen, making bets as to who would make it to the final, the young Pole or the German. We found out that the results were going to be announced and the prize-giving held that afternoon. We went back, of course, and Liz was right, the young German won and we watched as his mother wept with joy as he was showered with scrolls and flowers. Afterwards we successfully continued pretending to be relatives, consuming cheese, biscuits and red wine provided for the occasion, congratulating the participants and making off before we blew our cover.

On the way back from the Town Hall I had noticed a mournful, yet strangely beautiful, Jewish cemetery. It was overgrown and crowded with broken headstones. By its side was a museum. I climbed the steps to the entrance and walked into the first gallery. Grey stone walls were hung with drawings and paintings by children who had been imprisoned in the concentration camps. Some depicted remembered scenes of sunlight, birds in leafy trees, cottages with smoking chimneys and dogs lying on the doorstep, sunflowers and stick figure mummies and daddies; others showed a solitary child pinned against barbed wire, black charcoal skies, lightning and rain pelting down and violent abstract slashes revealing despair and misery. I found them deeply moving. When I came out I sat silently in the cemetery and had a cry. Liz, who had refused to go into the gallery, appeared by my side.

'Don't be so sentimental, Hilly.'

I didn't think it was in the least bit sentimental to be tearful. 'We're talking about children's drawings, Liz, and you didn't even see them. I found the misery and trauma they conveyed touched me deeply.'

Liz wandered the museums and art galleries in Prague by herself. They were the last word in dreariness, she said, far from user-friendly; she found walking round them funereal. The guardians were for the most part elderly, well-girthed Prague ladies who, although not in uniform, conducted themselves as though they were in the military, telling Liz to follow the signs and not to take shortcuts even when Liz explained to them that certain exhibits were not of interest.

The day after Liz had been on one such excursion we woke to grey skies. I looked out of the window and it was pouring with rain. Liz refused to get out of bed or speak. I was so used to Liz being in charge of making the plans that I was surprised at this turn of events. It was a Liz I hadn't encountered before.

'What are we doing today?' No answer.

'What's up? Are you ill?'

'No, just leave me alone.'

'But I depend on you to plan our outings.'

'It's pointless: I'm bored out of my brain. The museums are complete duds, the food's shit and why would I want to go out in the pouring rain?'

She was right—the food was appalling. I had happily set out to discover whether the food in Prague was as poor as I had been told and found that it was the pits. I scoured cafés and delicatessens and they were woeful. Only at the central market could I buy fresh vegetables and fruit for our picnics, and even then the choice was limited. But it wasn't like Liz to care about food, and I decided she must be depressed by the English weather.

I finally managed to coax her out with the promise of fresh coffee and a taxi ride to the Strahov Monastery, with the medieval library I knew she wanted to see. Once absorbed in the books, she became her cheery self again, particularly when we explored the incredible Prague Castle complex afterwards. It was a jumble of cafés and art galleries surrounding the Gothic cathedral. The basilica, palaces and a row of cottages where once musicians and soothsayers had worked the streets now housed up-market bijouteries into which I happily plunged while Liz explored the castle.

More stalls for tourists were to be found on the Charles Bridge, a cobbled corridor across the Vltava River. Twisted, blackened statues of saints and angels looked down quizzically from pedestals along the wall of the bridge. They observed a continuous performance of pantomime and music from itinerant vendors, musicians and actors down below. All this against the backdrop of the castle glowering above.

Liz took a photo of me on the bridge and insisted on posing me pointing at the castle. A few months later I found out why when she sent me her *Karachi Evening Star* articles. On the front page of the travel section dedicated to Prague was the photograph of me, prominently displayed with the caption: ELDERLY PRAGUE RESIDENT PROUDLY POINTS OUT HER CITY. There I was, the 'elderly Prague resident', clothed in shapeless raincoat and scarf leaning against a lamppost and pointing across the bridge up the hill! It was Liz at her amusing best and I dined out on the joke for months.

Liz's articles on Prague and Morocco each took up the full back page of the paper's weekend supplement. They were liberally illustrated with my uncredited photographs, and I complained bitterly. Soothing apologies followed, and my name promptly appeared in print. Liz was now beginning to worry that it appeared as if she was travelling alone in her articles. There were no personal stories or interaction with any living person and she began to understand what her editor had been complaining about.

'Never mind. I'm sure that if we continue travelling together a few personal touches will creep into your writing,' I said reassuringly.

'Don't count on it, Hilly,' she warned me. 'I've never liked intimacy, I avoid it. I really don't know what it is. I enjoy gossip, but if I sense anything personal is creeping in, I stonewall. It's too disturbing and I get agitated. I'm a fair-weather friend, Hil, remember that.'

'I'll bear it in mind, but I'm unconvinced,' I said.

Picking a travel companion is a risky business. At best it can be brilliant, at worst a misery. After the two holidays together, I was beginning to wonder whether Liz as holiday companion was going to work out. Her sharp comments about late-night television and my excessive food intake were tedious. And her habit of ranting on about politics, art, history and anything else that took her fancy could be wearing.

But, by the same token, I was a ready sponge for her encyclopaedic knowledge. Liz was infinitely better than a guidebook. She was such an enthusiast; she would get me instantly interested in a place, and I'd long to go there immediately. I managed the practical arrangements and Liz went along with them, and this set-up, though I was loath to admit it, underpinned most of my more successful relationships. But most of all, we shared the same anarchic sense of humour and relish for the bizarre—throwing in a splash of fantasy for good measure.

For her part, Liz said I was the perfect travelling companion.

'You see, while you rest I can get on and see stuff for myself in my own time. And I love all that mad laughter we go in for.'

She added that she liked the way I didn't plague her with the personal. 'Both mine and yours,' she said.

'Long live the "damaged" newly-old,' I said cheerily.

2

Responding extravagantly to South America

Morocco and Prague had whetted my appetite and I wanted our next journey to be a truly extravagant one. Excitedly I started to research a six-week South American 'intensive'. What could be more intoxicating? I had heard and read so much about this ancient continent, its turbulent history, Spanish conquistadors rampaging through a unique Incan civilisation, condors floating on air currents over austere Andean mountains, llamas pounding across bleak plateaus, and those masters of poetry and prose, like Pablo Neruda and Gabriel García Márquez. I wanted to plunge in one fell swoop—from Patagonia to the Galápagos Islands, from Quito to Machu Picchu and everywhere in between. Liz was apprehensive.

'What about floods, political upheaval, theft, abduction?' she had asked me nervously.

'There's no point in giving them a moment's thought. We'll be in the hands of the gods. That's half the excitement of travel,' I replied.

'True,' she said, as game as ever.

*

I contacted three travel agencies specialising in South America. I quickly warmed to a quirky company run by Billy Owen, who had offices in the unlikely town of Wyong on the central coast of New South Wales, ninety kilometres from Sydney. So intrigued was I that I decided to visit him. When I arrived the office was empty save for a blonde office receptionist with long black talons for fingernails who was holding the fort by answering multiple phones with great difficulty while stuffing information into backpacks. She proudly told me that Billy had driven a double-decker bus round South America for several years and knew absolutely all there was to know about the place. I instinctively decided that Billy had to be my answer. He subsequently choreographed a kaleidoscopic journey around the continent for us. We would visit five countries in six weeks and feast on a smorgasbord of adventure.

I emailed Liz with the itinerary.

> Lizzie, hold onto your hat. Here it is. Hil xxx-x

She was in New Zealand at the time, hanging out with her niece. She replied:

> smashing. See you in the Quantas Lounge at Auckland
> Airport, at four on the day.

Liz was never big on spelling, grammar or clarity.

*

Three weeks later I flew into Auckland and Liz found me in the duty-free wool shop, drooling over some fleecy-lined ugg boots which I had just bought for mooching around hotel rooms.

We flew from Auckland to Santiago and from there took a four-hour flight to Punta Arenas in Patagonia. We were heading for the eco-friendly Explora hotel in the Torres del Paine National Park. I felt a momentary pang of guilt as I thought of the two plane trips we had already taken just to get to Punta Arenas. We then spent a relentless three hours driving in a gas-guzzling van to reach our ultimate destination, often on single dirt track roads through countryside which transformed from plains and fields to snow-capped mountains and icy lakes. Through the windows we saw herds of guanacos—small grey llamas native to South America.

We finally arrived at Explora, a sort of hunting lodge perched on the edge of an icy grey-blue lake opposite the jagged central massif of the Torres del Paine mountains. On the afternoon we arrived the mountains appeared in relief against a piercingly blue sky. There was a view of them from every room in the lodge, including the loos. Explora was austere from the outside, its lines not unlike those of a battleship, with long, low horizontal features hugging the landscape. Inside the lodge the style was simple: mellow wooden furniture and floors, with huge comfy sofas.

Explora was the brainchild of a millionaire Santiago business-man called Pedro Ibáñez who made bags of money from supermarkets and other commercial concerns and built Explora to fulfil his own fantasies and private passions. He wanted his eco-tourist guests to reconnect with the environment, to enjoy a landscape of astonishing beauty and experience a lifestyle far removed from their normal everyday life. And it worked. Our days were filled with trekking, and we returned to the lodge in the evening to soak in an open-air heated spa bath and swimming pool, looking up at the night sky with its infinite stars. Most nights there would be a brief rain shower. While steam rose from the heat of the bath below, rain poured down on one's head. It was a hedonist's dream.

Pablo was our personal guide at Explora. He had long eyelashes and spoke softly. Every evening he would tell us the options for the following day: a trek to the grey glacier, a close-up of some of the peaks across the lake, a whole-day trek with a picnic lunch, cross-country skiing or riding treks with a gaucho.

The most exciting option for me was the riding trek. I hadn't ridden since I was a kid, and then only two or three times. But doe-eyed Pablo enlisted the help of a silent gaucho called Diego, who saddled up a gentle horse called Maya for me. Liz had bowed out. The two men, each with their hands under my buttocks, heaved me groaning onto Maya's back (maybe they were groaning too!) and we set off trekking across the *campo*, splashing through streams, weaving through woods, brushing tree branches and climbing mountains while mists descended and condors rested lazily on the wind currents above us. It was sublime and I felt pure joy—it was an elemental time in which I lost any form of desire. Throughout all four hours of the trek I pranced along perfectly, even cantering on the way back, but once over the final stream Maya accelerated to a gallop towards the finishing post, pulling up abruptly when she saw the other horses coming to a halt. Needless to say, I fell off. Pablo helped me up, tenderly enquiring as to whether I had any broken bones. Diego, a smile passing briefly over his granite face, remained silent and apart. He then removed the saddles from all the horses, and, with a final flourish, released them. Maya and her sisters, snorting with pleasure, took off at full speed across the plain, manes dancing, breath steaming, determined to be the first to reach home.

I remember thinking quite clearly, *This is as good as it gets*, and *Gee, that Diego's a hunk!*

The first trek Liz and I took on foot was a miracle of care and concern on Pablo's part. He walked at our pace, carried our clothes when we got hot and discarded our outer layers, fed us energy bars, nuts and raisins when we flagged and chose the perfect scenic spot for our picnic near the top of a hill overlooking an icy waterfall with the mountains in the distance. He even found us a cave in which to shelter when the wind freshened and a drizzle started.

'Honestly, Hil, I'm overwhelmed,' said Liz. 'There's too much beauty. You know I spent my childhood in an incredibly beautiful part of south-west Wales, but after fifteen years of it I was glad to leave. I never thought I'd want to breathe an iota of fresh air or see another blade of grass or gaze at yet another umbrella of blue sky again. But this Patagonia is something else again. So marvellous you arranged it all. A-mazing. Truly. I must be Plato in his cave looking at mirages rather than the real thing,' she sighed.

'Liz is away with the pixies,' I explained to Pablo.

'What is this "away with pixies", Hilary?' Pablo asked, perplexed. 'Plato said many wise things like Liz. He said, "Necessity is the mother of invention." Did you know that?'

I shook my head.

'But do you know the best thing he said? Plato said you can discover more about a person in an hour of play—'

'—than in a year of conversation,' chimed in Liz with delight.

Pablo must have noticed my surprise at his Platonisms. 'I have been studying philosophy in Santiago by correspondence, you understand,' he said by way of explanation. Squelch.

And he went on effortlessly to explain and describe the history, geology, botany and birds and beasts of Patagonia as he packed up our picnic and we continued our walk along wild, untouched stretches of this amazing continent. Pablo was not a local boy. He and the other staff lived hundreds of miles away and had to be trucked in on fortnightly shifts in the same gas-guzzling vans that brought us.

Back at Explora we tucked into delicious three-course meals, simply prepared from snap-frozen fresh food brought in daily by refrigerated trucks from Santiago. The sous-chef baked a variety of breads daily in the kitchen and the wine cellar was fully stocked with local and French wine.

On one very special day we were treated to a *quincho*—an authentic Patagonian picnic—at Laguna Azul. Before we set out, Pablo told us to watch out for pumas—the elusive, black, shiny cats that roamed around the area, quite capable of snatching chicken legs from our hands, stealing babies from prams and purring like kittens when their bellies were full. Liz was so alarmed that she refused to walk or ride with the rest of the party, and had to be driven to the picnic separately.

The picnic site was an octagonal wooden pavilion overlooking a deep gorge. Inside, the staff had prepared a central log fire with lambs' carcasses hanging over it like bats, dropping sizzling fat onto the embers. Local red wine flowed freely. Gorgeous Pedro and another equally handsome gaucho, both dressed in full riding gear, brought out long knives from their boots and cut hunks of delectable meat straight onto our plates. I couldn't resist trying my Spanish and said to Pedro, '*Quisiera algo para beber, por favor.*' (I would like something to drink, please.)

'*Le daré vino tinto local. Es muy bueno.*' (I will give you local red wine. It is very good.)

'*Gracias tanto.*' I became bold. '*Siéntese aquí.*' (Sit down with us.)

It's amazing how the Spanish flows when there's a good-looking bloke in one's sights. Somehow speaking in Spanish loosened my tongue and gave me courage. In a foreign language it did not seem to be me talking; I observed this fearless woman with amazement.

'You're getting a bit beyond yourself,' said an astonished Liz. 'He's working.'

'I'm having fun,' I said, brushing her comment aside.

Pedro went off to the bar and reappeared with a large carafe of red wine and two glasses.

'*Gracias tanto.*'

'You must excuse me. I have to work. I see you later.' Pedro gave a slight bow.

'Of course. You are busy.' I was embarrassed. Liz was right.

After lunch a guitarist and a gaucho playing a small harp struck up and to loud clapping and shouts of enthusiasm the guides and the gauchos started the 'Cueca' (national dance of Chile). It depicted the elaborate rituals of birds' courtship. The boys selected partners from the female staff and we watched them weave elaborate patterns around each other with their red handkerchiefs, staring piercingly into each other's eyes. As the music intensified the couples sized each other up and performed more intricate steps: first the boys advanced, heads held high, chests out, boots stamping, while the girls held their ground in a flurry of swirling skirts and sturdy ankles. I was suddenly aware that Pedro was striding over towards me. I felt my face flush and my heart pound like a teenager. He bowed, held out his hand and I took it and rose slowly. Everybody in the room stared at us delightedly and erupted into applause, banging their hands on the tables and hollering. I was extremely relieved that I had worn a skirt and could do a lot of skirt swishing and stamping, concealing zero footwork, while he performed like a peacock. However, it was the eye contact that was all important and I had no difficulty there! We danced until I was exhausted and flopped onto a bench.

Pedro smiled, *'Felicitaciones. Baila muy bien. Es una Chilena verdadera.'* (Congratulations. You dance very well. You are a real Chilean.)

'Well, you've won a heart there,' said Liz.

'I wish.'

'Why are you on your own?' Pablo asked Liz some time later.

'Hilary's ridden off with Pedro. Who knows where they've gone.'

Pablo smiled. 'Well, Leeez. You and I will go together. Don't worry, Pedro will look after Hilaria.' And Pablo smiled again—'Just another old dotty falling for the Spanish charm,' Liz imagined him thinking.

*

Santiago de Chile, where we went next, seemed old-fashioned and staid for all its romantic-sounding name. We touched down on Independence Day, which was a public holiday.

After depositing our bags at the hotel we ventured out to get a feel for the city. It was dry and dusty, the stone buildings seemed drained of colour and gusts of warm wind blew in our faces. I saw a lot of aimless tourists wandering through a flea market, rubbish swirling round their ankles, while weary locals picnicked in a small park under a sullen sky. No street sweepers on a public holiday. Liz had a totally different impression. She thought the locals were having a fine time, enjoying a cheery family Independence Day in a village atmosphere. It was curious that the two of us could read the scene so differently.

I pride myself on my powers of observation and intuition. Liz, on the other hand, comes to a situation with a kitbag of facts. I have always had an uneasy relationship with fact-wielding people—they so often use facts to exert power. Luckily, Liz doesn't use facts in

43

this way most of the time—she just uses them to get situations slightly skewed.

Liz found a statue of Bernardo O'Higgins on horseback in the centre of the square.

'Did you know, Hil, that Bernardo, the Irishman, led the fight against Spanish imperialism in Chile? Curious.'

'Can't say I did.'

After a futile search for open-air cafés we gave up and returned to the hotel. The dark brown regulation decorations in all the open hotel spaces made me lethargic so I lay down for a snooze. Liz meantime discovered that the Museum of Colonial Art was open and reported back that the gloomy interior was stuffed with grim religious paintings—no less than sixty-four depicting the life of St Francis. In the evening we ventured out again to find a meal. The only place nearby was a milk-bar-cum-café where, hopefully, I could practise my faltering Spanish.

'*Dos sopas de pollo con fideos, por favor,*' I said, squinting at the pronunciation guide in my phrasebook. (Two chicken soup with noodles, please.)

'*No hay sopa de pollo que se acabó,*' said the teenage waitress. (The chicken soup is finished.) She looked anxiously at Liz, who was flapping her arms and darting round the café making chook noises by way of explanation.

The owner, Bruno, came out of the kitchen just as Liz, in her rooster glory, crowed loudly, pummelling her chest with her fists. Bruno stared at her in disbelief, then chuckled as she produced a few follow-up cluck-clucks in his direction.

'*Está loca,*' I said, laughing and 'bravo-ing' Liz's performance. The waitress giggled as she explained the chicken soup problem to her boss. Bruno disappeared briefly and returned with two thick bowls of mud-coloured sludge.

'*Se trata de una sopa muy buena de la región, sea de su agrado,*' said he, all enthusiasm. Then, noting our confusion, he valiantly translated, 'Eees good soup of the region,' smiling at Liz through brown, broken teeth.

We made a point of finishing the fairly revolting soup, assured Bruno that it was '*muy deliciosa*' and paid the bill. '*Hasta luego,*' I called cheerily as we bolted out of the café—See you later! It wasn't a brilliant culinary start to our trip but we could see there was fun to be had with the language and we were able to order room service back at the hotel.

We were picked up the next day by our guide, Valentina, a glamorous cougar. She took us first to the Club Hípico—the racecourse. The most significant thing I learnt about racing was that in Chile the horses race counterclockwise, like water down a plughole. She pointed out the magnificent grandstand, built in 1892 by an English architect; it was framed by the snow-clad Andes. But when she launched into the history of Santiago, I found myself switching off. She was smart enough to get the message that I, for one, wanted to meet some locals and so, instead of taking us to the nearby cathedral, she adjusted her program and took us to a '*café con piernas*' where excellent coffee was served by waitresses dressed in G-strings. I chattered to one of the girls, who was decked out in tassels and five-inch heels. As she poured the coffee, she told me that she made a good living, $300 for a five-day week, only six hours a day, no evenings after 9 pm and no alcohol. 'The worst thing is the shoes,' she told me. 'Sometimes the patrons are aggressive but the managers have very firm rules.' She was very chatty and I boldly asked her if she was obliged to sleep with the patrons.

45

'No,' she said. I wasn't convinced and wanted to continue, but she was more interested in finding out about us. Apparently there are hundreds of these *cafés con piernas*, which serve coffee all day. *Con piernas* means 'with legs', because the waitresses in these cafés have beautiful legs and wear next to nothing. The coffee is cheap and there is no cover charge because the establishments do not have liquor licences. They are a Chilean phenomenon.

'*¿De dónde eres?*' she asked me.

'Sydney.'

'*Ah, Sidenie, puente del puerto.*'

I had a vague idea that *puente* meant 'bridge', so drew a vast semicircle over my head.

'*Muy bonito,*' she said with a smile.

I warmed to her. 'What *es tu nombre?*'

'Conchita.' *Perfect*, I thought, and wondered whether it was her stage name.

'What is your name?' asked Conchita, practising her English.

'*Hilaria.*'

'*Muy bueno.*'

'*¿Trabajas* here *todo el tiempo?*' (Do you work here all the time?)

'*No, soy una especialista IT,*' she said. (No, I'm an IT specialist!) 'But I need *dos puestos de trabajo* to 'elp *mi família.*'

I could have happily gone on all day in the dark café, but Liz decided we should see the modern Barrio Suecia area of the city (the Swedish neighbourhood).

'Let's take Conchita and Valentina to lunch and abandon the formal tour.'

Conchita had no trouble obtaining an early mark from her manager.

'I am very lucky. Carlo, my manager, is a very good friend to me and my baby girl.'

'Oh, you have a baby? How old?'

'Two years,' said Conchita. She pulled out a photo from behind her tassels and showed me a formal studio headshot of a small baby with a large pink bow on top of her head.

'That's my Emilia,' she said, smiling.

'Does your husband look after her while you are at the café?' I asked.

'I am not married, but Carlo looks after me. He gets very jealous if the customers flirt with me.' And that was as close as I was able to get. Her body language filled in the rest. Carlo was probably the father but was not, for whatever reason, in a position to marry Conchita.

When we got back to the hotel, Liz said quite cheerfully, 'I think you're hijacking this holiday with all your chat to the locals. You remind me of that chap in Lermontov's novel, *A Hero of Our Time*.' She opened her notebook and read, '*I wanted dreadfully to get some story or other from another person—a desire common to all travellers and writers.*'

'So what do you think we should be doing?' I asked.

'Don't get me wrong, Hil. Despite myself, I'm quite enjoying the chats and laughs you inspire. You see, I normally concentrate on the facts: ghastly oppressive Spanish rule for three hundred years; freedom; and now the Allende–Pinochet years.'

*

When we reached Quito, Ecuador's sky-high capital, we made a point of concentrating on facts for Liz's benefit. Fifteen kilometres outside Quito was the midway point between the northern and southern hemispheres, and if you place your foot on a marked spot, you could be standing with one leg in each hemisphere.

'Apparently you weigh less. That'll be good for you, Hil.'

I got on the scales nearby. 'No discernible difference, I'm afraid.'

We went up the 200-metre-high hill known as El Panecillo, or 'small round bread', because of its shape at the top. In 1976 an aluminium statue to the Virgin Maria was erected there. From this height we could see beneath us the source of the Amazon River and the colonial city of Quito, which had been largely swamped by recent modern architecture. Clara, our local guide, had a history degree and a further certificate in tourism; she was an anxious woman in her early forties. She pointed out the cathedral and the convent of San Francisco and told us many tales of explorers long gone. She was a mine of information, never drawing breath, and Liz listened with rapt attention, even taking notes. I could feel my head swimming and it wasn't only due to the reduced oxygen in the atmosphere.

'Are you married?'

It just popped out of my mouth—a very basic attempt to bring the Clara 'fact machine' to a halt so that I could pause and enjoy the 360-degree view in peace and quiet. Clara needed no further prompting: she dropped the history of her country like a hot brick and started to pour out the story of her unfaithful husband, who had run off three weeks earlier with her best friend, leaving Clara to cope alone with their three children. She didn't know where he was, why he hadn't phoned or why he hadn't given her money for the children. To top off her woes, she was fearful that she might be pregnant and confused about what she should do, because it was against her religion to have an abortion. It was impossible to ignore the raw anguish of her story; tears poured down her cheeks and saturated the tissues I offered her. Her despair was rather more than I had bargained for and the rest of our stay in Quito was largely dominated—once she stopped crying—by her rage against the perfidy of men and the plight of abused women. She spent every coffee break attempting to brainstorm what action she should take next.

Poor Liz—we passed by all the fine examples of Spanish colonial architecture with hardly a second glance. Liz gradually withdrew from any engagement with Clara and looked around the museums and churches on her own. Clara grew increasingly clingy as our brief stay came to an end. On the day of our departure she insisted on accompanying us to the airport.

'Take it easy if you can, Clara. I am sure it will all work out for you,' I said, without much confidence that it would. But she was a good-looking woman and would probably find someone else. At security she hugged us both, handed us each a key ring with the emblem of Quito and waved her sodden handkerchief as we fled through the embarkation doors. As we sat down and listened to the plane's safety instructions my neck muscles loosened. The willy-willy had passed.

'You do a good job, Hilly, with the needy Claras of this world. Maybe it's because you're needy yourself?'

I wondered whether this was a dig, and if Liz was finding me emotionally too demanding, but remembered that she was enjoying the 'people' gossip and, provided I didn't involve her in any 'in-depth probes', there was no problem.

'Quite possibly. I certainly empathised with the chaotic mess she was in.'

*

We were flying to the Galápagos Islands, 900 kilometres off the Ecuadorian Coast, to join a boat trip. It was the most convenient way to see the extraordinary flora and fauna which existed on these pimples of volcanic rock strung out along the equator. Of course I was interested (at least to begin with) in our fellow 'boatees'. Liz warned me not to plunge into premature relationships.

'People frequently turn out to be Big Bores,' she said.

Our boat was small; there were twenty-two of us and a crew of seven. How we all fitted into the tiny space was a mystery. But we all had hot showers, narrow bunk beds, lashings of food three times a day and daily briefings about our hectic schedule, which often began at first light.

We ate our meals around a small horseshoe table, in such close proximity that it was hard to avoid forced intimacies. There was a young Dutch couple on their honeymoon; there was Dinah, who cried every time children were mentioned; there was one unfortunate woman who was seasick the whole time and rarely appeared—so no chance to befriend her. Her husband kept disappearing to administer acupuncture, in vain it seemed.

John, our guide, was employed by the Galápagos National Park Service. On the first day we were approaching the shore of one of the islands in a small dinghy when Jim, the honeymooner, impulsively leapt overboard and started wading ashore. This was despite strict instructions from John minutes before.

'You will *not* disembark until the boat has been beached, and you will *not* wander anywhere without permission, as you could disturb the fragile ecosystem,' John had said sternly.

'Come back now . . . I mean NOW,' John shouted at Jim as he took off.

'Fuck off. I don't take orders from you,' said Jim, fuming.

'If you don't come back, I'll have to put you off at Puerto Ayora.'

'I don't appreciate your manner,' said Jim. His newly minted wife was desperately shushing him from the boat.

They narrowly avoided blows. Two alpha males. The rest of the boatload became very quiet; it was a nasty beginning.

Liz and I debriefed later.

'He should have left Jim alone, he's on his honeymoon. John's overreacting,' said Liz.

'Come on, he really cares about the environment.'

A typical day began with a small boat journey to the beach. Was it to be a wet or dry landing? This became our most pressing problem as we struggled with cameras, shoes and bathing costumes for the few hours ashore. Often the sea was quite rough, so getting in and out of the dinghy onto the beach could be a hazardous affair. I found this out on the second day when I lost my balance and fell flat on my face in the surf. I lay motionless for a moment in the wet sand trying to decide if I was hurt. There was a terrible silence in the boat, but the hundreds of sea lions ranged along the beach honked happily. I rolled over and buried my embarrassment by laughing along with them.

That day we spent with the marine iguanas—black, scaly creatures who basked motionless on sun-drenched black rocks. We would come across hundreds of them almost underfoot. Every now and again one would move, slowly clambering over any of its mates who were in the way. Then it would settle down to sleep with a clawed arm resting comfortably on the mate's back. We saw several piled on top of each other in an orgy of closeness, or lining up as though posing for a family photograph. Their tiny, scaly eyes seemed to take everything in as they looked at us looking at them looking at us.

The land iguanas, huge lizards who flopped about on the ground, basking in the sun's rays, didn't go around in crowds. We found one slowly propelling itself out of the scrub on its thick, ungainly feet, its stomach barely off the ground, swishing its long tail slowly from side to side.

But the high point of the day came when I spotted a giant tortoise lumbering down the path towards us. His little ET face peered at us from beneath an enormous mottled shell. He had the longest, thinnest neck I had ever seen.

'It's Lonesome George!' I cried out to the group.

'I don't think so,' said John. 'George is housed and protected by the Charles Darwin Research Station and isn't allowed outside their grounds. He wanders around there all day, a happy chappie. We have to protect him because he's between seventy and eighty years old and the only surviving member of his species. And he's a confirmed bachelor.

'But if any of you,' John grinned wickedly, 'can find him a mate, you'll win a reward of $10,000! I warn you though, he's very choosy.' John went on to tell us all that George had knocked back all 'tortoisian' blandishments thus far—not so much as a whiff of enthusiasm had he shown for anyone!

'Is he so old that his genitals have shrivelled up?' I asked.

'Get him onto Viagra,' suggested Liz.

'I can't see a problem, Lizzie. If this isn't George, we've gone one better; this is Pepita, destined to be the light of George's life.'

Pepita wasn't exactly looking red hot at this moment; she had gone to sleep in the shade of a bush.

'Pepita will be perfect,' I said. 'She'll perk up when George comes rumbling up to her, high on steroids, beating a mating drum roll on his shell. What d'ya reckon?'

'She's IT!' cried Liz. 'Let's take her to the station and claim the reward.'

'You try carrying her,' said John. 'She'll weigh a ton.'

'No worries, John, you'll lend us some rope, won't you?' I wheedled. 'And we'll lead her on a leash to the superintendent's office.' Our group were by this time quite bemused but still wanting to hear the end of the story. 'It will be love at first sight,' I told them.

Liz jumped in. 'George will attempt to mount the coquettish Pepita—'

'Who will be torn between eating her carrot and enjoying George's embrace—'

'George will cling to her scaly shoulders like a tortoise possessed and, groaning under the magnitude of his task—'

'Will finally deliver the *coup de foudre*—'

'And the prize will be ours!'

'AND John will be crowned Galápagos King of Sustainability, Biodiversity and Eco-Tourism,' Liz and I chorused triumphantly, and all our fellow cruisees clapped. John grinned, taken with the fantasy, although I could see that his literal mind had found it difficult to imagine two elderly ladies trudging up the path towards the superintendent's office, triumphantly leading a reluctant Pepita.

'And we'll be George Junior's Honorary Godparents!' we added, squealing with delight. But this was a step too far for our fellow cruisees, who now wanted to get back to the tour.

*

When we got back to the boat on our first evening, Liz and I changed into bathing costumes and flung ourselves off the deck into the sea.

'This is so gorgeous after gazing at all those dotty animals,' said Liz, splashing around.

We never gave a thought as to how we would get back on board. After a while we called, 'Ahoy, there,' hoping we were being suitably nautical, and crew members came to the side of the boat. We swam to them and grasped their hands, but our weight was too much for them and we fell back into the sea. By now our fellow cruisees were lining the deck, highly amused.

'What now, Lizzie? I'm getting a cramp in my leg.'

We were motioned to the back of the boat and a rope was lowered so that we could heave ourselves up to a level where the crew could get a better grip of our shoulders. With difficulty they lugged us out, gasping for breath, until we lay spread-eagled on the deck like beached whales. Our fellow cruisees burst into laughter, but despite the humiliation of their response to our aged bodies, we didn't care; we were the ones having fun and we insisted on repeating the swim every evening.

After our evening swims John served us sundowners while the boat moved swiftly to its mooring for the night. His speciality was the delicious Blue Footed Booby cocktail. After we had become suitably lubricated with Boobies, John would relax, and confided in us that he was not looking forward to turning forty.

'Half my life gone,' he said in his cups one evening.

'What you need is a good woman,' I said.

He nodded. 'Yes, but where on these islands will I find one? They all leave.'

As we did the next day.

*

There is a postscript to this adventure. John was a wildlife photographer and published postcards and a calendar of Galápagos mammals and birds for sale in tourist shops. I couldn't find the calendar when we were there and asked if he would send me one. Months passed. No calendar—but finally a postcard of a Blue Booby arrived, with the cocktail recipe printed on the back and the news that he had got married: 'You said I needed a good woman!'

* * * * *

Blue Footed Booby Cocktail

Serves 1 or a miserly 2

Ingredients

30 ml rum

15 ml blue Curaçao

45 ml lime juice

syrup to your taste

soda water

ice

slice of lime, to serve

Preparation

Mix and serve in a cold glass, decorated with a slice of lime.

* * * * *

It was dusk when we arrived in Lima. We had been told that it was a highly dangerous city, but didn't dream for a second that we would be exposed to any harm. Catalina, our local guide, met us at the airport and shepherded us into the agency van that was to take us to our hotel.

We had pulled up at traffic lights in what the driver said was a middle-class area of the city. Liz said afterwards that she glanced out of the window and saw a man sprinting across a small park towards our van. He smashed the van window with a spark plug, put his hand through the jagged glass and grabbed my handbag, which was open on my lap. In one fell swoop he got everything—cash, credit cards, jewellery, make-up, my diary, address book—the lot. Only my passport was safe; in a wallet around my waist.

To claim insurance I needed to report the theft to the local police. In Lima there was a special police office which dealt with tourist thefts, a testament to the thriving thievery trade. It was housed in a dismal, rundown shanty building, where we spent three hours while they copied out the list of items stolen into a large ledger. This was then typed out three times on a computer. My statement (in English) about the circumstances of the theft was then taken, and translated into Spanish. Even with translation assistance from Catalina, this took forever: I had to convince the police that the theft had taken place, even though there were three witnesses. When I was handed back the statement, now in Spanish, to sign, I asked Catalina how I would know that my words had been accurately translated. She didn't have a satisfactory answer. She was out of her depth and made it clear that she wanted to go. She said her boyfriend was waiting for her. She departed, leaving us alone with a sorry line of robbed tourists who trailed through the door of the ramshackle office. They sat disheartened on rickety benches, each with a tale of horror to tell worse than the one before.

The next day Liz and I vented our frustration on two police persons in the main square who had ENGLISH SPOKEN written across their highly decorated chests. Eventually, Liz pointed out, politely, that this statement was incorrect. But the two were unmoved, their impassive faces as wooden as the choir stalls in the nearby cathedral. They did not seem to understand or care that the system they were part of was so hopeless.

I suppose, given the circumstances, it is not surprising that we disliked Lima. The poverty and neglect were overwhelming.

Fortunately our visit was partially saved that afternoon by our travel agent Billy's special connections. The Pedillo family harked back to the original conquistadors who had come out from Spain to conquer, sequester and exploit the people and the continent. Liz was thrilled, since she is an empire buff. We were taken around the house the family had built shortly after arriving in Peru five centuries ago. It was just off the main square and, like many houses in Spain, its entrance was just a door in the busy street. Inside were tiny rooms crammed with centuries of bric-a-brac, each room opening out onto a shaded courtyard full of succulents in pots; we could have been in Seville. Catalina gave us the names of each Pedillo family member in respectful tones. Inside the small family chapel, Liz found a picture of the baby Jesus and said, 'Pablo Pedillo Junior?'

Catalina was not amused.

The family was now adapting to the modern world and embracing tourism to increase their cash flow. When we visited the Sacred Valley a few days later we were taken to the Pedillo estate there, where we joined a van load of up-market tourists for a lunchtime spread. The meal was served buffet style from tables groaning with the most delectable food. I picked out a raw fish dish (raw fish has always been a favourite) —a beautiful Chilean ceviche—which went superbly with a crisp South American white wine.

*

As far as I was concerned Lima was a dead loss and I was delighted to leave at four in the morning for Cusco and the Inca heartland. At Cusco we stayed in a monastery that had been converted into a comfortable hotel. Liz found it 'gaunt', but I enjoyed the high ceilings, shaded corridors and limited light coming through high windows. I didn't mind the holy pictures, but Liz could have done without them. The air was thin in Cusco, as we were over 3000 metres high, and I had a headache when we arrived so went to lie down. Liz woke me in midafternoon.

'You haven't been asleep all this time?' she said, frustrated. Liz had sussed the place out and was eager to show me the sights. She took me to a café in the main square, where she was in her element railing against the conquering Spanish who had crushed the culture and religion of the Incas. The café was full of hippies, some of whom were listening idly to Liz.

'I'm going back to the hotel,' I said.

'Why?' she replied. 'We've only just started. There's so much to see.'

'You go,' I said, to which she replied, 'I've seen it all. I want *you* to see it.'

But with my head still throbbing, all I could see was a scruffy square with an overdecorated cathedral at one end. Young tourists swarmed everywhere, while locals in peasant costume shuffled around selling postcards. It all looked to my aching eyes distinctly unattractive. I wanted to be back in the cocoon of the monastery hotel. *Best give this day a miss*, I thought.

I made an effort nevertheless that evening. Dinner was served in the beautifully restored refectory. Liz gave me a blast of Inca/Spanish history and a diatribe on the iniquities of imperialism. My brain was feeling like my handbag, no longer my own. When I gently mentioned that I was feeling a bit wan, she said, 'You've got all the symptoms of altitude sickness. You're not eating and God knows that's unusual; the next thing will be a nosebleed, diarrhoea and swollen hands and feet. You'd better go back to bed.'

Liz didn't seem to realise that just as you can have too little oxygen, you can have too much information.

Mercifully the next day the headache had gone and I was 'all go'. There were a million babies to snap as we left Cusco and went through the Sacred Valley, stopping off at various village markets. I was in heaven—the markets were awash with Quechuan ladies dressed in brightly coloured wide skirts—several layers seemed to be de rigueur—with bowler hats jauntily perched on their heads. Most of them had a baby or shopping slung in a shawl on their backs. Small children milled around holding tiny lambs or llamas, prodding my side and begging to be photographed. One of the photographs I took, of an old, wizened Incan woman holding a lamb, found its way into Liz's *Karachi Evening Star* articles. Liz had captioned it: HILARY, THE WRITER'S COMPANION, DRESSED UP IN LOCAL COSTUME.

The market stalls sold everything: textiles, alpaca jumpers and hats, fake archaeological artefacts and even a whole lot of nineteenth-century Spanish ecclesiastical books. And then there was the food: maize in all the colours of the rainbow; many different types of potato, some dehydrated for easy storage; and inviting vegetables I couldn't even identify. There were sacks of spice and aromatic herbs, and natural dyes, echoed in the vividly coloured clothes the Quechuan women were wearing. And finally we found the local doctor's surgery, where on open stalls there were medicinal plants and sinister-looking dried animal remains. Quechuans still adhered to old Incan practices and believed that the natural world was imbued with spirits. In deference to these spirits that lurked in their produce, the stall holders kept a respectful silence as they waited for customers. In this quiet corner of the market there was no bustle or barter, which felt strange, and I was glad to return to the clatter and confusion. Liz preferred to keep faith with the spirit world.

The Sacred Valley was fertile and green, narrowing and losing vegetation as we neared the mountains. The last town in the valley, Ollantaytambo, played host to an Incan archaeological site, which gave the townsfolk access to tourists. Ollantaytambo, itself dating back to the fifteenth century, had some of the oldest continuously occupied houses in South America. Most of the houses were pitifully poor, clumps of decaying stone with open sewers. We wandered along the narrow alleyways followed by a cluster of children whose number grew when I pulled out the pencils I had brought from Sydney with kangaroos and fluffy koala bears attached. Wide-eyed with delight, they lined up with their hands outstretched, thrilled when they scored a prize pencil. One little boy who was particularly cute pushed his way to the front of the queue and grabbed a koala.

'No, back in the queue,' I said, snatching his koala back. 'Wait your turn.' And then I felt small-minded and mean when I ran out of pencils and he was left empty-handed, looking desolate. 'What was the point of trying to impose my western idea of manners on this young kid? How petty and ridiculous,' I said to Liz.

'Well, at least you didn't take the food out of his mouth,' said Liz. 'Lighten up, it's not the end of the world.'

From Ollantaytambo we took a train full of tourists like us to Aguas Calientes, a small town below the great Incan site of Machu Picchu.

The train was slow and it was impossible to see more than the occasional glimpse of mountain peaks, so I began chatting to three teenage musicians who had a gig coming up in the big hotel at Machu Picchu.

Liz started up. 'Here you are travelling to one of the most incredible sights in the world and all you can do is chatter on as though you were on a Sydney bus. Do you realise that this railway track was specially carved through the jungle to take us tourists to Machu Picchu?'

'Listen, Liz,' I interrupted, 'you don't have to rant on. I've read about Machu Picchu. I can't believe that they started building it in 1400 and the place is still virtually intact. We still don't know why it was abandoned a century later at the time of the Spanish conquest. It's incredible to think that the city remained hidden and wasn't found by the Spanish invaders. I know it was known about locally, but the outside world didn't know anything until Hiram Bingham discovered it in 1911. I suppose it must have helped that the site was surrounded by mountains and ravines.'

Liz just looked at me, apparently staggered by my amazing erudition, and disappeared into the corridor to look at the view.

Every man and his dog has a theory about Machu Picchu. That night at the hotel in Aguas Calientes, Liz met a man called Bernardo who maintained that the city had been built after the Spanish had set foot in South America. He said that the Incas had built it as a decoy so that when the marauding Spanish arrived, they would be conned into thinking that they had reached the capital of a mighty kingdom and would not bother to go any further into the jungle. Meanwhile, deeper in the rainforest, the Incas remained undisturbed for another two hundred years. Spectacular remains had recently been found which proved, he believed, the accuracy of his theory. Bernardo gave Liz a map of Machu Picchu on which he marked seven significant places to visit which would prove his theory.

The next day we took a bus up the zigzag single-track road to Machu Picchu. At the entrance we were met by Carlos, our guide. Liz could hardly wait for him to get the necessary passes and documentation to enter the site. Once through the gate, we were faced with a narrow path cut into the rock, with a very steep fall on one side. This proved a nailbiting moment as Liz edged forward, gripping Carlos's hand tightly, vertigo beginning to take hold.

Once standing firmly on the very small area of level ground, she gave Bernardo's map to Carlos and told him she wanted to see the spots marked on it. Carlos looked at the map intently and set off, ignoring Bernardo's map and taking us to points of interest on his own prearranged list. These invariably proved to be perched on the edge of a precipice with spectacular views deep down into the depths of the valleys. Liz would tremble and stop in her tracks. Carlos and I would hold her hands, give her a pep talk and reassure her, but our efforts failed. She gave up after a couple of these experiences and just sat on a rock with no view at all while Carlos and I continued walking around this extraordinary place.

'It's mind-blowing, the incredible beauty of those deep ravines rising up to jagged, tree-covered mountain tops. It's breathtaking,' I said, when I returned to Liz. 'Forget the mystery behind the abandoned ruins and the stones scattered over the ground. Estate agents say it about Sydney Harbour views; Machu Picchu is just the same—location, location, location.'

Back in Cusco after the Machu Picchu expedition, we took a daylong special tourist train to Lake Titicaca. The train trundled along at an agonisingly slow pace. The first six hours we wound our way up a valley beside a roaring river, bare mountain slopes on either side. We passed an occasional village, a few tiny dots surrounded by green fields. After an enormous effort the train pulled out of the valley and made its way over a bleak and desolate plateau. We stopped in the middle of nowhere and were served a sumptuous lunch, at the end of which one hundred or more Incan women suddenly appeared, gesticulating and waving at us through the windows. They were festooned with dolls, babies, rugs and knitwear. Everybody got out of the train and bargained happily for the crafts. The women then evaporated. But where did they go? There was no sign of human habitation anywhere around. The train started again and appeared to pick up speed. It was scary; the ground below us felt loose and I kept thinking we were going to leave the track.

We reached Puno after dark, in the middle of a thunderstorm. We walked to the hotel, which was nearby, and arrived wet but relieved to have made it. The next morning we awoke to see through our window a huge expanse of sparkling water that stretched as far as the eye could see. It was Lake Titicaca, the highest navigable lake in the world.

The storms had gone and we embarked on our trip across the lake on a brilliantly sunny day. As the catamaran sped towards Sun Island we were given a great lunch of freshly caught fish and salad. Our new guide, Mateo, told us about the history of the Incan empire and its origins. He was a serious history student who came from La Paz.

'The Incan civilisation had its origins in the highlands of Peru sometime in the early thirteenth century and legend tells us that it all began with the creator god Tici Viracocha rising up from Lake Titicaca. Tici Viracocha was enraged because his neighbours had insulted him, so he turned them all into stone. Pleased with himself after this success he created the sun and the moon and a string of humans, including his son, Manco Cápac, who also emerged from Lake Titicaca and headed to Cusco with his brothers and their wives via underground caves. He then fought his three brothers, defeated them and turned them to stones as well. He kidnapped their wives and with his sister-wife, Mama Ocllo, became the first ruler of the Incas (or 'Children of the Sun', as the Incas are known) and founded the city of Cusco. His empire went from strength to strength until the Spanish arrived in the early sixteenth century and wiped it out almost completely.'

Mateo ended his speech with a warning: 'If someone falls into the lake, be it fisherman or tourist, it is still traditional not to rescue them, but to let them drown as an offering to the Earth Goddess Pachamama. So watch out!' he concluded, grinning from ear to ear.

On arrival at Sun Island we climbed a hundred steps and at the top found a fountain, a fabulous view, several indigenous Amerindian ladies with llamas pestering us to buy knitwear and a couple of naughty boys who held their hands out for money.

We moved on to a pavilion where we were given water and greeted by a witch-doctor type who blessed sweets, herbs and a stick or two before throwing them all on a flame. He then tossed water drops on us and gave us certificates saying we had been blessed, Inca style. Around us were an assortment of alpacas, vicunas, a man making a reed boat and women weaving.

'This is a completely sanitised construct,' said Liz in disgust, 'made up by the tour company.'

'It may be, but some people on the trip think it's authentic. Anyway, does it matter? The locals get to make a bit of money and that has to be a good thing.' I broke off and stared at the glistening blue lake. 'If you don't like the sideshow, try a spot of meditation and let the wind ruffle your hair.'

'Have you no interest in the truth?' insisted Liz.

I made one last effort. 'All I can do is treat the people here with respect as fellow human beings, buy the souvenirs and tip them for service. That's really all I can offer. We're just passing through, Liz.'

'You are totally ignoring the reality of people's lives.'

'Maybe you're right. But I prefer not to be characterised as a bleeding heart,' I said impatiently. I looked over at the Amerindian women weavers chatting happily and became silent. It was pointless to continue the argument.

An hour or so later the catamaran took us to another island and landed us at a poor, rundown village. We were met on the quayside by the villagers, who put garlands around our necks. A band appeared to lead us through the village to another, smaller beach, where we were helped into rowboats. Ancient grandpas, straining at the oars, rowed us to the other side of the island. It was a long way—where were the strapping lads? They must have left the village to search for work on the mainland.

We landed on the other side and clambered up a steep cliff. Over the brow of a hill we were shown the barely visible remains of an Inca settlement. It was beautifully positioned to give us a 360-degree view of the lake. We paused for a while to absorb the scene and then walked back to the village through neglected fields and piles of stones that had once been houses. It was picturesque but sad, and we grieved for the community's loss of the certainties of lake life.

'You see, Hil, this was once a thriving community, but now it has declined into poverty, when faced with globalisation.' I was not very sympathetic to Liz's approach to the world's woes. She liked to analyse, explain and then blame—usually some big 'ism', like capitalism. I became exhausted by Liz's description of the enormity of the world's problems and too worn out to be drawn into discussion.

That night we ate a large dinner by candlelight in the catamaran, moored by the village quayside. The village band came aboard, multi-tasking for the night as the catamaran dance band, and entertained us with music and dancing. At one point Mateo called us to the window, where he pointed out a file of villagers traipsing along a path. 'They're off to worship the Inca god of the earth,' he murmured confidentially.

Liz was up early next day and went for her morning walk along the same path. It led to some badly farmed fields. On her way back towards the catamaran for breakfast she passed the same villagers Mateo had pointed out the previous night.

'They weren't off to worship the Incan gods last night,' said Liz as she tucked into her porridge. 'They were on their way back from toiling fruitlessly in barren fields. Today they're off to slave away again,' she added triumphantly.

But I refused to bite. I preferred Mateo's story. Poor Lizzie, always trying to unearth some ghastly reality and shove it up people's noses. No one at the breakfast table wanted to know. I was more than happy with my own experience on Sun Island, even if it was a fantasy.

*

La Paz was our last port of call. La Paz is the highest capital city in the world and 64 per cent of the population of Bolivia live below the poverty line. As we hastened towards La Paz we first drove through El Alto, a town perched on the hill overlooking La Paz in the valley below. One million people lived in El Alto (about the same number as lived in La Paz), 30 per cent of them in abject poverty. There was no greenery; it was a dust bowl, with dirt tracks and ragged children. At any time I could imagine the inhabitants rising up, streaming down the mountain and entering La Paz, seeking work and justice and causing riots and revolution. The difference between La Paz and El Alto seemed, at first sight, stark.

We drove into the centre of La Paz, with its leafy streets and high-rise hotels, and the comparison was odious. We dropped our bags at the hotel and set out to walk the streets and get a flavour of Amerindian life. In La Paz, roughly 30 per cent of the people speak either Aymara or Quechua, making up a sizeable percentage of the city.

We wanted to find the Calle de las Brujas ('the Witches' Street') which was uphill from the historic San Francisco church. At first sight it looked like yet another cobblestone colonial street full of shops and stalls selling woven bags, hammocks and alpaca sweaters. But when we went behind the shopfronts we entered another world. Looking closely, we saw signs of the mysterious and ancient pulse of Bolivia. Burnt offerings, llama foetuses and dried frogs were for sale for Aymaran rituals. Llama foetuses were also sold for burial in the foundations of new buildings to bring luck. This ritual had to occur on the first Friday of the month. Most indigenous people in Bolivia believe in Pachamama, or Mother Earth, a hungry goddess who is a potent primitive force of nature and needs constant attention and care. On her special day of worship people make offerings of leaves of cocoa, cigars, walnuts and llama wool. They will even part with their guinea pigs, pictures of family members and images of Catholic saints as burnt sacrifices. They make rectangular tablets of sugar as offerings, each one with a symbol on it in the shape of a dollar bill, star, book, condor or even a house. And they toast the insatiable goddess with beer. There are an equally large number of people who believe in the Catholic Church but mostly manage to combine their faith with white magic, black magic or superstition, call it what you will.

'Here's the perfect potion for you, Hilly—some lovely powdered dog's tongue which you could add to your next lover's food to make him loyal to you.'

'Lovers are a thing of the past, Liz, more's the pity. What I need is a potion for my knees.'

We saw shamans there too. In pre-Catholic Andean culture they were intermediaries for good between humans and the gods but, with the rise of Catholicism, shamans were now frequently associated with the devil and witchcraft and could as easily destroy your wellbeing and your business as restore you to health.

Finally we found Sofía, tiny and only nineteen. She sold small figures of condors promising a good trip, amulets of the Inca sun to bring energy, and desiccated frogs for good luck. She didn't see herself as a witch, but as a helper. She did a brisk trade in small charms, which appealed to tourists more than a canister of herbs, a large statue of an Aymara god or the dried llama foetus hanging over her head. Liz and I couldn't leave without a memento and Sofía insisted on selling Liz a packet of the herb tyanthus. She assured her that it was an aphrodisiac and would give both her partner and herself sexual potency. Liz didn't like to disabuse her of this notion. For me there was a bottle of the sweet-smelling essence of *posanga*, which she said would bring me good luck. I wonder if she knew that after six months I would get my insurance claim from the Lima incident back in full.

On our return to the hotel we noticed a parade marching past and asked the concierge what was going on. Not one member of the hotel staff had a clue what the festivity was about. In the middle of the road on a grassy verge, jammed between a lolly stall and a souvenir seller, a woman had set up a stand and was displaying her paintings. There was one landscape which had real quality, I thought: a stretch of poor country road with fir trees clumped together, a dirt foreground with boulders and a wall and nondescript building in the background. No people. It would have been depressing were it not for the sky, which was azure blue with large fluffy clouds scudding past. I asked her how much it was and paid what she asked. She looked surprised at such an easy sale; I asked if she was the artist. She shyly said, '*Sí.*' I tried to ask her where she had written her signature but I had lost confidence in my Spanish so suggested in mime that she write her name on the back of the picture since I could see that she had not signed it. Once she had added her signature, she smiled and looked really pleased and it seemed as if for the first time she was taking pride in her creativity. It was a poignant moment—small but significant. The picture hangs in my living room, a vivid reminder of a poor but proud country and a living memory of a magnificent holiday.

At El Alto International Airport, we planned to go our separate ways, Liz to London, me to Sydney. As we said our goodbyes, Liz declared, 'This holiday has been a Hinge Moment in our travelling relationship, don't you think?'

I hesitated, not sure what she meant. Liz saw that I was looking a bit anxious and smiled at me. 'I think we've come through the High Challenges, including the Andean ones, with flying colours.'

'I agree,' I replied.

3

A disgracefully huge holiday in Southern Africa

Liz emailed me:

> Why don't you come to South Africa? What are you
> doing?

She was heading there for a nephew's wedding and was wondering what she would do when the 'jollifications' were over. All the other guests seemed to have plans and no one seemed to be springing up with an invitation for her to join them.

I emailed back:

> Great idea. I've been wanting to go back there for years.

Her reply came quickly:

> What on earth for? I've never thought of South Africa
> as being a country which really beckoned. Beaches
> and buffaloes, that's all there is, for goodness sake.
> Apart from a political history so hideous that only a
> committed humanitarian would even want to think
> about it. If it weren't for the wedding, I wouldn't set
> foot there.

Liz was staying in Ireland at the time, where emailing was a hassle—it was cold, too, and she was quick to tell me that sitting under the stairs plugged into an ancient phone held little attraction for her. I persevered, though, getting very excited and pestering her for dates—did she have any particular places she wanted to visit, or sights she wanted to see?

All I got was a brief reply:

> I'm sure you'll organise it perfectly.

I had met a *simpatica* American called Clara on a trip to Antarctica the previous year, during which she and I spent happy hours outdoing each other with descriptions of our latest travel adventures. I was particularly enthralled by her romantic description of a safari camp near the Kruger National Park lit entirely by lanterns. Clara had relied on a US travel agent called Bart who really knew his Africa. Instinct told me that I was getting good advice from Clara and I made a note of Bart's email address. I love an expert.

When silence from Liz greeted my persistent questions I decided to press on without her input. I emailed Bart in the United States and he and I were in almost daily contact for weeks, working out a Huge Fantastical Holiday. No matter that he lived in America, the emails and phone calls flew across the globe—it was as if Thomas Cook had got hold of David Livingstone. Bart and I finally decided on a thirty-three-page itinerary, which I sent to Liz. It was so long that the printer she was using ran out of paper and her host was furious.

She emailed back:

> A holiday indeed, it's an assault course! Do you realise
> we will be travelling for six weeks during which we will

be visiting twenty or so places, none of which we will stay in for more than three days, and many for a single night. And no less than eight safaris. Really, Hilly. I'm speechless. I can hardly read the text it's so closely packed and most of the places I've never heard of and haven't a clue where they are. It had better be good: it's going to cost me the best part of a year's pension!

My covering email encouraged her to change anything she didn't like and to suggest any additions:

But let me know quickly because Bart my heavenly 'expert' will need to book everything in the next week to make sure we get the small plane connections.

Again, Liz was quick to get back to me:

I've tried to relate your journey to my atlases which are all pre second world war. The countries are coloured pink and have old fashioned English names like Rhodesia. It reminds me of my stamp collecting days which is reassuring. It's freezing here: I'm going to take the dog for a walk.

I sensed she was not a happy person. Fortunately her tone changed with the arrival of a second email.

The dog and I have just walked over the fields. A few birds flitted across the relentlessly grey sky, nothing moved, the trees were bare and the grass was scant. Biff sniffed madly among some pathetic remains of bracken and brambles, a rabbit came out startled, its eyes round with fear, dog and rabbit looked at each other. I looked

at them. It was a practice run for all that animal
watching we'll be doing on the holiday.

It's incredible to think that in a month you and
I will be plunged into a pulsating world of excessive
animal and plant life, wandering through lush forests
and savannah land. And with the heat of the sun to
cap it off. How did you come up with this amazing
marathon? It all looks fab. Oh, by the way, I'd like to
see Sun City while we're at it—it's on the way.'

I flew into Cape Town two days before Liz was due to arrive. I had
booked us into a house in Camps Bay, overlooking the beach,
which was lined with palm trees and glitzy restaurants. It reminded
me of Sydney's northern beaches. By contrast, nothing really
prepares you for Table Mountain, which rises up from sheer cliffs
and dominates, shelters and infuses every moment you spend in
the city. I could hardly wait to get to its flat top and did so almost
immediately—by cable car, of course. Up there the views were
breathtaking: to the south and west the sea, to the north and east an
endless, pastel-tinted countryside rolling on and on into infinity.

The next day I wanted to visit the Khayelitsha township, forty
minutes outside Cape Town. It is the home of a million black
South Africans who live there in poverty. The housing is atrocious,
mostly lean-tos made of tin. Unemployment is widespread and
AIDS and other diseases go largely unchecked. I visited a primary
school: the children were on their best behaviour. They looked so
clean and neat in their school uniforms as they sang their school
song for us. How did their parents keep their uniforms so clean
when the water was putrid and dust swirled like a willy-willy
round their shacks? I felt quite choked up as I wondered what

additional deprivations their parents had suffered to make sure their children were looking 'just right' for the tourists. It was impossible to reconcile Khayelitsha with the prosperous life being lived in Cape Town itself, a mere thirty-five kilometres away. My guidebook did not even mention the township, although if you do your research, guided tours are now on offer and one enterprising resident even offered bed and breakfast in her shack. As Nadine Gordimer observed, 'Being a tourist in South Africa is like having a picnic in a beautiful graveyard.' I came away reeling.

That evening I watched the local news on television and phoned Liz.

'You're really missing out—there's a large-scale power cut here. None of the restaurants can serve hot food, a Dutch tourist has fallen off Table Mountain, an American has been knifed in the art gallery and a tourist helicopter has crash-landed at Cape Point. That's in one day. Come quickly!'

And the very next day she did, as planned.

We hadn't seen each other for over a year, not since the South American holiday. In a strange way our meeting again now in South Africa was just like that meeting in Sydney with Miranda— long-lost friends getting on like a house on fire. We chatted and screamed with laughter about nothing at all.

'Guess what, Hilly—when I arrived they took me straight from the airport to a frock shop and poured me into a "smart" outfit. You see, I was required to read a lesson at the wedding ceremony.'

My mind boggled—was I hearing correctly? Liz dressed sedately, in a church, standing at the pulpit reading from the Bible. Amazing.

I thought we should celebrate her arrival by booking tickets for *Umoja* ('The Spirit of Togetherness'), an all-black hit musical that was playing a return season in Cape Town after touring the world for several years to sold-out audiences. *Umoja* was the creation of two long-time friends, Todd Twala and Thembi Nyandeni, who met growing up in the township of Soweto during the time of South African apartheid. *Umoja* told in dance and song the story of black South Africa, hideous stories of subjugation and cruelty, followed by the collapse of apartheid in 1994 and the dawning of democracy and hope. Todd and Thembi had travelled round the townships to audition underprivileged kids who they could train up to become professional performers. The show was an explosion of raw energy, sexual heat and athletic dancing to the beat of the African drums. The infectious rhythms brought Liz and me to our feet, jitterbugging up and down the aisle. The show was as ebullient and high voltage as I imagine it must have been on the opening night. Liz, who normally only likes Opera, was on cloud nine and she reached a frenzy of excitement when the glistening male gumboot dancers advanced down the aisle towards her, feet pounding, beaming from ear to ear, and abs pulsating as their sweat sprayed like a sprinkler around her. But Liz was not to be outdone; she shimmied seductively round the gumboots and burst into a faux cancan to the amazement of the boys! It was the perfect launching pad for our African adventure. I bought the CD afterwards, and we played it whenever we found a CD player as we continued our journey through South Africa.

Bart had arranged for us to be driven through the Cape winelands, stopping off at Franschhoek to sample the fine wine and cuisine. This area had been settled and developed three hundred years ago by the Huguenot settlers. For miles and miles over gently folding mountain slopes there was hardly a grape out of place. We stopped at two of the more than 360 wineries in the area. The buildings were gracious, Dutch-gabled and oozing old-world charm.

In the evening we reached Franschhoek, a very 'bijou' town cupped by the surrounding hills, and with more tourists than residents, or so it seemed. Liz took off to check out the information centre and returned with warnings that it was not safe to walk the streets at night. Our hotel was a haven and we had picked the perfect night to stay; an eight-course tasting event with matching wine had been scheduled for the evening of our arrival. The sommelier had picked his favourite wines from South Africa and around the world—La Motte shiraz, Stony Brook semillon and Cabrière's Pierre Jourdan Blanc de Blancs. We also tried the Boschendal shiraz—they were all fabulous. Then came the dinner. Again Liz egged me on, going for the wild game tapas of warthog and wildebeest while I tried the springbok and impala. I remember also choosing a chicken breast on a lemongrass skewer, served with creamy yellow polenta and slivered almonds, marmalade and thyme butter; Liz more cleverly chose fresh kingklip with orange-scented barley pilaf, pineapple salsa and a cumin paprika cream sauce. I can't remember the puds but know that we tried them all.

So overexcited did we become that by the end of the night we were both completely drunk. We left the restaurant, tottered into the garden and arm-in-arm fell into the fish pond. Squealing at the sensation of slug-like goldfish swimming between our legs, we grabbed the hands of burly security guards who unceremoniously pulled us out and escorted us mortified and dripping to our room. I spent the next half-hour picking green weed out of my hair while Liz laughed loudly.

'For God's sake, be quiet, Liz—the walls are paper thin. Any minute now we'll be thrown out.'

Before we set out on our Safari Extravaganza we flew to East London, where Bart's colleague and representative, Kutz, met us at the airport. Kutz was short and stocky, a member of the Xhosa, a tribe speaking Bantu and living in south-east Africa. He had formerly been employed by the local government tourist board, but had recently set up his own tourist agency to concentrate on tailor-made local cultural tours. The Eastern Cape had not yet been overrun by tourists, so when Bart suggested that we might like to take one of Kutz's tours, we both thought, *Perfect.*

East London was busy and clogged with traffic and seemed down at heel. Kutz proudly pointed out a Mercedes-Benz factory. 'A proper working town with no frills,' Liz commented. It was very hot in Kutz's immaculate but shabby van, but eventually we were able to leave East London behind and sped across Xhosa land towards the Mgwali cultural village, where I hoped to see some local craft. As we bounced over the potholes and stopped for the sheep we were able to get a feel for the vast African continent—the low, rolling grasslands, with hills and valleys disappearing into the distance beneath a cloudless blue sky. Kutz filled us in on the history of the area. He told us in vivid detail about the nine frontier wars fought between the Xhosa, the Boers and the British. The ghastly Brits had finally beaten the valiant Xhosa and called the area, in their insensitive way, British Kaffraria. Liz listened to him completely rapt, particularly when we sped past one town where she saw a rundown barracks building with 'Mauser Sniper Rifles' embossed over the lintel. I confess to having fallen asleep, much to Liz's irritation. Kutz had apparently been looking quite anxious when he realised that fifty per cent of his tour party was fast asleep. Liz kneed me in the ribs several times.

'Wake up and take an interest,' she hissed.

I rallied as Kutz told us the story of a young Xhosa woman in 1857 who had a vision that the Xhosa people would be reunited with their spirit world if they destroyed their cattle and crops. This they did and then died in tens of thousands. As she listened to this tragic tale Liz had tears in her eyes. I feared that she was about to go into a huge decline; it seemed time for me to take over, after my earlier (sleeping) fall from grace. I tried to change the subject.

'How's your business going, Kutz?'

'Not many tourists come to the Eastern Cape,' he replied. 'They prefer to visit the Garden District—the coastal area running from Cape Town to Port Elizabeth.'

'That's very brave of you, setting up on your own after having a secure government job.'

'I love my country and its culture,' he said simply. 'And I want people to know about it.'

'Good on you,' I said, and then worried that I sounded patronising.

'We are heading for Mgwali village, which was one of the first converts to Christianity in South Africa,' Kutz said, back in role again as tour guide. 'When the Xhosa homeland Ciskei was set up, the white South African government wanted Mgwali village removed because it was a "black blot" in a white corridor which they wanted to retain. The people of Mgwali resisted and eventually won. Now it has been designated a cultural village and receives government funds to maintain and develop handicrafts and Xhosa traditions.'

After five hours' drive without a break we arrived at Mgwali, a group of scattered settlements consisting of small, brightly coloured cottages, some with thatched roofs. There was a large garden area around them, mostly filled with tall wild grass with the occasional brave flower trying to peep through.

Kutz pulled up and Liz bounded out, while I descended rather more gingerly. We both went into a flurry of hand-shaking with an eager group of ladies who were waiting to meet us on the outskirts of the village. They were led by the amply bosomed Tyhilelwa Bolana, a formidable force of nature and chairperson of Mgwali village. She stood next to us as her ladies busied themselves around us, smiling and laughing while we tried to repeat and memorise their names. Then, on cue from Tyhilelwa, they launched into a dancing-singing-swaying routine that could have used a proper director. We saw few signs of the ladies' natural spontaneity; Tyhilelwa had whipped them into an awkward ensemble for tourists. When the dance fizzled to a stop, Tyhilelwa led us to a fenced-off area that looked like the decaying remains of a once-hopeful aid project.

There was a large barn, falling apart, sheltering some vandalised tractors and vans. We were shown around a dusty room masquerading as a museum, but it was hard to summon up interest in the few yellowed photographs stuck on the wall and dreary artefacts of village life. We were then taken behind the 'museum' and ushered into an empty room, where a table was set for our village meal. Liz and I were seated while five or six of the women clustered around. Tyhilelwa stood beside Kutz watching over her ladies like a hawk as they spooned huge helpings of maize and potato onto our plates; all eyes were on us as we ate. Liz wolfed hers, while I pushed the maize around on my plate. As soon as I tactfully could, I nudged Kutz and we were finally able to escape with him without being impolite to the ladies.

Later Kutz asked us, 'Were you happy with your visit?' He was plainly worried, and with good reason. Bart had plans to send thirty American Baptist ladies to Kutz, who was to escort them to Mgwali and supervise their experience of actually living in the village. I worried about how Kutz's business and reputation would survive and took him gently to one side. 'I think you will have to have a word with Tyhilelwa; she will need to give her ladies more help and instruction. Americans are used to trips going like clockwork and to receiving a certain level of comfort: you'll need more craft for sale, well-sprung beds, locally made tablecloths, flowers and more variety in the food.'

Kutz's face fell.

'I know this is a tall order,' I said.

It was obvious Kutz sensed an uphill battle lay ahead—it was pioneering stuff and he was on his own. But he was a very determined person and was not going to give in without a fight. Between him and success stood the redoubtable Tyhilelwa. She was meant to be working with him, but she was ambitious and seemed to have her own agenda.

We rejoined Tyhilelwa and walked towards the festivities she had devised. She couldn't wait to tell us the story of her life. Tyhilelwa was thirty-six with three children from three different men. She had quickly cottoned on to the fact that 'culture' was the way out of poverty for herself and her whole family. While she had taken on responsibility for providing the 'cultural visits' for Kutz, she had also organised for herself a constant round of symposia and seminars to attend all around the country. She had grants coming out of her ears and was clearly a brilliant politician and, one imagined, utterly credible outside the village. But her powers of persuasion and leadership with the female villagers did not appear so successful. It seemed to me that the ladies resented Tyhilelwa. As she herself admitted, her bead-making and sewing classes were poorly attended and few of the women continued for any length of time. The next day we were shown their work and it was not up to scratch; even I was hard pressed to find anything to buy.

Tyhilelwa continued her story as we all walked to another part of the village to visit a traditional rondavel—this was a thatched roundhouse where everything took place: cooking, sleeping, sex, laughter and gossip. We burst in on a Saturday night 'hop': there was chatter and laughter and above all singing and dancing. It was a ladies' night and no men were invited. Liz couldn't wait to join in and was soon part of the fun. She whirled around like a dervish, whooping and clapping, gathering up the 'oldies' and insisting they danced with her. She outdanced them all and they finally collapsed exhausted like ninepins in a heap on the floor. During the breathless interval which followed, the women asked us a lot of questions about where we lived, our families and why we were travelling, and I in turn quizzed them about their lives. They were quick to tell us how treacherous their men were and how they felt trapped in the village and longed to get away. From time to time hens and dogs wandered in and chased each other around the mud-packed floor. A clutch of overtired children clung to their mothers' skirts, wanting food and attention.

Later, as we padded through the silent village, the moon smiled gently on us from a cloudless sky and guided our footsteps towards Tyhilelwa's house and into her sitting room, which was full of second-hand furniture covered with dust. It looked as if it had all been stored together in one room in case one day there might be a need for it. We squeezed past the chests of drawers to find two small beds. I tentatively asked Tyhilelwa where the bathroom was.

She did not respond, but when I asked her a second time she took me outside and pointed with a torch towards the vegie patch. She then wished us a good night and departed.

'Hilly, you're a nutter,' said Liz after she'd gone. 'The loo's a hole in the ground. You can't possibly use it in the middle of the night. You'd fall in. You'll have to use the bucket. It's at the bottom of the bed.'

Later that night I felt a sense of achievement as I peed into the bucket, waking Liz when the urine pinged as it hit the metal surface. No loo paper to be seen. I wondered how the thirty Baptist ladies would handle it.

Tyhilelwa's uncle was the bishop of the Bantu Church of Christ the King and there was a magnificent photograph of him hanging in our 'bedroom'. I imagined him relishing the moment as he gazed down on my bare bottom.

*

Kutz drove us the next day to bear witness to the stories of South Africa's recent political struggles. We were shown Steve Biko's grave in a cemetery on the outskirts of the town where he was born and placed a pebble on the grave in accordance with Xhosa custom. Kutz told us how Biko had risen suddenly to prominence when he led marches against the hated identity card system, and about his ignominious end, beaten and killed in police custody. We went to visit his simple house, which is now a national monument. A local came out to tell Kutz that Biko's brother had just died, and we read in his obituary the next day how much Steve owed to his elder brother for his radical ideas.

We drove across pure Xhosa countryside, a gently rolling, grass-covered landscape dotted with rondavels painted in cheerful colours. Kutz at one stage said we were passing through ex-President Mbeki's village and then, bursting with pride, announced that we were coming to Nelson Mandela's village. The field by his house had several marquees in it and was buzzing with activity. We stopped to investigate and were told that Mandela's favourite grandson was getting married. While Kutz hung back in deference, we tried to gain entrance, pleading the vast distance we had travelled in the hope of seeing the father of South Africa. A young woman smiled warmly and said, 'I'm so sorry, but I'm afraid that this is a private occasion. Where do you come from?'

'Australia.'

'You have come a very long way . . . You are most welcome to South Africa. I wish you a contented holiday.'

It's amazing how swiftly good manners disarm even the most obdurate. By way of compensation Kutz took us straight to the Nelson Mandela Museum, where we saw a comprehensive record and testimony to his ceaseless struggle against the apartheid regime. It was all there, his twenty-seven years on Robben Island, his dramatic release, his appointment as head of state and now as world statesman.

'He's a once-in-a-lifetime miracle,' I said and Liz nodded.

Our few days with Kutz had welded us into a team, so much so that we were sad to say goodbye. Just before he delivered us to the airport, Kutz took a small detour to give us coffee at his home, where we met his wife and small boys. It was such a gesture of friendship. All too soon, though, it was time to go, and we headed off to catch our flight.

'Goodbye, and all the best of luck with your business and the Baptists,' I said, shaking his hand warmly.

'I hope you will remember my Xhosa culture,' said Kutz.

'We certainly will,' Liz and I chorused.

Kutz stayed there, waving, right till the last moment, when we disappeared through security.

*

It was now safari time, and the moment I had been waiting for, with camera equipment poised and a newly acquired long lens for animal close-ups. Bart had convinced me that eight safaris were quite in order. 'Every safari will be different,' he said. 'The terrain changes and invites different animals and birds.'

We started out with a safari camp next door to the Kruger National Park.

'Kruger covers two million acres and is one of the largest game reserves in the world. It has 147 species of animals and mammals,' Liz told me as we flew out of East London. 'Isn't it amazing to think that in the nineteenth century hunters came to Kruger to kill the "big five"—lion, rhinoceros, buffalo, leopard and elephant— and now here we are coming not to kill them but to follow their footprints in a four-wheel drive and gawp at them. Listen to this, Hilly—' Liz pulled out her notes and read: '*My joy may therefore be imagined when I saw the most superb specimen that I have ever seen lying dead before me.* This,' she said, 'was written by a chap called F.C. Selous, describing, in 1870, his reaction to killing one of the last white rhinoceroses.'

'I've got my doubts that anything has really changed,' I said. 'We talk about conservation, but people's bloodlust remains, I fear.'

Liz droned on, fact after fact, figure after figure, but I tuned out, and thought instead about all the new varieties of food I had read about that we were going to try on safari. I was even keen to sample the starchy porridge known as *fufu*, if only for the name, and I wondered whether I would like the flavour of red palm fruit oil, which I had been assured was full of beta-carotene and antioxidants.

The oil lantern and candlelit Umlani camp I had heard about from Clara consisted of a dozen or so thatched chalets joined by tiny paths to a central dining room with an observation deck overlooking a dry riverbed. There were no fences or boundaries. A small swimming pool had been carved out of rock, which in drought conditions attracted elephants, who would wander into the camp in search of water.

Our hosts, Kathy and Brian, had left high-powered jobs in Johannesburg to run the camp. With their African chef, Willie, they devised wonderful meals, including a wild venison curry and a delicious West African prawn soup with tamarind, lime, ginger and chilli. I got to know Willie and asked him if he could cook us one of his favourite South African dishes. He decided on *bobotie*, which he and his wife, Sarah, ate at home—a delicious dish of minced meat baked with an egg-and-milk mixture on top. *Bobotie* probably originated in Indonesia, during colonial times, but was brought to South Africa in the seventeenth century, and there are many variations. Willie made a simple version but he added mango chutney and berry spices, which gave it a sweet-and-savoury flavour. Sarah served Willie's *bobotie* with pride in a silver dish on our second night at Umlani. I thought it would be fun when I returned home to serve the same dish stuffed inside a large cooked pumpkin. I would accompany it with *blatjang*, a fruity, jam-like condiment that is often served alongside *bobotie* in South Africa, as well as, or instead of, chutney.

* * * * *

Bobotie

Serves 4

Ingredients

2 slices wholemeal bread

2 onions, chopped

25 g butter

2 garlic cloves, crushed

1 kg lean minced beef

4 tbs madras curry paste (less if you don't like spicy food)

1 tsp dried mixed herbs

3 cloves

1 tsp allspice

2 tbs cranberry or mango chutney

3 tbs sultanas

6 bay leaves

1 large pumpkin (par-cooked separately)

150 ml full-cream milk

1 large tub of yoghurt

2 large eggs

grated pecorino cheese, to taste

blatjang, to serve (best prepared at least one day in advance)

Preparation

1. Heat oven to 180°C. Pour cold water over the bread and set aside to soak.

2. Fry onions in the butter, stirring regularly for 10 minutes until they are soft and starting to colour.

3. Add the garlic and beef and stir well, until it changes colour.

4. Stir in the curry paste, herbs, spices, chutney (but not the *blatjang*), sultanas and 2 of the bay leaves with 1 tsp salt and plenty of ground black pepper.
5. Cover and simmer for 10 minutes.
6. Squeeze the water from the bread, then beat into the meat mixture until well blended.
7. Tip into an oval ovenproof dish. Press the mixture down well and smooth the top.
8. Beat the milk, yoghurt, eggs and pecorino cheese with seasoning, then spoon over the meat.
9. Top with the remaining bay leaves and bake for 20 minutes.
10. Spoon the mixture into the par-cooked pumpkin and bake for half an hour.
11. Serve with *blatjang*.

* * * * *

Blatjang
Makes 3 jars

Ingredients

250 g dried apricots, chopped

250 g seedless raisins

3 litres grape (wine or cider) vinegar

4 large onions, finely chopped

4 cloves garlic, crushed

500 g brown sugar

200 g flaked almonds

2 tbs salt

3 tbs ground ginger

2 tbs ground coriander

2 tbs mustard seeds

2 tsp chilli powder

Preparation

1. Combine the apricots, raisins and vinegar in a 5-litre saucepan. Soak overnight to plump the fruit. Alternatively, if time is tight, simply cover, bring to the boil and set aside for about 2 hours.

2. Add the remaining ingredients, and cook uncovered over medium heat, stirring occasionally at first, then constantly towards the end of the cooking time, until the *blatjang* has reduced to about one-third, and is beautifully thick. It should take 1½–2 hours. To know when it is ready for bottling, test the consistency by putting a little in the freezer to cool.

3. Pour into hot, sterilised jars. Seal and store in a cool, dark cupboard for up to 3 months.

* * * * *

After dinner that night there was a strange howling noise, which was promptly identified as a wild dog. Brian told us excitedly that there were only 247 of these dogs left in the park and that we should leave immediately to find it. We all made for the four-wheel drive and Kathy sat on a special seat on the bonnet, sweeping the bush on either side with a huge flashlight. Impala stared at us, paralysed by the light, a couple of zebras bounded out of the way and, best of all, a porcupine waddled along in front of us, quills quivering. We never found the wild dog, but our hearts pumped fiercely in the blackness of the night as we cascaded through mud, swerved to avoid an unidentified shadow and zoomed along unseen tracks, feeling the scrutiny of all the shining eyes staring at us in the darkness.

We were back in our chalet when a thunderstorm erupted and huge rains fell; the river next morning was a raging torrent and an old bull elephant had come down to drink. Brian told us that the old fellow had retired from herd duties and was well on his way to wearing out his sixth and last set of teeth, after which, Brian said, 'the poor old boy will die of starvation'.

The floodwaters had also attracted a cacophony of birds—hornbeams, African snow eagles, red-breasted rollers, not to mention the dread vultures flying menacingly overhead. My long lens was in constant use.

It took two plane rides and a four-wheel drive to get us to our next safari in the Okavango Delta in Botswana. The delta is one of the world's largest inland water systems and over 200,000 animals and mammals live there in largely unspoilt wilderness.

We stayed at three different camps in Botswana; each one mimicked the set-up at Umlani (except for the oil lanterns). There were beautifully appointed chalets linked by walkways to a central pod that housed a dining and lounging area. There were no locks on the doors of our chalets, no phones, no television and few reminders of the world outside. There was always an outdoor shower open to the elements, which I loved, but Liz declined to use. She was not, as I had discovered, keen on exposing naked flesh, even to monkeys.

The daily routine of the camps was remarkably similar, starting with an early morning safari from six to eight, looking for 'the big five', then breakfast and rest. Sometimes there was a safari after lunch, although the heat of the day was not the best time for seeing animals; they wisely stayed deep in the bush in the shade. The safari at dusk was the most fruitful—the animals were out having a ramble or looking for food—and the evening meal was the highlight of the day.

The camps were similar in format, but each had a flavour which depended on the personalities of the people in charge and the mix of animals that surrounded them. At Chitabe in Botswana we were looked after by some real charmers. One of them, Moise, told us, 'My name means "Oh dear, not another girl" in Botswanese.' She was eighth in the family, and they never managed a boy.

On our first morning at Chitabe, Jimmy, our guide, suggested a ride in a *mokoro*, a wooden dugout canoe, which he propelled through the thick reeds of the flooded river with a pole. There was an uneasy silence broken only by the slurp of the water and the swish of the reeds as the boat passed through.

'Keep your eyes open for hippos,' said Jimmy. 'If we run into one, it'll overturn the boat.'

Perfect, I thought as I scanned the surface, very conscious that the tall reeds would conceal all but the largest hippo. Liz sat frozen in her seat.

'There—see—TWO of them!' called Jimmy, and I made out two large, ugly shapes only three lengths of a *mokoro* away! (*This is IT*, I thought, *we've had it*—and imagined the two of us thrown into the water and the huge jaws of one hippo closing on my thighs while the other swallowed a screaming Liz.) Jimmy, meantime, calmly angled our boat away and we passed the hippos, who were now no more than sixty centimetres from the boat, but apparently unmoved by our presence.

'Are they friends of yours?' I spluttered. Jimmy laughed. It was his job to make sure that all the tourists got a 'scare' so that they had dinner party conversation for the next year in the withdrawing rooms of Kensington.

Savute, our next camp, produced an elephant family with two babies barely able to totter to their feet. The mother elephant appeared in our path, its ears flapping.

'Look, Hilly, babies, just for you,' shrilled Liz. 'Where's your long lens?'

'I'm hopeless, it's back in the cabin.'

But I was waiting for Mombo, which had been recommended as the best safari camp of them all. And it certainly was super-comfortable, and the food five-star. But there was no means of contacting anyone from our chalets except by blowing a foghorn and we were told not to leave our quarters until we were fetched.

I noticed a temporary piece of railing on one of the walkways and my fantasies took wing.

'Imagine this, Lizzie: a drunken old banker is lurching along the path, hears a snort from below, leans heavily against the rail and, weighing 140 kilos, breaks it and topples into the bush below. He calls for help, but the only response comes from a pair of hungry warthogs, eyes glinting, snuffling as they sniff his face, licking their chops and preparing for a top feed. How about that!'

At Mombo we met Bob and Bobbie, a middle-aged, recently married couple who were travelling the world on honeymoon. He was a retired businessman in his sixties; and elegant, younger Bobbie was a successful interior decorator. They were amusing, and we teamed up with them for the scouting trips. Setting out in our Land Rover we were confronted with the reality of bush life when we came upon a leopard spread-eagled along the branch of a tree, pulling pieces of flesh off a wretched impala impaled on the branch. He gnawed away, occasionally looking up and guarding his prey. He must have dragged the impala up the tree in the first place—it would have been heavy and a horrible sight. While Liz and Bobbie shuddered at the thought, I snapped away, feeling like a voyeur at a road accident. It was a strange, somewhat macabre scene, a group of Land Rovers containing tourists surrounding a tree observing a large spotted cat eating its dinner.

Our next safari camp was in the Serengeti National Park. We arrived on a dirt runway in a tiny plane which had to brake abruptly to avoid a couple of zebras who seemed disinclined to move their fat bottoms. Our guide, Joseph, wanted to get going rapidly as he knew there were lions to be seen nearby. We found a whole pride lying under a tree, panting and swishing the flies off their mangy coats with their tails. They were very near our camp, which had no fences or boundaries: we became used to being warned not to come out at night. Our cabin was a long way from the main buildings.

The camp was on the banks of a small river which was covered in bright green weed. Camouflaged beneath the weed we spotted at least twenty hippopotami, who peered at us through tiny pinhead eyes. Occasionally they would raise their heads above the water, open their enormous mouths very slowly and produce a succession of sneezes and grunts before shaking their heads and disappearing again beneath the surface. In the evening they would wend their way downstream and lever themselves up onto the bank, where they would spend the night munching enormous quantities of grass. Full to bursting, next day they lurched back down into the river again, burping with delight at the thought of another day to be gently whiled away in the cool waters.

During our first morning game drive, Joseph gave us the facts.

'Serengeti National Park is very big—thirteen thousand square kilometres. There are two million wildebeest, half a million Thomson's gazelles and a quarter of a million zebras living freely. It is one of the wonders of the natural world.'

He was right—we saw buffalo, zebras and wildebeest spread out across the savannah as far as the eye could see. It was weird—I kept blinking and expecting to see cows and sheep. But no, we were in Africa, watching buffalo and zebra grazing. They were hypnotic and mesmerising as they moved methodically from one patch of grass to the next, their great jaws masticating the grass, savouring each mouthful.

That evening Joseph took us for a drive and noticed vultures circling. He made for the spot and pulled up abruptly beside a repellent sight. A gazelle was lying on the ground, its stomach being torn open by an ugly vulture. The lappet-faced vulture is the only vulture with a beak strong enough to tear flesh, so it was having first go while other birds looked on ghoulishly. There was something grimly compelling about the sight of vultures in the trees looking on (not entirely unlike us watching the leopard earlier), and still more standing by, sometimes moving closer with outstretched wings, uttering terrible cries. Beyond the vultures were the marabou storks, hideous birds with big beaks and red necks. All of them scavengers. Joseph pointed to a wire attached to the gazelle's leg. It had been trapped by a poacher, but the vultures had got there first. It was a clear reminder that nature is savage, and not to be soppy and sentimental.

Sensing that we might like a cheerier change of scene, the following day Joseph suggested that we visit Lake Victoria. It was two hours away and we stopped on the way at a small fishing village beside the lake.

'This is a new village; the old one was drowned ten years ago,' Joseph told us.

Fishermen were leaving their dhows, taking the catch to the village and selling it under the trees to a crowd of locals. Nearby an orderly queue of cattle waited for their turn to drink at the water's edge. We wandered around the village and into the only shop, which was owned by a man named Pastory China, who sold cards and pictures of village life spiced up with supernatural images. He turned out to be a teacher from a nearby primary school and actually painted the pictures himself. We were very impressed and we both bought a picture. Pastory obviously hadn't had a big sale for many months and when I asked for some cards as well he immediately gave them to me as a gift.

'You have already paid a lot,' he said.

As he wrapped my picture in newspaper his biro accidentally slipped and made a mark in the blue sky of the painting. Without a pause, he flattened the painting out and, picking up the biro again, he drew a bird flying in the sky over the offending spot. I liked the picture all the more for this unique feature.

That night back at our camp we dined on chicken piri piri with a West African bean cake called *moy moy*, which is particularly delicious when sliced and pan-fried on each side until crisp and golden, then eaten under gleaming stars, listening to the distant roar of the lions.

At the end of the meal we had a two-grappa nightcap and wandered back to our tent singing a full-throated version of 'Danny Boy' and urging Bruno, the houseboy, who was escorting us, to join in. No luck there.

We crawled into our swags and I covered myself with insect repellent. Peace descended. Sometime later Liz nudged me.

'Can you hear that snuffling noise, Hilly?' she said, her voice quavering.

'Yes, I can.' I got up and peered out of the small window on the side of the tent.

'*Wow!* There's a *lion* outside the tent, Liz. I can see him clearly.'

'*What?*' Liz sat bolt upright.

'He's scuffling and digging near the tent pole. I reckon he's drooling at the thought of the scrumptious feast that awaits him only centimetres away.'

'You're not serious, Hilly?'

'Certainly am.'

'What shall we do?' Liz's voice was a high, parched whisper.

'Say your prayers and go to sleep, I suggest.'

'You're such a nightmare, Hilly.'

Liz had finally decided that I was joking. I screamed with laughter; Liz joined in weakly. Both of us gradually settled down again. After ten minutes or so the snuffling started again, this time louder, nearer and more urgent.

'Ignore it, Liz, there's nothing we can do. Go to sleep. You don't have to worry, I'll be taken first. I'm nearer the tent flap.'

'I never know when you're being serious, Hilly . . .'

'That's the general idea, dear girl.'

*

By the time we had finished our safaris I had taken over a thousand photographs and was looking forward to Sun City, which is a vast casino and over-the-top luxury resort, two hours' drive from Johannesburg. I would be able to download my photographs onto the computer while Liz gorged on the sights. We had been told to look out for the Valley of Waves, which boasted a huge man-made wave for would-be surfers, tantalisingly described as

95

'an adrenalin junkie's fix'. Liz took off immediately to explore this phenomenon.

'I bit off rather more than I could chew in the Roaring Lagoon,' she said on return. 'There's no way you could do it, Hilly. You're so unfit and fat, you would have drowned. The first thing I knew was a warning siren sounding over the loudspeaker. Before I could think of running away, a wave over a metre high grabbed me, turned me upside down and pounded towards the beach at thirty-five kilometres an hour, dragging me along under water and dumping me and a hundred screaming children on the sand. We swallowed gallons of water and were gasping for breath. Terrifying.'

Despite this ordeal Liz had soon recovered and was off again to check out whether Sun City's brochure's boast that it was 'more like a mini city than a theme park' was true.

On her return I bombarded her with complaints about the place being decidedly decadent, not a patch on Las Vegas, and grubby.

'How would you know?' said Liz. 'You haven't left the room.'

'I can smell the bedroom carpet reeking of stale smoke and can imagine the wine spillage, hastily cleaned and sprayed with the cheap scent of tropical flowers.'

Liz was full of a story about a woman she had talked to, looking over the back fence of the compound. The woman told Liz that she worked from six in the morning until six at night for a pitiful wage and then had to pay forty rand to return to her township, which was two hours away. She had two sick children, her husband was out of work due to injury at the factory and she had no family living nearby who could help.

I couldn't wait to leave Sun City. I found it a joyless, greedy confection dreamed up by a multi-national conglomerate intent on pursuing every last dollar in profit. I couldn't even laugh at it, but I could see that Liz was disappointed by my negative reactions. After all, she had suggested it be included in our itinerary.

'You see, I'm a bit of a tourist and recreation buff,' she said.

'What does that mean?'

'Well, I've got these friends who are consultants in the tourism industry and I tend to look at visitor attractions like Sun City through their eyes.'

'And how did you view it, through their eyes?' I said.

'I saw it as a very successful place. You may not like it, but the people I spoke to were enjoying themselves no end. They loved the large range of facilities and things to do, and it was cheap for them.'

*

I have a friend who had recently visited Zanzibar and Lamu. She got my juices going by relating tales of beautiful nineteenth-century Stone Town, a UNESCO world heritage site. It was only a couple of plane rides to Zanzibar. My friend suggested that we book into the Emerson & Green Hotel, which had been carefully restored to echo the cool, dark interiors of the town's prosperous Arabic history and boasted antique furniture and hand-painted walls featuring flowering vines and peacocks.

Out in the streets it was a different matter. Hideous smells assaulted us, and many of the houses near the hotel were now decaying and barely habitable. One of the larger houses, with only its outer walls surviving, was stuffed with plastic bags bursting with household waste falling into the alleyway beneath. Mangy cats mewed, nibbled and tore at the grisly remains.

Music, we discovered, was very much a part of 'Zanzibarian' life and the Dhow Musical Academy in the refurbished Customs House was just along the seafront from the Mercury Restaurant, named after the rock star Freddy Mercury, who was born on the island. As you passed through the entrance of the music academy, sounds of Arabic instruments, the *oud* (a pear-shaped lute), the *daf* (oriental tambourine), the *kamanja* (violin), *ney* (bamboo flute) and *darbuka* (drums) wafted down into the courtyard and a caretaker sprang forward, eager to show us over the building. We talked to the students, who told us about their instruments, and about *taarab*, Zanzibar's most popular music. *Taarab* reflects the influences of many cultures, including Arab, Indian and Egyptian, and was first introduced to Zanzibar in 1870 by Sultan Seyyid Banghash, who brought Egyptian musicians to his court and sent a Zanzibari musician, Ibrahim Muhammed, to be trained in Cairo. On his return in 1905, Muhammed formed the Zanzibar Taarab Orchestra.

One of the teachers spoke about Bi Kidude, the 'Little Granny of Zanzibar', also known as the 'Queen of Taarab', who was born in the village of Mfagimaringo, the daughter of a coconut seller. Bi Kidude is now around ninety years old; when asked her age, she replies: 'I cannot say that I know myself, but my birth was at the time of the rupee.' (The rupee was introduced to Zanzibar in 1908.) She still sings occasionally and has achieved almost mythical status performing everything from cultural drumming through classic Zanzibari *taarab* to modern Tanzanian 'dansi' jazz.

We longed for Bi Kidude to join us the next evening on the roof of our hotel. Beneath the stars we listened contentedly to the gentle *taarab* singing of a graduate of the academy and ate a traditional meal. Liz started with *shorba bulur* (wheat soup), while I took the softer option of *supu ya kuku* (chicken soup). I went on to *mchuzi wa samaki* (a beautiful fish curry) and Liz tucked into a sweet-and-sour goat casserole, which she pronounced 'delicious'. We finished off with *tufaa* (apples with rambutan cream) for me and *kaimati* (sweet dumplings) for Liz. The air was balmy and the sun set in glowing oranges and yellows over the bay. A meal to remember.

*

We didn't give Lamu a fair go. There had been a mistake with our flight so we missed a day and only had one night on the island. The island had been popular in the sixties and there were still a few hippies hanging around in their old age. Liz befriended a few and spent time with them drinking coffee in the hotel.

We watched two obese Kenyan businessmen arrive at the jetty. They were dressed in shiny suits and white loafers, with a lot of gold around their fat necks, and they struggled to find their feet on land while the pilot tried to stop the motorboat from lurching wildly. 'They're certain to be developers and crooks,' said Liz. 'Lamu is fast becoming an up-market tourist destination and there are new condominiums going up all over the island.'

On our return journey the next day our friends the developers were seated in our six-seater plane. Both of them needed two seats each.

'See, Hil, ugly people making money out of Lamu.'

'Shush, Liz, I don't need an altercation with those two.'

They continued to talk on their mobiles after the pilot had asked that all electronic devices be turned off.

'I will not be leaving until the phones are off,' said the captain. Once we were airborne the thinner of the two awkwardly climbed into the co-pilot's seat, grabbed the pilot's earphones and continued an animated conversation with him for the remainder of the flight. As we taxied towards the terminal the two Kenyans were back on their mobiles and I distinctly heard one of them say, 'The cufflinks are with my secretary and can be collected any time.'

*

Bart had responded perfectly to my fantasies about Africa and never more so than when he talked about Namibia, sending me snippets from early travellers to this remote and desolate land and, in particular, its notorious Skeleton Coast. One of these travellers had written: 'A shudder, amounting almost to fear, overwhelmed me when Namibia's frightful desolation penetrated my consciousness. I imagined that death would be preferable to banishment in this country.'

Namibia sounded both exciting and romantic and I was determined to get there. I was also keen to go to the most northern tip of the country, just opposite Angola. I thought we would escape a lot of the tourists there. Tourists like the idea of travelling to places where there are no other tourists, in theory, but forget that the reason there aren't any other tourists is that the destination is hard to get to, and that it may have hidden dangers or discomforts. Nevertheless, I felt that we needed to run the extra mile—and it was the right decision. Namibia remains for me the most vivid memory of the whole trip, and the sensation of remoteness is a potent part of it.

We flew over bone-dry gravel plains bisected by petrified riverbeds; canyons carelessly gouged out of the earth. Land like this supported very few animals and plants and those that did live here had adapted impressively to cope with the harsh and waterless environment. We landed on a dirt strip and left without delay in a Land Rover across the desert; the journey took two hours. We were to have three days in a safari camp so remote that it took two days for the trucks with provisions to get there. Water was motored in every two days—it took four hours there and back to fetch it from the waterhole. The set-up was simple: a timbered main room with old wooden furniture and a long bare table where we had our meals. There were cabins dotted around among small sand dunes and tufts of grass. We were beside a dry riverbed, behind which rose a vast dune. It was supernaturally quiet; there were no people or villages, or even traces of people, for miles and miles around. Just us.

The camp was managed by Joel, a young 'whitie' from Windhoek. He had apparently once been taken to New York by an American visitor to the Skeleton Coast as a private chef and general bottle washer, and now had yearnings to open a bar there. Having sampled the high life he had hoped that his benefactor might finance the bar, but this had not come to pass and he had returned to the Skeleton Coast and was saving to open an up-market bar in Windhoek. Windhoek is the capital of Namibia, and tourism, he reckoned, was on the increase: the international airport, for example, handled 400,000 people a year and Brad and Angelina had helped to put it on the map. I wondered how many of the tourists stayed in Windhoek for more than a night—it seemed to be the transit point for other, more interesting places. But I kept my thoughts to myself, not wanting to dampen his enthusiasm.

Joel chose the menu and supervised Bluey, our black African chef, as he prepared our (mostly frozen) food, simply cooked and served by the staff, who quickly became friends. Joel was tense and driven, and we had to work hard to get him to relax, but once he had downed a few drinks he became calmer and exhibited a rather arch sense of humour. On the first night he and his team came with us for a walk along the dry riverbed. I suppose they thought we might get lost. There was a full moon and we climbed up the less steep side of the dune and stood on the top looking out at the midnight blue horizon stretching into infinity, the sky just a shade lighter than the dunes and twinkling with stars. The moon was shining brightly;

it was a miracle of beauty and peacefulness. We broke the silence with a yell as we followed Joel's lead and leapt into the air, landing squealing on our backsides, then slid down the other side of the dune on our bums, collapsing in giggles at the bottom.

Liz had studied dunes in the plane on the way to Namibia. '*The crests of dunes have clean knife edges to them,*' she read, '*and are often highlighted by a faint purple dusting of garnet sand. Dunes may be coloured by other minerals, so moving among them they can change colour slightly from yellow, through greys, greens, even to purple.*'

We went out with Kel, our guide, one day and noticed that sand dunes are the strangest things, shifting imperceptibly while the tiny grains of sand whistle in the wind as they rub up against each other. We threw ourselves against the slopes of sand, tentatively at first, but they were soft, warm and inviting—even magical. Kel fancied himself as an entertainer: he searched the smooth surface of the sand with careful exaggeration and then plunged his hand in and brought out a gecko. Kel, the prestidigitator. And then, to top that trick, he drove up the almost vertical face of one dune and, once at the top, careered at full speed down the other side to our accompanying shrieks of horror.

And then there was the 'roaring dune experience'. We stood on the top of a dune looking down, so far down that when we took off our shoes and tossed them to the bottom they looked like beetles scuttling around. Urged on by Kel, we took off, sliding down on our backsides, slowly at first, then faster and faster until we could hear deep rumbles erupting from the sand. We gleefully pretended the sounds came from our bottoms—huge flatulent farts slicing the silence.

Next day it was the turn of the Skeleton Coast to amaze us. Four hundred kilometres of untamed beach littered with the bones of whales, dolphins, innumerable fish and seals. The wind was wild and thunderous seas pounded the beach. It was hard to keep our balance. Gleaming, smelly seals (200,000 of them, Kel told us) shuffled, sunbathed and waddled as far as the eye could see both in and out of the water, and Kel raced the van along the beach beside them. We became hypnotised by the rhythmic pounding of the waves, the incessant howl of the wind and the intense glare of the sunlight. Kel set out chairs, a table and a picnic and we sat down to eat. We tried to believe that there were people and towns not too far away across the dunes but we knew there were not; we were the only human beings in this turmoil of sea, sky and air.

I say that there was no one but I discounted the Himbas, who lived not far from the airstrip—a tribe still clinging to a semblance of traditional life but increasingly buttressed by government hand-outs and tourist tips. We were taken with a Canadian couple to their village, which was little more than a stockade—with a plaited fence to keep out predators. Inside, at discreet intervals, there were very small thatched huts. We were taken into one where a naked woman was sitting by herself, very dignified, covered in ochre paste and dandling a baby on her lap. We whities sat uncomfortably on the floor, sweating profusely, and the Canadians launched into a series of inane questions: 'How do you get food?' 'Do your kids go to school?' 'Do you have a doctor?'

After a few awkward minutes we moved on to the next hut, where one of the Himba women showed us how the ochre paste was mixed. Liz could be contained no longer and rushed forward, lathering her face and arms with the paste. She then squatted beside the mother and chatted to her about how cool and pleasant the paste was. Of course, the Himba lady couldn't understand a word and looked uncomfortable but the Himba ladies looking on offered her no support. They simply collapsed in laughter. Although I was mortified at the time, I acknowledged later that Liz's strategy worked. The whole atmosphere in the camp relaxed and Liz became the Himbas' best friend. We then talked with the headman, who spoke good English, and told us that he had recently arranged a Himba wedding for an American couple. He described the party which followed as 'Plenty music, singing, dancing. Bridegroom paid price of two cows for ceremony.' Later we heard that the bride and groom had stayed at our camp and the bride intended to write an article for *Vanity Fair* entitled 'My Bridesmaids Were Topless'.

That evening Kel suggested we go out to see the sun set among the sand dunes. 'Fabulous idea,' we chorused. We drove out into the desert and Kel found the perfect spot, with a 360-degree view of dunes. Once the Land Rover's engine had stilled, we sat quietly looking out at miles and miles of nothingness. There was sand and more sand and no living creature to be seen, although our guide told us to look and listen carefully and after a few minutes he pointed. We followed the direction of his finger and there was a solitary deer so beautifully camouflaged that it was barely visible. It stood alert, ears twitching, poised to take off at the slightest sound. Kel also spotted a family of meerkats, whom we found difficult to see, their colour being the same as the sand. Finally, with the aid of binoculars, I was able to make them out clearly, the cutest small squirrel-like creatures with huge black eyes and pointed noses standing on tiptoe, bolt upright, miniature sentinels guarding their burrows and looking out for predators.

Our eyes drank in the sky above us, vast and all-encompassing, shadows of purple and deeper purple moving over the sand as the light faded. I got out my camera and tried for the millionth time to take the perfect sunset shot, so elusive and hard to capture with the changing colours and mood of the light.

Once the sun had finally set it got dark quickly and became cold as the wind whipped round our ankles. I suggested that it was time to go, but Liz was not happy.

'We can't leave now; we must enjoy this intense experience to the full.'

'Well, I'm freezing and it's nearly time for dinner,' I said, making for the Land Rover.

As we drove back to camp I chattered on about how many grains did we suppose there were in a single dune and wondered what we might be having for dinner. Liz was silent.

'You're very quiet,' I said.

Liz let fly. 'I can't believe that you could be so insensitive to the beauty of the dunes out there—how you could break the mood so easily and then lapse into banal chat. You talk about loving peace and quiet but when it's staring you in the face, you just want to take a photo and leave.'

'Well, if you wanted to stay you should have said so loud and clear and we would have stayed.'

'All you could think about was your next meal. Nothing would have induced you to stay.'

'That's not true,' I said, adding after a pause, 'You're probably right. It's true that I was cold and hungry.'

When we arrived back at camp, Liz got out of the van and marched towards the dining room in silence. I followed her. 'I'm sorry, Liz, I was insensitive.'

Liz ignored me; she didn't speak at all during the meal and hardly ate anything. As we walked back to our hut she said, 'It's no surprise. It's just you.'

Her comment was fair enough; I had trashed her moment in the dunes. I recognised that I am often so busy taking photographs that I forget to stop and allow the beauty of my surroundings to sink in. Too much living at one remove.

I didn't sleep much that night: were the cracks appearing in our relationship going to grow? I hoped I hadn't blown it. But mercifully the next day the storm seemed to have abated and Liz was her usual cheery self.

I was frankly amazed: Liz was behaving as though nothing at all had happened the night before—there had been no 'drama in the dunes'. But I was more than happy to follow her lead and leave the whole sorry affair well alone.

I realised later, much later, that Liz has a real horror of revealing her inmost feelings; in fact she maintains she has very few of them. So for her that night on the dunes, letting rip was a truly frightening event she wanted to obliterate from her mind as quickly as possible. That was why she returned to her usual cheery self the next morning. Thank goodness.

*

Our Huge Holiday Number Two was nearly over, and we were staying in the Saxon Hotel in Johannesburg before returning home. Strangely, the atmosphere in the hotel was almost as removed from the real world as the safari camps in the dunes of Namibia. Security was so intense that only a few people were able to penetrate the hotel, with the result that it was virtually empty. The staff were completely idle and stood around chatting, getting no practice in memorising orders or fulfilling the most basic requests. We sat near the swimming pool and attempted to order lunch. The still water arrived fizzy; the tomato juice became mango, and when we sent it back was replaced with orange; and my pumpkin soup turned up as a shellfish risotto.

The waiters looked on bewildered. Then one came forward with a bottle of French champagne in a bucket. 'What's this? Don't tell me the management are making a peace offering,' we chortled. The waiter pointed to a table on the other side of the pool. We looked in the direction he was indicating and there, to our amazement, were Bob and Bobbie, the American couple we had met in Botswana. We fell into each other's arms.

'I told Bob it couldn't be anyone but Hil and Liz,' said Bobbie, 'when we heard the gales of laughter.'

'Tell me, I just have to know,' I asked Bobbie, 'were you the Himba wedding couple?'

'Certainly were. It was swell. I even forgave them covering my white wedding dress with ochre!'

4

Time for reflection: fallout in Turkey

By now Liz and I had notched up ten countries and twenty-eight destinations. I had 5234 photographs to show for it and Liz had twenty-six articles printed in the *Karachi Evening Star*. I felt I still had a lot of catching up to do, even if it meant gorging on new experiences. Liz thought the speed of our travels was fun but disgraceful. She would have been happy enough to return to countries she had been to before and enjoy them again.

We didn't have much time to 'hang out' while we were travelling. We were always on the move from one place to the next; it was incredibly stimulating. We had barely enough time to wash our knickers. We were as naughty as we wished to be; we talked to any stranger we liked the look of, and if they turned out to be boring we knew we'd be leaving the next day. We hardly had time to talk to each other but, as Liz said after our first trip, she was glad I didn't Plague her with the Personal.

For differing reasons both Liz and I were wary of close relationships. This was not surprising in my case, since I was an only child and never knew my mother. She died six days after I was born. Maybe I grew up associating closeness with loss. My father remarried during the Second World War but I didn't live with him or my stepmother until I was eight. They both worked in London during the buzz bombs and decided that I should be kept as far away from them as possible, so I was evacuated to Cornwall with an elegant nanny called Jill Gill. She had coils of hair over her ears like a pilot's earphones and thought that living in Newquay, Cornwall, and looking after her old arthritic father, harbourmaster of the Newquay lifeboat, and me, was not where she was meant to be. She should be back in Hong Kong living with diplomatic expat families with little to do apart from organising embassy cocktail parties, ferrying children to and from school and bossing the servants around.

I was uprooted from her care when I was eight and went to live with my father and stepmother in London. The first thing my stepmother did was to cut off my long corkscrew curls, carefully engineered by Jill. I was blinded by tears and rage; it seemed such a betrayal of Jill's love and care.

Only twice during my childhood was my real mother ever mentioned at home. The first time was when I was fifteen, during the Christmas school holidays. I had spent my first term at Cheltenham Ladies College in Gloucestershire as a boarder. I hated it. So I spent the Christmas holidays crying every day. On the twenty-third day (I was fairly hoarse by this time with the effort of keeping the crying going!) my father mounted the stairs to my bedroom.

'What's up?' he asked.

'I don't want to go back to Cheltenham,' I replied.

'Why not?'

'I'm lonely there.'

My father looked at me but his expression was distant.

'When your mother was alive, we had two babies before you were born. They were both born dead. When you arrived, your mother died six days later.' He paused. 'She did manage to hold you and said you were "a sweet little thing".' There was another long pause. 'So, Hilary, I know what loneliness is.'

The tears in my eyes froze in their ducts and I felt the portcullis come down on my heart with a clang. I returned to Cheltenham without another word. It was the first time he had ever spoken to me about my mother and the first time I had heard the story about my two dead siblings.

The second time was on the occasion of my twenty-first birthday. I was preparing to go out for the evening with friends. My father knocked on my bedroom door, walked in and said, 'I think it's time for you to have this', and handed me a parcel wrapped in brown paper.

He stood there silently, which I took to be a cue for me to unwrap the parcel. Inside there was a box and, inside the box, tissue paper. I unwrapped the tissue and staring up at me was a sepia photograph of a smiling woman in her late thirties, sitting in a wood. Her smile was open and generous. I thought, *Good God, it's my mother*. With extreme awkwardness, I asked my father, 'Is that Mummy?' I found it incredibly difficult mouthing the word 'Mummy'.

'Yes,' he said.

I started to unwrap photographs of their wedding, a small box of jewellery which I took to be hers and finally a leather-bound book with an inscription on the front: *A.L. 1938*. I was totally numb by this time. I turned the pages and realised that the journal was written in my father's handwriting. It was his memories of my mother, and of their relationship together, written six weeks after her death, when his grief must have been at its sharpest and most profound—written as a gift to me, so that I would know her a little. The opening page read: *Aileen—for her daughter, Hilary Margaret Aileen Linstead.* Aileen was my mother's Christian name. I couldn't go on reading in front of him and I couldn't think of anything to say; there was silence. Finally, after what seemed like an eternity, I said, 'Thank you,' and he turned and left the room. He never mentioned my mother again.

*

Liz's childhood, by comparison, was as she said, 'extremely ordinary'. But, she added, 'Small towns breed small minds and give you tiny, if any, experiences at all. And my mother curtailed my life even further by imposing a domestic regime more reminiscent of a nineteenth-century workhouse than a modern twentieth-century existence. We would be up, dressed, washed and fed between 7.30 and 7.45 am. I was allowed to walk alone to school but it was back home to lunch—two courses eaten in eight-and-a-half minutes. Tea came at 4.30 pm, and supper was from 7.15 to 7.30 pm, and then bed at 8 pm. And this went on until I was sixteen. I didn't visit a cinema until I was nineteen.'

'What about friends?' I asked.

'They weren't encouraged, and I suppose when I finally rubbed up against people it was really exciting but also bewildering, because I had very few social skills at all. As my housemistress said in a school report, "Liz has an unfortunate manner", which led to all sorts of misunderstandings early on when I left my workhouse environment and entered the Big World of cities, where I was to spend all my life.

'I loved the *idea* of people,' Liz said, 'and would eagerly embrace them at first meeting but my "unfortunate manner" would put them off. So I learnt to restrain myself and I suppose in the end decided they were a bit of a waste of time. I decided, I suppose, on a Non-People Path.'

'But were there any bruising encounters with people, any traumatic occasions to set you on your Non-People Path?' I asked.

'Not that I remember,' she pondered. 'And people are so needy . . .' She eyed me fiercely. 'Nothing in my childhood prepared me for the neediness of people and my real inability to respond. I had no experience, so was unable to develop strategies to deal with it.'

I should have listened to Liz more carefully before suggesting that two old friends of mine join us on our trip to Turkey. My friends Robbie and Ron were easygoing and intrigued by the itinerary I had prepared. They were keen to meet Liz. 'She's a hoot, one out of the box,' I had told them, and then stopped short. It was impossible to describe Liz; they would have to see for themselves. And Liz was curious to meet them.

Liz had been to Istanbul thirty years earlier and had developed a crazy passion for the Ottomans, and I had forgotten that when Liz has an obsession she needs to share it with the world, whether the world is interested or not. She had already started burbling on to me about it before we left, even though I wasn't listening and was busy dreaming about the food forages that Robbie and I could go on in Turkey.

'Do you realise that the Ottoman Empire was the centre of interaction between the East and West for six centuries? Suleiman the Magnificent was extraordinary. His empire spanned three continents, controlling much of South-Eastern Europe, Western Asia and North Africa . . .' and on and on she went. She was outraged that I had only programmed four days in Istanbul before we took off for Cappadocia.

'We can't begin to do justice to Istanbul in four days,' she said, claiming my attention.

'True, but I think we should at least catch a glimpse of Cappadocia—I've heard it's extraordinary.'

We flew from London to Istanbul and got a taxi to the Yesil Ev Hotel to meet up with Robbie and Ron.

From the word go I could see we were in for trouble. Liz had scarcely shaken hands and exchanged pleasantries before she and Ron began a fierce discussion of Middle Eastern politics. Liz was not anxious to pursue the subject for long, though, as she swiftly decided that Ron was not sympathetic to the terrible and complex plight the Iraqi people were currently enduring in Baghdad as they waited—once again—for the inevitable invasion of their country by the United States.

'And how do you fit Saddam Hussein, a former ally of the United States and a sadistic Arab fascist, into this picture?' asked Ron. 'A man who regularly tortures and murders anyone who opposes his authority. You seem to have conveniently left him out.'

Ron was irritated by what he thought was a simplistic, cartoon version of history and treated Liz to a ten-minute rant about the horrors of Saddam Hussein. It became clear to me that this was a 'no go' topic as far as Liz was concerned and the two of them fell into a long, uncomfortable silence.

Liz got going again when she decided that Ron was totally ignorant about Turkey's great past and needed a lesson on the wonders of the Ottoman Empire. She plunged into one of her raves on the subject, words tumbling out of her mouth in a torrent. I called it 'Ottomania'. Ron listened politely, but I could see that Robbie was longing to get settled, unpack and have time to adjust to her surroundings.

'Our hotel used to be the imposing townhouse of a successful nineteenth-century Ottoman merchant, which gradually became a neglected ruin,' Liz told us. 'But now it's been transformed into a tasteful home-away-from-home for the "discerning" traveller. Most of the "must-see" monuments are close by, so the three of you can see them without being jostled by Real Life Istanbul.'

I thought Liz was being a shade provocative and patronising and that Robbie and Ron might be irritated, but they both kept their counsel. Ron is a brilliant production designer and cartoonist and the two of them had travelled all over the world when Ron was on location working on films, with Robbie acting as Ron's manager. Robbie loved spontaneous travel decisions and they both had a broad knowledge of the politics and history of Turkey.

Liz babbled on. 'It's changed so much—all for the worse. More traffic on the roads and the bazaar's become a shopping mall. It used to be so exciting, a mass of scurrying people buying and selling from thousands of stalls spilling out onto the cobbled alleyways, lit at night by flickering gaslight. It's lost its authenticity. But the most unpleasant transformation is around here—the Topkapı Palace, Blue Mosque and the Hagia Sophia area. These monuments have been humbled into a theme park. I can't believe that every-thing has been sanitised—newly laid cobbled streets, refurbished hotels, innocuous carpet bazaars and an endless retinue of tour buses disgorging insatiable, gawping tourists.'

I could see that Robbie wanted a break from the babble.

'We're as keen to find the authentic Istanbul as you are, Liz,' she said.

I stuck up for the hotel, which had been well restored and was very conveniently situated.

'You don't have to label me Insensitive Tourist just because I enjoy a measure of comfort,' I said. But Liz was hankering for the chaotic, raucous street scenes of thirty years ago and could not see past her own memories.

The first night, when it came time to decide where to go for the evening meal, we all seemed in agreement. None of us wanted 'international' food or 'tame' curries, we all wanted genuine Turkish nosh. Robbie is a fabulous cook and once ran her own restaurant. She has an encyclopaedic knowledge of food, so was the first to follow Liz down alleyways in search of a genuine Turkish meal. They found a café which looked perfect.

We ate mixed meze followed by *manti* (delicious stuffed pillows of a spicy meat mixture) with yoghurt and garlic, *kavurma* (a pork stew with veal liver and vegetables), *güveç* (another meat stew with olives and mushrooms) and *maqluba* (a lamb and eggplant dish)—all delicious. Robbie has managed to come up with her own version of *maqluba* for her friends in Sydney, drawing on her memories of our meal in Istanbul.

* * * * *

Robbie's Maqluba

Serves 4

Ingredients

> 3 large eggplants
> olive oil
> ¾ cup rice
> 1 onion
> 3 cloves garlic
> pinch thyme

a couple of large pinches of allspice

500 g lamb (left-over slow-cooked roast lamb is ideal;
     otherwise use cooked lamb mince)

50 g almonds, blanched in boiling water and skins removed

1½ cups beef stock

yoghurt and green salad, to serve

Preparation

1. Slice the eggplants the thickness of a little finger, brush them with olive oil and bake in moderate oven until lightly browned.

2. Soak the rice in water for about an hour.

3. Sauté the onion until soft, add finely chopped garlic, then thyme and allspice.

4. Layer the eggplant in a baking dish. Add a layer of meat, then sprinkle it with chopped almonds and onions. Repeat layers until you have used all the meat and eggplant.

5. Drain the rice and spread it over the top.

6. Pour over the meat stock, cover with a lid and bake in a moderate oven for about an hour.

7. Invert into an ovenproof dish and cook a further 10 minutes, until the rice is cooked through.

8. Add more beef stock if it seems dry. The proportions can be varied as long as there is enough stock to ensure it does not dry out.

9. Serve accompanied by yoghurt and a green salad.

* * * * *

Ron, once he had a good meal inside him, fired up and started to challenge Liz's 'Ottomania', bringing her into the twenty-first century by asking searching questions about human rights and the status of women in Turkey. I decided that as the mood was fast becoming prickly, the restaurant uncomfortable and the atmosphere not conducive to relaxed discussion, I suggested that we should move on for pudding. Liz agreed and dragged us up the hill in search of a café where she insisted she had eaten a delicious Turkish dessert called *kazandibi* thirty years ago. 'It's a Turkish version of a crème brûlée—much better, because they add pistachios and flavour it with rosewater,' she said.

'How on earth do you know that? I thought you weren't interested in food,' I said.

'Turkish food is an exception,' responded Liz.

We must have walked for a quarter of an hour before Liz located the dreary, uninviting café. It was hot and airless inside. Robbie tasted the *kazandibi* and pronounced it bland. 'Bland. What we should be trying is *aşure*. It's a wheat pudding which I've heard is delicious.'

'Next time, definitely,' I promised.

I leant over to Liz. 'Could you please bear in mind that Ron and I are not rock wallabies. We walk slowly and we don't go great distances. I'm not sure the pudding was worth the effort.'

Everyone was now tired and testy and it was obvious that Robbie and Ron wanted a break. Back at the hotel I decided to forestall further fallout with Liz. Before bed I suggested to her that she should listen more to what 'R and R' had to say.

'You'll have to ease up, Lizzie, and let R and R decide what we do for some of the time—there will have to be a bit of give and take or there'll be blood on the carpet before the first week is out.' I could see Liz was bewildered.

'I don't know what you're talking about. I listened all night to Robbie talking about food.'

'We all need a good night's sleep; hopefully, it will be better tomorrow,' I said, bringing the conversation to a full stop. As is so often the case, I could see both sides of the argument and only wished that Ron and Liz could accept each other's point of view. Having grown up in a family in which we never raised our voices and never indulged in fierce argument over dinner, I was unused to public spats and disliked them intensely. Of course, if it was me doing the shouting, it was fine, provided no one came back at me!

The next day Liz was up at dawn and darted down to the Bosphorus. She had put the chill of the previous evening behind her and was bubbling over with enthusiasm when she joined us. We were having a leisurely breakfast.

'Come on, we can't waste precious time in the hotel. There's a ferry going up the Bosphorus now. We must leave immediately.'

The three of us reluctantly abandoned our second cup of coffee and followed Liz, who was straining at the leash. Down at the quay the crowd was thick and Liz disappeared.

'Oh God, where's she gone now?' said Robbie.

'Here we are,' announced Liz, appearing moments later triumphantly brandishing tickets.

She led us through the melee up the footbridge to a ferry, which proved to be the wrong one—our ferry wasn't going for half an hour, and hadn't even arrived. Liz had not yet absorbed that Robbie and Ron did not like having their holiday pace dictated to them and I found myself in the unwelcome role of meat in the sandwich. But since I had suggested the group in the first place I felt obliged to explain my friends to each other and try to keep the peace.

I could see that Liz was really trying to be helpful.

'We'll have some coffee—real Turkish coffee,' she said, and led the way to one of the many busy stalls. 'Four coffees,' she shouted to one stall-holder and he passed them to us over the heads of the crowd. Liz gulped hers down while we all dumped ours in the nearest garbage bin. It was acrid and far too strong. It was very clear by now that R and R could only take Liz in small doses and I was beginning to dread the fortnight ahead.

We finally got on board the right ferry. Liz took up her Ottoman refrain but Robbie and Ron exchanged exasperated looks and ceased listening, happy to be distracted by the activity on the water and the billowing domes of successive mosques etched against the sky. The ferry chugged up the Bosphorus, stopping at tiny villages as we moved towards the Black Sea. At lunchtime we got off and ate under a tree in a simple café. The conversation was stilted, but Ron cheered up when he was befriended by stray cats, who clustered around him hoping for the remains of his fish. Liz shuddered at the sight of their mangy bottoms. Still, lunch in the open air provided the setting for an interim truce. Robbie was delighted to taste fresh anchovies for the first time and the local beer relaxed us all.

That night Robbie and Ron took charge of our eating arrangements and insisted on dining at Rami, the restaurant next door to our hotel. We got the last table, but before we had even had time to look at the menu, Ron launched into a rave about the stupidity, fecklessness and sheer brutality of the Turkish aristocracy. Liz was dying to have her say and burst in with a tirade on middle-class aspirations, greed, the iniquities of individualism and the breakdown of moral responsibility.

'The problem with the middle classes is that they are no longer frightened of the aristocracy, who had always given them a sense of right and wrong,' she said.

Ron took the bait and protested to Liz that the middle class had never been subservient to the aristocracy. The two ranters carried on throughout the meal at the top of their voices, without a thought for Robbie or me, let alone anybody at the adjoining tables. When we were finished, Robbie hastily called for the bill and as we left the table she took me to one side.

'Liz is insufferable. Can you please pull her into line? She's upsetting Ron.'

'Can't you see that Liz has her passions like anyone else and she, like Ron, has strong views? She'll have no idea she was being rude. She'll be horrified to hear that she has hurt Ron's feelings. Unfortunately, the two of them are on parallel tracks destined never to meet. But I will certainly speak to her. It's terrible sitting there listening to two people going gangbusters along two non-connecting tracks. I reckon everyone is going to have to take a deep breath and calm down.'

'Well, it's up to you,' said Robbie. I could see that she was unconvinced by my defence of Liz.

When I got back to our room, I sat Liz down in a comfortable chair and told her with some trepidation that Robbie and Ron were utterly fed up with her. They found her rude and overbearing.

'You'll need to back off the Ottomans and stop ranting about middle-class greed.' Liz started to defend herself, but I cut her short.

'I understand where you're coming from, but they don't, and I'm not going to spend my holiday explaining you to them. You know that I love your enthusiasms, but the fact is that I know you very well and can tell you to shove your rants up your bum if I get bored. We will not survive this holiday if you don't give ground—think what misery it will be travelling in a tiny little car together on the next leg of the trip!'

Liz was completely dumbfounded. So much so that for the next two weeks she restricted herself to three sentences at a time and certainly not a word about the Ottomans or the middle class. I had punched home my lesson. But I regretted that she felt muzzled. I missed her jokes and her eclectic take on things. I continued to feel on edge, though: would Liz 'go Ottoman' again or would she manage to keep up her silence? My nervousness grew when we went to see the harem quarters of the Topkapı Palace. Would Ron or Robbie bring up women's rights again, and would Liz rush to the defence of the Turks? Fortunately not. Liz merely pronounced the harem's living quarters 'attractive and domestic' and that was that.

We followed our guide into two sumptuously decorated rooms in which, we were told, the Crown Prince was confined during his entire youth. And then on to the extensive torture chambers, which displayed a hideous group of torture weapons. No human rights here.

Robbie and I took off for a brief period of relaxation at the *hammam* (public baths). The baths we chose were built at the height of Ottoman power: high ceilings, domed roofs, a huge central marble slab where we lay like dead fish on a chopping block. Antique crones wearing grey bloomers and dirty singlets lumbered up with filthy face cloths and slapped us about with soap, shampoo and buckets of water. They followed this with a massage. The women heaved their pendulous bosoms in front of our noses as they crouched on all fours beside us. We thought we would choke as we breathed in their sour breath while they pummelled our bodies. I felt as if I was in a Fellini film, extricating myself slowly from their grasp and standing on the lush marble floors, rinsing my face in the shell-shaped basins.

We found the Whirling Dervishes that afternoon. They are part of the Sufi sect, one of the most mysterious and mystical sects in the Islamic world.

'They have fascinated outsiders for hundreds of years with their white concertina-like costumes and ritualistic dance. But now,' the guide told us, 'there are signs of conflict. For generations the Dervishes have lived in a segregated world, but now one group of believers has begun mixed-sex dancing, and the traditionalists are scandalised. "The sexes must remain separate," they say. "Men and women are not to be distracted by the smell, by touching, even by the breathing of each other."'

No one could tell us where they were holding their ceremonies. 'They move around. You just have to get lucky,' confided a fellow tourist. 'Go over near the river and start asking where you can buy tickets.' We followed these instructions and were pointed in many different directions by many different people. In the end we followed the most canny-looking local down a narrow laneway. Liz marched the three of us past a queue of at least fifty people to the front, where she lucked out and got the last tickets from a harassed attendant. Once we had the tickets in our hot hands we pushed through the door and moved rapidly towards the chapel. The Dervish performance provided both an intense and meditative experience—mesmeric, highly focused and skilfully performed. The men twirled around and around in the same direction at ever-increasing speed. I kept expecting them to be so dizzy that they would fall over. But no, it was a highly choreographed performance.

When we flew out of Istanbul I wrote in my diary that the Dervish performance, the *hammam* bathhouse and a delicious grilled fish roll, bought from a boat on the harbour and sprinkled with lemon and pepper, were my favourite memories. Liz said hers were, naturally, the romantic shadows of the great Ottoman past as represented by the brooding presence of Suleiman the

Magnificent's mosque, visible from almost everywhere in the city.

My original idea was to hire a car in Istanbul and drive to Cappadocia, but Robbie and Ron had read their guidebooks and been horrified by the traffic accident statistics: for every one person killed on the roads in America, there were twenty-two killed in Turkey. Moreover, coach travel in Turkey had a particularly bad safety record.

I looked at their alarmed faces as they recounted the figures at breakfast. I was also more than aware of the potential for rows in a car and decided to consult the friendly travel agent in our hotel. He arranged for us to fly to Cappadocia and have a car meet us, with a guide to show us the sights. And it was not much more expensive than hiring a car would have been.

We were picked up at Kayseri airport by a fellow called Hasan, who introduced us to Turkish driving. Hasan believed in sudden acceleration and equally sudden braking. He was a guide rather than a driver, we decided, and was probably multi-tasking for the first time. But we rose above our terror when captivated by our first sight of Cappadocia. A mountainous volcanic moonscape stretched out before us, with giant mushrooms of rock rising up on either side and hobbit toy houses gouged out of the cliffs.

Hasan drove us to Göreme, home of the 'fairy chimneys', so called because the locals thought them so magical and strange that they must have been created by fairies. We passed through the appropriately named Love Valley, with its penis-shaped yellow cones and dunes suffused in shades of pink and brown. The whole area was made more dramatic still by the long shadows cast by the dying sun and the leering pockmarked cliffs. We visited the Ihlara Valley, where we came across churches carved into soft rock faces, many with elegant facades and frescoes. Some of the cliff-side burrows still housed people, while others had been abandoned or turned into dovecotes, housing flocks of doves who had made their home in this unwelcoming environment. The Cappadocians used the birds to send messages between towns, and saved their droppings for fertiliser. I suppose they ate the birds in the end; nothing was wasted.

Hasan was a lugubrious young man but proficient in English. He became more and more depressed during our three-day stay when we refused to stop at the tourist shops to buy the ever-present carpets, dolls, onyx and, of course, plaster casts of the landscape. We redeemed ourselves in his eyes only on the last day, when rain drove us into a spanking new carpet emporium. First of all we were shown all the stages of carpet making—the spinning, dyeing and weaving. We were told that most of the carpets were still made by hand but that increasingly the factory was turning out machine-made items. We were guided through an arcaded courtyard, where we sat and drank delicious cups of mint tea and fruit juice.

Then came the hard sell—a series of carpets was displayed with much ceremony in front of us by charming, shiny-suited young men who told us where each carpet was made and the story behind its design. Robbie and I succumbed, weakened by the insistent patter. We opened our cheque books and bought one carpet each, with the promise of delivery to our front door in Sydney. We were completely taken in when they assured us that we would not have to pay a penny of duty. Hasan was wreathed in smiles—he had hit the jackpot at last.

Of course, it was not to be; not only did we both have to trek out six weeks later to customs at Sydney airport to take delivery but we also had to hand over hundreds of dollars in duty. But, that said, the carpets sit happily in their new homes, admired by all.

I had read about the excellence of the local red pottery, so our next stop was Avanos, where, in rooms carved out of the rock, there was a marvellous collection of locally made pots and an active workshop. I looked carefully at the exhibition and paused excitedly in front of a large red dish.

'*No, Hilary*, you are *not* buying *anything*,' said Liz. 'Have you thought how you'd lug it round Turkey?'

'Maybe they'd send it to Australia ...' I said, trailing off and following Liz out of the burrow.

Very peculiar was a Museum of Hair attached to the pottery. Tens of thousands of locks of hair covered the walls and ceiling of the room. Each had a card with the name and address of the donor. Liz and I chased each other around the room brandishing scissors, attempting to cut off a lock of each other's hair to add to the collection. R and R tapped their feet impatiently as they waited for our antics to finish.

Hasan drove us to several of the ancient underground cities, including Özkonak, which was only fourteen kilometres from Avanos and had been discovered in 1972. Although there are thought to be one hundred or more underground cities or villages in Cappadocia, only six are open to the public.

We went on to Derinkuyu, one of the underground cities dating back to the Bronze Age which had been carved out of volcanic deposits, initially to protect the inhabitants from the attacks of wild animals, but later acting as refuges for the first Christians, who were trying to escape persecution by Roman soldiers. There were seven levels to this town from ground level downwards—passageways and living quarters intricately carved at different depths. It was no surprise that Liz disappeared to one of the lower levels, causing Hasan acute anxiety as he chased her down passages in which she played hide-and-seek.

'Did they bring all the animals down here?' she asked, when Hasan caught up with her.

'Yes,' replied Hasan, puffing, 'there are records dating back to 4 BC that say that there were goats, sheep, cows and poultry living here.'

'The smell must have been putrid,' said Liz.

I found it claustrophobic creeping along endless winding passages and peering into different spaces, at kitchens, stables, wine presses, depots for cereal, meeting rooms, churches, saloons and loos, all connected to the surface by a single shared tunnel. Despite the ventilation chimneys, I felt a sudden wave of nausea coming on, usually a precursor to a panic attack, and had to make a dart for the surface.

After Cappadocia we flew to Antalya, where we found a boutique hotel called La Perla. It had once been an elegant house with an internal courtyard, but had been declining over the years. Carla, the owner, had been the first in the area to open a hotel but now boutique hotels had mushroomed and Carla was not handling competition well. There was only one other visitor, Carla's lover Joachim, an out-of-work architect who appeared to have no responsibilities other than to pleasure Carla. Every evening the two of them hosted drinks and took dinner with the guests and encouraged us into extravagant behaviour and games. Liz was really in need of a blow-out. On our last night she became extremely drunk, dressed up in Ottoman clothes and danced with Joachim, who seemed to take a fancy to her. As a final flourish she jumped into a cupboard. Encouraged by Carla, the waiter locked her in and we all hooted with laughter—except R and R—and drank more champagne as she pounded her fists on the door. Finally Joachim came to the rescue and unlocked the door, whereupon Liz fainted into his arms. Robbie and Ron were unimpressed by this performance and went to bed. Carla sat at the end of the long dining table, drinking champagne and smiling; I worried for a moment that Liz might be in trouble. But Carla was queen of her castle. She knew her inamorato well and, after a beautifully judged pause, sashayed up to Joachim, took his hand and led him away with all the promise that her heady perfume and seductive décolletage offered.

Next morning I could have been excused for thinking that the previous night had been a dream until I saw a chipper Joachim in the courtyard garden enticing the tiniest of tortoises to eat a lettuce leaf. Carla was nowhere to be seen but calm had been restored and we ate a beautiful breakfast of olives, cheese and freshly baked bread with an array of homemade jams under the lemon tree.

R and R made no mention of the previous evening's events, but were anxious to get going. We set out in an exceedingly small, cheap hire car to drive around the south coast and back to Istanbul. It had very poor suspension, so that we jolted over any pockmarks in the road. I remember little of the journey—a blur of sea on the left and a few subdued moans from 'vertigo Liz' as we gazed down at the Aegean from dizzying heights. We had to keep stopping to stretch our legs, complaining in turn about the cramped conditions. But at least the 'breathers' helped to keep the peace.

We made a detour to visit the ruins of Miletus, dating back to the fifth and sixth centuries BC. Although the city was rebuilt more than once, the Turks had settled into the city in the twelfth century AD and used Miletus as a port to trade with Venice. The Ottomans, too, used the city as a harbour during their rule in

Anatolia but as the harbour silted up, it was abandoned. What remains today are the ruins of the vast theatre, and we wandered through a maze of broken stones trying to make sense of what had once been a powerful city. Nowadays, the flood plain of the Meander River is covered in cotton fields, so it's extremely difficult to imagine ships docking right in front of the theatre.

Later we pulled over to the side of the road to have lunch. Liz stood well away from us, eating her food. Robbie said, 'What's up now?' I walked over to find out.

'Did we have to leave Miletus so quickly?' said a tetchy Liz.

'We were hungry and we've still got a long way to drive. We've got a plane to catch. Remember?'

We got back into the car and she piped up, 'Recent research tells us that Egyptian Pharaoh Ramses II probably died of tuberculosis, but how could that be? The tuberculosis bacillus was only discovered by Robert Koch in 1882.' I didn't know what she was on about. There didn't seem to be any connection between Ramses and Miletus.

Despite the smallness of the car and the frayed tempers, some-how we got to Istanbul airport without further incident and, after mildly strained farewells, Liz and I boarded a plane to London. Robbie and Ron were off to Los Angeles a few hours later.

After we'd settled and Liz had stopped peering out at views of the Bosphorus and all things Ottoman, I said, 'Phew, that was an ordeal.'

'What do you mean?' said Liz. 'I enjoyed myself no end. I thought your friends were fun and I certainly saw plenty of non-Ottoman Turkey.'

I looked at Liz. Was she joking? Had we been on the same trip? Liz saw my look of disbelief.

'Well, of course I realise I overdid it early on and you were right to shut me up. I was overexcited.'

'I was grateful you behaved well for the rest of the trip.'

'It was fine,' she replied. 'My childhood got me used to living an oppressed half life, although I've never experienced it before travelling with you.'

As we landed at Heathrow and headed for passport control we could contain ourselves no longer; we both let out a loud whoop for freedom and shouted at the tops of our voices, 'NO SMALL CARS, EVER AGAIN!'

5

Spinifex, spirits and songlines

I'd been to Darwin several times but never during the monsoonal wet season, which would surely qualify as an insane time to take a trip to the Northern Territory and the Centre. But Liz liked to avoid the cold European winter and I wanted to show her the 'real' Australia, despite the hot and humid midsummer weather.

I emailed her:

> I've heard that parts of the Northern Territory are under water, but never fear, pack your tropical insect repellent, water bottle and a hat (Alice will be over 40 degrees), and I'll guarantee spectacular thunderstorms and a lush and fecund Kakadu at this time of year.

(I thought a 'fecund' park would appeal to her.)

> Knowing your love of trains I've booked us on the iconic Ghan train journey from Darwin to Adelaide on New Year's Eve. We'll stop off on the way for a few days in Alice Springs to meet up with my friend Hilary. You'll like her. She's brainy, eccentric and has worked

with Aboriginal artists in the bush. What date do you
plan to arrive in Sydney?

She replied by return:

Are you dotty? We'll get swept down a storm water
drain into the mouths of crocodiles.
bestest lovest lizzest

No answer to my question, as usual. I replied:

We'll see the Hans Heysen retrospective exhibition in
Adelaide, which will get our eye in for the creek beds,
and then take the other iconic railway, the Indian
Pacific, to Broken Hill. I promise you time on an
outback station as well.

I was pulling out all stops.

And so it came to pass that we found ourselves squeezed into
seats on a chirpy Virgin flight to Darwin. We had a routine on
planes: Liz by the window for views and me on the aisle for leg
expansion and the loo. We usually had an innocent between us, in
this instance a pallid young man preoccupied with his iPod.

'What are you listening to?' I asked, seizing the opportunity to
practise communication with 'youth'.

'What?' He grumpily removed his earpiece.

Any confidence I had drained away as I repeated the question.
How presumptuous to think that a teenager would be remotely
interested in talking to an old fatty, fifty years his senior. I existed
on another planet.

'Ben Lee,' he mumbled, putting his earpiece firmly back in
his ear.

'Isn't he a bit of a wanker?'

The youth had had enough.

'No,' he replied, jamming his elbow over the entire armrest between us.

'Well, Hilly,' Liz observed, 'that little effort was an abject failure. You never know when to stop.' She grinned mischievously.

I ignored her. Liz turned her attention to a curly haired moppet tottering unsteadily past me towards her mother.

'Go on, Hilly. I dare you to trip her up,' she said wickedly.

It was pouring with rain when we landed. Liz made one of her maddening snap judgements.

'Darwin's a dump,' she announced.

We gingerly descended the slippery steps from the plane and walked across the shiny tarmac to the terminus, buffeted by rain squalls. In the transit lounge a slump of gloomy tourists, dripping onto turquoise plastic chairs, stared at us under the neon.

'What on earth are they doing sitting in Darwin Airport at 1.35 am?' I wondered aloud. 'They look badly in need of a cup of tea.'

'Goodness knows, Hilly. There's probably been a terror alert in Bangkok and their plane has been grounded. I'll get on the tannoy and tell them they're going to Port Moresby in half an hour.'

'Don't. You'll miss the bus.'

We climbed aboard the shuttle in oppressive heat. It was still raining. An Aboriginal girl, dressed in a faded pink shift, stepped in front of the bus as it drew away from the kerb, swaying and giving the driver the finger.

'The last time anyone did that to me I ran them over,' the driver commented dryly.

The following morning Liz was up at daybreak and had walked the length of the Esplanade outside our hotel before breakfast.

'How was it?'

'Great walk. Trees, manicured lawns and the names of hundreds of solid Territorians written on plaques describing their jobs—pastoralist, missionary, potter. I'm already amazed by this town. 'Here we are facing Asia, where you've got thriving cities like Kuala Lumpur, Shanghai, Singapore and Hong Kong. Yet what have we got here? Darwin—camping, out to lunch or simply relaxing, Aussie-style.' She broke off. 'Get up, it's breakfast time.'

I dressed and we set off in the rain.

I pointed to the first café I saw. 'That'll do.'

'No, it looks ghastly. They won't have decent coffee.'

'I don't care. I'm not walking in the rain and my knees ache.' I exaggerated my limp to ensure Liz got the message.

Inside the café Liz ate a banana.

After forcing down greasy bacon, sausage and eggs and a grey cup of something purporting to be coffee I developed instant heartburn. I paid the bill and trudged back to our hotel room, my clothes drenched. Throwing the *Darwin Advocate* and *Barrier Daily Truth* onto the bed, I kicked off my sodden shoes and collapsed.

I enjoy local papers. They are always full of death notices with touching expressions of love, often running to a whole page for one family. Page two of the *Advocate* featured advertisements for water and a sale notice for a three-and-a-half metre long pet carpet python. On the next page I found Cheryl—'New in Town, She's Hot'. She sounded steamy with promise. Also on the page was a desperate plea for the recovery of 'Humpty Doo', a male brindle lost in the city centre the previous day. I wondered how you would attract his attention—'Doo Doo, where are you?'

I was hard-pressed to find any interstate (let alone international) news. What had happened to the floods drowning the Northern

Territory? What news of the progress of war in Afghanistan or the global financial meltdown? And what about the failure after two years of the Australian Government's 'Intervention' to achieve any significant improvement to the health, education, housing or domestic violence issues in Aboriginal communities?

While I pored over the papers Liz padded off in search of the swimming pool, which she finally accessed through the basement garage of the hotel.

'It wasn't exactly inviting,' she commented on her return. 'But never mind. I kept thinking of cold, chilly Britain and how pleased I was to be here.'

Refreshed after her forty lengths, Liz was raring to go. She wanted to see what she called 'the remains of the Raj'; the old colonial buildings through which the Mother Country had exercised power in nineteenth-century Australia. Not much is left—modern development and Cyclone Tracy have seen to that. But there was Government House, the High Court, a police station and the Lyons Cottages. Liz loved them all and fantasised about architects in Whitehall sending out plans all over the globe which took little account of local conditions.

'You know, Hil, these buildings are quite like those in Karachi of a similar age.'

That evening we went to Fannie Bay for the obligatory sunset and seafood experience but the poor old sun was fighting a losing battle by the time we got there. Black clouds glowered and it wasn't long before the rain sheeted down again. The restaurant maître d' apologised profusely for the 'shocking night' but we assured him we did not hold him responsible. 'We're delighted with our personal firework display,' we chorused, pleasantly tipsy after several cocktails. As the thunder cracked in our ears and the lightning streaked across the bay we were enthralled by our very own *son et lumière*.

I was looking forward to the Kakadu 'outing'.

'It's going to be amazing, Lizzie. I have visions of swollen rivers and submerged eucalypts. There'll be spear grass two metres tall, magpie geese nesting in the sedgelands and even goannas and snakes sheltering in the trees.'

'Sounds really scary, Hil. I hope this is your well-developed fantasy world on full throttle because if Kakadu is remotely like that, I won't be getting out of the bus.'

Liz was in excellent form during the two-hour bus trip to the park. We would arrive at 'comfort stops' where she would gleefully point out the mouldy emu pens, curling postcards, the tragic deep green and brown bars and the cafés with stale buns and cloudy swimming pools.

At the park we made for the departure point for our river cruise. The rain had started again, dampening the spirits of our small band of fellow tourists. They hunched together as the rain pelted onto the canvas roof of our tiny flat-bottomed boat. My Japanese neighbour, who had introduced herself as Millie, had forgotten her mackintosh and squealed at her husband every time a flurry of rain blew onto her butterfly-sequinned T-shirt. I decided they were newlyweds and noted that her freshly minted husband failed to change seats with her, displaying a woeful lack of gallantry. Was he fed up with her attention seeking and wondering whether he had married a princess? I suspected he wished they had never left the honeymoon suite.

I joined a jubilant Liz at the front of the boat. Her mood had transformed. She was standing by herself like a ship's figurehead, her arms outstretched as though exhorting the water gods. We were both totally invigorated by the weather. The flood plains were full; we seemed to float over fields. A sky-full of migratory birds, everything from curlew and snipe to ibis and jabiru, squawked and screamed overhead. I had never seen or heard such a melee of birds in my life. Our guide, Bob, a dinky-di Territorian with slouch hat and ruddy face, pointed out the lotus bird, a whistling kite and a green pygmy goose nestling in the paperbark trees. His eagerness was infectious. He nearly fell out of the boat as he strained to show us the lemon-bellied flycatcher. Black-banded pigeons, white-lined honeyeaters, yellow chats—he named them all. His knowledge was encyclopaedic. And even I recognised the red-collared lorikeets prancing up and down the branches of the angophoras. My moment of greatest excitement came when Bob gleefully showed us a northern snake-necked turtle slowly making his way up the side of the bank.

'Normally they bury themselves in the mud towards the end of the dry season, so you're very lucky to see him.'

Everyone was hanging over the side of the boat trying to take the perfect photograph. Suddenly there was a squeal and there was Millie, camera poised, toppling over the side of the boat. I grabbed a handful of her T-shirt and hauled her back, narrowly preventing an international incident. The young groom bowed his gratitude and Millie sheepishly handed over her camera and sat silently for the rest of the trip.

'Good one,' said Bob, patting me on the back. I returned to the front of the boat and drank in the restorative power of the rain pouring down onto every root, leaf, blade of grass and clump of reeds, turning the park into a luscious, vibrant green and purple never-never land. The birds got it. They circled, dipped, wheeled and observed us—idiotic human beings so out of sync with our environment.

Northern bullfrogs and marbled frogs crouched on lily pads chatting to each other while red-beaked waders balancing delicately on spindle legs picked their way among the fuchsia-pink lilies. I was delirious—'Rain on, give us a storm!' I forgot the mosquitoes and the humidity. We reached a waterfall, its swollen waters cascading down the rocks and into the overflowing river below.

'Could you take us nearer? I want to swim behind the waterfall and see if I can stand upright under the rushing water,' Liz said to Bill.

'No way, Liz, there's a ton of crocs round here, ugly great brutes. You saw what nearly happened to the young lass. If she'd fallen in, it would have been good night, nurse.' Bill snapped his hands together as if closing his teeth over a choice piece of Liz leg.

Liz went a deathly shade of pale and sat down hurriedly.

Kakadu was a great success. Liz said on the bus back, 'I got a real feel for the vibrancy of the park and the wonderful birdlife. And the rain made it even better—brillio, Hillio.'

During breakfast next morning at the Wisdom Café, located in an old dental clinic, I was keen to take a photo of Liz navigating the thorns and pong of her durian fruit breakfast. Rummaging in my bag I felt a familiar sick sensation in the pit of my stomach. No camera. I called our waitress over. She picked up on my mounting anxiety and leapt into action. She traced the taxi in which we had travelled to the café and rang the driver. She was incredible; blossoming in the crisis.

'He's got it,' she called triumphantly across the courtyard. 'He was about to hand it in,' she bounced back to our table, 'but now, no worries. He said he'll drop it in here.'

'I feel like giving her the camera. You wouldn't get honesty and kindness like this in Sydney,' I said to Liz.

'True,' she agreed.

At the art gallery later that afternoon we saw a comprehensive exhibition of Aboriginal art and were particularly taken by a life-size pick-up truck woven in grass with a stick-like driver inside. We later learnt that the artist was the cousin of two of the Aboriginal artists from Ernabella whom we were to meet in Alice Springs.

That evening we chose a Moorish tapas bar for dinner. The owner, Carlos, had been in Darwin since 1971 and had gone through Cyclone Tracy.

'It destroyed my house. I had to wash in a wheelbarrow for months afterwards.'

'How was your tagine, Liz?' I asked at the end of the meal.

'A Moroccan school dinner. A stew in a pottery bowl,' she replied.

'You're an outrage. I notice you ate it all. My tapas were delicious.'

'But we all know you'd eat anything—sweet-and-sour wombat, if it was on the menu.'

'It's a pity the Mindil Beach markets aren't on in the wet season, Liz. You would have loved it. The whole of Darwin turns up for a picnic.'

'Every night?'

'No, Thursdays and Saturdays—men and women from their offices, families with small children, lovers, migrants, loners, losers. Some lug card tables to the edge of the beach and sip cheap champagne from plastic flutes; others stand with their stubbies watching the sun set. Then they follow the spicy smells of the Asian food stalls set up just behind the first line of palms, and choose their dinner from steaming woks full of stir-fries, sweet and sour pork, fish curries, gado gado or kebabs.'

'It sounds fun, but you know I'm not keen on large displays of food,' said Liz.

'It was fun eating ourselves to a standstill while the kids built sandcastle cities, and dripped ice-cream onto the turrets.

'I remember so clearly one time seeing a little old lady sitting alone on a tartan rug silently staring out to sea. A lone Aboriginal man sat next to her, muttering to himself and playing on his message sticks. I sat down beside them and the three of us became still as he played and together we watched the glowing orange orb in a bougainvillea orange-pink sky deepen and sink suddenly on the horizon. I remember feeling at peace with the world.

'One year, Lizzie, they had a festival with tall wooden pylons planted in the sea, covered with brightly coloured paper flowers and sea monsters. Boatmen rowed out to set them alight. They burst into flame and formed a glorious series of water bonfires while a long multicoloured paper dragon snaked his way along the shore.'

'It sounds brillio. With things like that going on here I'm surprised Darwin isn't booming. I'd expect developers to be having a field day. Multimillion dollar townhouse complexes mushrooming, way outstripping town planning. Overheated foreign investment going through the roof.'

'Maybe the stuffing was kicked out of the place by Cyclone Tracy.'

'But that was forty years ago.'

Next day we packed our bags and found a taxi to take us to the much-anticipated Ghan. We had high expectations both the Ghan and of the Indian Pacific.

'Did you know that the Ghan was named after the camels from Afghanistan, Hil? They carried goods and passengers part of the way from Adelaide to Darwin in the mid-nineteenth century.' Liz was bubbling with excitement.

I had noticed the envious expressions of friends when I mentioned our forthcoming trip. They were all hooked by the mystique surrounding train travel. I had talked myself into the belief that our every whim would be catered for. Highly trained staff would guide us to our carriage and respond to any call for help, however minuscule.

A misplaced hope. We departed from a muddy wasteland south of Darwin. No inviting café or shop to visit prior to departure. It didn't augur well. The train pulled unceremoniously out of the siding and the suburbs receded in a cloud of drizzle.

We had booked into 'gold' class. I had expected a wood-panelled bedroom with goose down pillows. That was the first of several fantasies dashed. The cabin was cramped, the bathroom the size of a shoebox and the window small and dirty. In spite of its gold status, the loo had to be pulled down from the wall and then, when finished with, pushed back into place. The problem was that the bowl was very shallow, like a bedpan, and water in short supply, so you had to press the button repeatedly. You could hardly turn around in the shower and there were no sewing kits, shampoo or lavender-scented soaps wrapped in tasteful sachets to dissuade us from our conclusion that the service barely warranted two stars. For once I joined Liz in showerlessness and vowed not to wash until we arrived in Alice Springs.

I selfishly bagsed the lower bed, regressing to boarding school behaviour, and assigned the upper bunk to Liz, pleading 'bad knees'. She was on to that scam in a trice and my girlish wheeze nearly came to naught when she discovered that she would have to climb up a ladder to get into the bed.

'What about my vertigo?' Her voice rose to a wail.

'Don't be ridiculous. You're barely off the ground.'

'Who designed this train? Clearly someone who gave no thought to the comfort or mobility of seventy year olds.'

'Look at this!' I was incredulous as I thrust my pillowcase in front of Liz's nose. 'Can you believe it? That's ironed-on blood. Unbelievable! There must have been at least four checkpoints between the laundry and the train for someone to make this discovery.' I stamped off in a rage and showed the filthy bed linen to a female attendant who, beside herself with apologies, was way out of her depth. She rang a bell, desperate for a supervisor to rescue her, but help came there none. By this time the poor girl was babbling incoherently and Liz and I were beginning to feel sorry for her. I finally spoke to the duty manager on the train and followed it up with letters to the chief executive of the Ghan and the Minister for Transport. I received a grovelling letter from the Ghan and a letter of acknowledgement from the minister with a promise to look into it and get back to me. Neither he nor his office got back. The only thing I received, six months later, was a promotional flyer inviting me to travel on the Ghan. I scanned the page but did not see the words 'complimentary' or '50 per cent off'.

We put the episode behind us and made for the bar for a few stiff drinks. We were sitting in a red plush booth, becoming pleasantly sedated, when the music started up. Cat Stevens. I had read about his comeback album, but this was certainly not it. Was there no popular classical music that could have filled the bill? What about *Eine Kleine Nachtmusik* or *The Four Seasons* or, as an Indigenous solution, Gurrumul Yunupingu's hit album *Rrakala*? Both Liz and I tried and failed to get them to turn Cat down. We would have been content with a didgeridoo or a meditation tape of bush and bird sounds, or even better, nothing. Liz took to looking out of the window, gazing at flat, thinly grassed land stretching as far as the eye could see, and I tried to read my book.

Dinner was served in two shifts in the Queen Adelaide restaurant car.

'Why would anyone be impressed by eating in a dining car named after a little-known British queen?' remarked Liz.

There was a definite sense of urgency about the service from the outset. A thin maître d' with a pink nose and sparse whiskers like a white mouse supervised podgy waitresses with lace décolletages who waddled between the booths pouring water, followed by waiters with bowls of soup, as the train swayed between the tracks.

The first sitting had to be brisk to accommodate the second sitting and the second sitting knew that they too had better hurry: the staff positioned themselves at our elbows ready to clear the tables as soon as Liz had swallowed her last spoonful of sticky date pudding.

We were seated for the New Year's Eve dinner in a booth opposite an elderly man and woman who had met for the first time at the lunch sitting. The booth was decorated with pale blue balloons already losing their air and hanging limply, suspended with pink ribbon from the ceiling. The couple were both white South Africans from Zimbabwe and both shared the distinction of having looked after ill spouses over a long period of time. The man had cared for his wife with Alzheimer's for seventeen years. She had recently died and he looked as though he had just emerged from a broom cupboard, blinking at the light. The woman had looked after her husband with Parkinson's disease for twenty-seven years and felt guilty because she had finally succumbed to her children's pleas and put him in a home, where he promptly died.

Their stories of self-sacrifice and dedication were quite confronting to Liz and me; we seemed to have waltzed through spectacularly fortunate lives. Once Adam had warmed up, he was unstoppable. I had once worked as a family mediator and, to my surprise, suddenly found myself drawing on some long-forgotten training.

'My wife used to repeat herself over and over again until I wanted to explode,' he said.

'You felt as if you were about to burst,' I ventured.

'Yes, yes—sometimes I wanted to hit her.'

'You were at the end of your tether.'

'What on earth are you doing?' Liz hissed at me, and dragged me off to the bar.

'I was just trying a spot of active listening,' I replied, once out of earshot of Adam and Gay.

'What on earth's that? You were winding poor Adam up.'

'It's a counselling technique. You listen carefully to the speaker and then reflect the emotional content of what they've just said in your reply. If you get it right you help them to release some of the stress and strain they've been bottling up.'

'Well, I'd be very careful if I were you. You sounded very strange to me—you need a refresher course. And the way you're going, you'll be trapped all night and there's no way I'll be staying around. It's New Year's Eve, we want a bit of fun. I'm going to find Graham, the forklift driver we met at lunch.'

Graham had diverted us with stories of his life on building sites.

'The boss let us go home if it rained for two hours straight,' he told us, 'so we used to hose our newspapers and then show the soggy pages to him as proof. The scam always worked—it was a good life.'

I went back to sit with Adam and Gay while Liz went in search of Graham. I was plunged again into more stories about Adam's life with his sick wife and came to the conclusion that Liz was absolutely right: I needed a refresher course. I wasn't helping him, I was just being sucked into a whirlpool of his pain. Best get out before it was too late. He and Gay were much more comfortable with each other.

'Please would you excuse me? I'd better go and find Liz. Happy New Year!' I said, and extricated myself uncomfortably.

Liz had spotted Graham sitting at a corner table by himself and was ensconced in lively conversation. He had abandoned his lunchtime red and yellow hibiscus shorts and replaced them with a shiny grey suit several sizes too small, a polka-dotted bow tie and a tight pink shirt, the buttons straining over his stomach.

We consumed two more bottles of champagne, some grappa and beer and became instant best friends. Just as well that Liz had brought the grappa with her because the Queen Adelaide dining car had never heard of it. Despite the best of intentions we couldn't last beyond 11 pm, so we exchanged Happy New Year greetings with Graham, bidding him sweet dreams, and escaped to our carriage.

Outside the window the stars were glowing pinpricks of light a million miles away in the vast night sky. Dark shapes rushed past, the wheels of the train clattered and hummed and we picked up a faint chorus of 'Auld Lang Syne' down the corridor. Liz and I found two polystyrene cups and drank a grappa toast to the new year and our continued travels.

We arrived in Alice Springs twenty-four hours later. It was stinking hot, but the dry heat was far removed from the debilitating humidity of Darwin. The light here was fierce and relentless; it throbbed through the tinder-dry air. My friend Hilary was waiting on the platform. I had known her for many years and we had often been called 'Hilary 1' and 'Hilary 2' when we worked together in our youth. She looked worn from her long years working at Ernabella in the bush, but still stood tall and impressive. Her hair was pulled back and she wore a crisp white shirt and faded blue jeans. Smiling warmly, she grabbed our bags and whisked us away to our hotel in her open all-purpose van.

'What was the trip like?' she asked.

'Not at all what we expected,' I said. 'The views outside were terrific. But inside it wasn't great—more like camping than the luxury train that they advertise.'

'Why can't Australians embrace modernity?' Liz asked Hilary.

'We're ambivalent about it,' she quipped back.

Pukatja, also known as Ernabella, is 440 kilometres south-west of Alice Springs, in South Australia, and is home to 500 people. Hilary had spent seven years as Coordinator of Ernabella Arts Inc., employed by the Women's Community Arts business. The Arts Centre was sixty years old, the oldest of its kind in Australia. Many of the artists were well known all over Australia and internationally for their batik work, painting, printmaking and pottery. Hilary ran pottery and printmaking workshops and toured exhibitions of the women's work around Australia and overseas. She grew very fond of the women; they became her family and she used to go rabbiting with them at the weekends.

Our first day in Alice coincided with a public holiday weekend, so Hilary was free to take us to the Telegraph Station Historical Reserve for a spot of history and picnicking. The telegraph station was the first site of European settlement in Alice Springs, where it was in service for sixty years, largely under the control and mentorship of Charles Todd, after whom the Todd River was named.

Sir Charles Todd KCMG was a remarkable man, born in London in 1826, the son of a grocer. In December 1841 he started work at the Royal Observatory, Greenwich, and moved to Cambridge University Observatory in 1847, where he stayed until 1854. I became fascinated with Sir Charles, who seemed to have had courage, passion and imagination. He always kept the big picture in his sights and he had the determination to stick to his goals.

Todd met his wife, Alice Bell, in Cambridge when she was twelve and he was working as Assistant Astronomer. She was young, innocent, and captivated by his energy and zeal. It was a schoolgirl crush but one which was to last. For his part, he was bowled over by her beauty and completely spellbound when she promised to marry him when she grew up. Six years later, when Alice was eighteen, Charles reminded her of her promise. She needed no further urging; she had kept his image in a locket round her neck in the intervening years and was giddy with love. They married in April 1855. He had been offered a job in South Australia as Superintendent of Telegraphs and Government Astronomer. He filled her heart with his dreams of providing direct telegraphic links between England and Australia. Alice was carried away by his vision and happily agreed to follow him to the end of the world— or so Australia must have seemed to a young English rose.

They set sail for Australia in June, 1855, and arrived in Adelaide five months later. *What a mixed blessing*, I thought, *that the same journey can now be done in twenty-four hours.*

Years later, after Alice had brought up six children—a task which could not have been easy for her, with a husband often away and preoccupied with his own ambitions—she appears to have warmed to her adopted country. I like to imagine that Charles named the town Alice Springs as a gift for her forbearance.

After more than twenty years, Charles's greatest dream finally became a reality in August 1872, when the first single international telegraphic link from Australia to the rest of the world was opened.

'Take a look at this dear little morse code machine tapping away,' called Liz from one of the small stone rooms in the telegraph station.

'I can't get my head around the immensity of the communication revolution we've witnessed in my lifetime. And now there's the internet and everything that flows from it. How are we poor little humans going to keep up?' I said to Hilary.

Charles died in 1910, aged eighty-four, having been a public servant for fifty years. He was buried beside his wife.

'All power to the dreamer and obsessive,' said Hilary.

We left the telegraph station and carried our picnic to the banks of the Todd River, which was in full flood thanks to recent rain. Hilary pointed out a group of Somali and Sudanese picnickers.

'There are not many Somalis in Alice but I think there are about 200 Southern Sudanese who fled the civil war and live here. Some of them work in the supermarkets,' she said.

'Why did they choose Alice Springs?' asked Liz.

'I don't really know, but I read somewhere that the landscape is similar to the landscape round Juba, South Sudan's capital,' Hilary replied.

'You have camels round here, don't you?' I asked. 'I heard that you can buy camel lasagne, which intrigued me. I'd love a few camel recipes—I'm joking!'

'I don't know anything about camels,' said Hilary. 'I know you can get a ride on one—that's all.'

'Did you know that camels have three eyelids for each eye?' volunteered Liz.

We sat on a large square mat and spread out our picnic. An Aboriginal woman with two young boys recognised Hilary and sat down to chat. I looked on silently from my corner of the mat. Kids were clambering over rocks and diving into the water, or squealing, pushing each other off stony ledges. Liz took the boys down to the water and splashed around with them, enjoying their fun. When she returned an hour later, much to her amazement I was sitting stock still on my corner of the mat exactly as she had left me.

'Why didn't you join in the conversation?' Liz asked.

'I couldn't think of a thing to say. I was shy.'

'Why?'

'I always feel overwhelmed by the gulf between Indigenous people and us westerners.'

'What rubbish,' said Liz, and proceeded to tell the woman she should warn her son to be careful in the water, as he was taking unnecessary risks, given that he could not swim.

*

The next day Hilary took us to Desert Park, a stretch of bushland in a bleached environment, with spinifex clinging to the arid soil and a backdrop of red rocks and kingfisher blue sky.

'The landscape reminds me of when I first came to Australia in 1960,' I said. 'I went round outback New South Wales in a bus, hired as assistant stage manager for an Arts Council theatre tour.'

'You've never told me that before,' said Liz.

'I loathed the bush and screamed when I saw my first goanna.

It took me at least four years to warm to gum trees, the red earth and bush flowers.'

Liz had been boning up on her bird book and thought she spotted a rufous owl, but when she went to check with the park ranger, he told her he was afraid she had only seen a dun-coloured sparrow. He ushered us into an open area and sat us down in a semicircle to watch as an eagle flew into the enclosure, where it broke open emu eggs with a stone and ate the contents. The bird arrived in its own time and departed without, it appeared, any intervention. I clapped: I was most impressed. Liz marvelled at my gullibility.

'You're so naïve, Hil, they've been trained by Bill. They're not real eggs. The manufacturers put a titbit inside each one so the bird won't feel betrayed.'

'How do you know that? You're wrong. It hasn't been trained; it's a naturally talented bird. It instinctively seeks out the emu egg,' I countered.

'You're such a sentimental old moll, Hilly.'

Hilary and the park ranger smiled their agreement.

*

We were now at Simpsons Gap, a gash in the MacDonnell Ranges. A few locals were taking an early evening stroll up the gorge, followed by a gaggle of tourists.

Liz was very taken with the scene.

'You know,' she said, 'these gaps in the landscape are very frequent in Europe. We take them for granted; but here somehow, because they are so few and far between, they have an almost mystical quality. And the presence of water, too, in this otherwise parched country gives it a special feel.'

'Would you like to go for a picnic in the bush tomorrow?' asked Hilary as we stood beside the cool water trapped between the starkly rising cliffs. 'My mob from Ernabella are here on holiday and want to go honey-anting.'

'Brillio,' said Liz, 'nothing could be better.'

'What can we bring?' I asked. 'We were going to hire a runabout to sightsee, so it would be easy to convert that to a Land Cruiser which would fit all of us. What do you think?'

'Great. Numbers are always a moveable feast,' said Hilary.

*

The following morning we picked up the cruiser and Hilary drove us around to the various hostels where the women were staying. We managed to cram the largest of them, Witjula, and Tina, her nine-year-old niece, into the front seat of the van while the remaining eight of us, together with a box of suppurating mangos, one lady with the flu, assorted kangaroo tails brought by the women, six frozen rabbits, two eskies, a crowbar and picks and shovels, were squashed in the back. The women indicated with a show of fingers that I should buy two more rabbits in addition to the six I had already bought but it was getting a bit pricey, so I let that slide.

It was about 11.30 am by the time we left Alice and the sun beat down on the van. I hoped we wouldn't be going too far. We were crammed against each other, sweat forming wide patches on our clothes, faces glistening, bare feet smelling. The ladies sat silently, neither talking to us nor among themselves but keeping a watchful eye on everything. As we left the main road and drove down rough tracks into the bush, arguments seemed to erupt. I said, 'They must be debating the best location for honey ants.'

'Not at all,' said Liz. 'They're arguing about who's going to win the 2.30 at Randwick Races.'

Eventually we arrived at a place which all the women agreed was a likely habitat for honey ants. We unpacked the eskies and Hilary spread a tablecloth and offered Liz and me olives and dips.

Meanwhile, the ladies dragged the kangaroo tails out of the van. Four of them wandered off purposefully with shovels and picks to start digging, while others gathered wood for the fire. On went the kangaroo tails and a few of the women settled down to watch the fire. Liz helped them gather wood.

Hilary had brought everything, from orange juice to loo paper. There were two picnics. Hilary had packed corned beef, crisps, salad and wholemeal bread for the women, while we ate baba ganoush, hummus, goat's cheese, salami, salad and rice crackers. I found it embarrassing to be eating a separate meal, but Hil assured us that she had especially brought the food her friends most liked to eat.

By the time we had finished eating, my knees were hurting and I was shifting from side to side in an attempt to get comfortable. I noticed one of the old ladies, tiny, with wispy hair and dark eyes, looking at me.

'This is Nura Rupert,' said Hilary. 'She's an elder and a healer.'

'Your knees,' Nura pointed towards my swollen joints, 'are hurting?'

'Yes, they are,' I replied.

She called over one of her friends and they planted themselves on either side of my legs and motioned me to lie back.

'Make you better,' said Nura, smiling gently.

And without more ado she spat on my knees and legs, called for 'butter' and sat waiting patiently until Hilary came running with a plastic container. Nura's friend then joined in and they rubbed my painful legs (one each) with a mixture of spittle, butter and grainy red earth. Up and down, up and down they went, in a slow, deliberate rhythm. They continued this steady action, singing as they massaged, and I gradually got used to the abrasive feel of their leathery hands and the grain of the earth. The process must have gone on for half an hour. When they had finished they called Hilary again.

'Paper.' And over came the Kleenex.

Nura asked, 'Feel better now?'

I nodded. 'Thank you so much.'

I'm afraid I was telling a white lie; I did not want to hurt her feelings. But the camaraderie I sought had begun to sink in and I felt a strong sense of wellbeing. Nura took my hand—my new friend Nura, the healer, in her pink and white floral dress covered with red dust—and we went walking in the bush. I thought she looked eighty, but was almost certainly wrong. Aboriginal women rarely live that long. We wandered silently, hand in hand, listening to the sound of the wind and the buzz of the flies, and I felt a great warmth towards her and peace within myself.

Liz had meanwhile joined the digging team. Pantjiti was using a crowbar to penetrate the powder-dry soil of the honey ants' secret chamber. She handed up shiny jewel-like spheres to two of the ladies, who had a collection of mugs into which they divided the baubles of honey equally. There couldn't have been more than twenty-five of the glistening beads, yet the women were quick to offer us both a bead. I tentatively put mine on my tongue and hoped for the best, relieved that there was no sign of the ant, just the sac or bubble behind his head; it was a bit like honey, or molasses, but I couldn't taste any of the nutty flavour I had been told about. Liz tried hers—'Bitter,' she pronounced. The digging was hard work and the women kept Hilary busy bringing bottles of water from the base.

Later on, Liz and I took off by ourselves for a walk in the bush. One of the women noticed our departure and warned us not to go too far. The bush was strange and hypnotic. Heat quivered in the air and the shade was flimsy as the leaves on the stubby trees hung downwards to avoid the sun. The ground was parched and our feet crackled on the crunchy leaves and twigs. There was a weird silence, punctuated by an occasional scurry of wind. There were no landmarks to show where we'd come from or what we were passing. In spite of the bright light it was impossible to see far ahead. The bush was featureless. We understood the women's warning.

'Only in Venice have I felt lost like this!' said Liz. 'Wandering the alleyways with little that I recognised. The walls and occasional glimpses of canals and bridges were so alike.' Liz's stark European comparison seemed a weird choice, but I could see her point. We had plunged for a brief time into another world, a world of spinifex, spirits and songlines, far from the sinking autumnal city of Venice, with its ancient waterways.

Later, when the wind freshened and the sun started to set, we happily scrambled into the Land Cruiser and the women sang on our way home. Even Niningka, who had bad flu, seemed to perk up after two Panadols and a sleep in the bush.

It was our last night in Alice and we wanted to try somewhere different for dinner. It was also Sunday, which meant that there were fewer options. We ended up in a tourist trap, the Overlander Restaurant, with crude representations of settlement and grazier life in the nineteenth century drawn on the walls. We had gone from the sublime to the 'gorblimey'. Liz ordered kangaroo, I had steak and Hilary had cauliflower cheese, from a menu drawn on a parchment map with carefully torn edges and a hillbilly typeface. We threw back the red wine and sang lusty drovers' songs with words writ large on a blackboard and Liz grabbed centre stage on the wobble board.

She summed up her feelings when we got back to the hotel.

'It seems strange that we spent a day with eight Indigenous women and learnt so little from them about their lives and problems. And they heard nothing about us either. But I suspect that their observations of us were a great deal keener than ours of them.'

We flew to Adelaide to connect with the Indian Pacific train on its day-long journey to Broken Hill.

During our half-day in Adelaide we went to the State Library to see the three carpets designed by the Ernabellians. We were also thrilled to see not just four of their batik paintings in the Art Gallery, but also three of their intricately designed pots, the most recent initiative of the Artists' Cooperative. Hilary had told us that the youngest of our ladies, aged twenty-four, who had been digging up the honey ants the previous day, was the cousin of one of the rug designers and was bringing up nine nieces and nephews as well as her own child as a single mother.

'How lucky he was to have gum trees to paint all his life,' said Liz as we walked around the Hans Heysen retrospective exhibition. 'And no Robert Hughes telling him that the trees resembled Rembrandt's nudes.'

That night we caught a train to Broken Hill. We were going to continue our holiday with a taste of station life. I had found Widgery Station on the internet and it looked promising. I booked for a couple of nights and arranged for us to stay on the way at a Broken Hill hotel called the Royal Exchange, with a distinctive Art Deco facade. Liz found it stuffy and when I went to bed she descended the grand staircase in search of the bar. In the small hours she staggered back to our room and attempted to wrench her bed from its position next to mine. (In all the hotels in which we shared a room Liz always moved her bed as far away from my snoring as possible.) This time she broke the bedhead and left two deep gashes in the wall. Not at all contrite, she laughed and laughed.

'You must tell the manager in the morning,' I said angrily, knowing better than to attempt a rational discussion while she was drunk.

'You'll have to tell them,' said Liz. 'I'll just laugh.'

I snorted crossly and covered my head with the sheet.

The following morning Phillip Jones, the fifth generation Australian owner of Widgery Station, pulled up in his four-wheel drive to collect us. Before he arrived, Liz informed the hotel management about her fall from grace as she paid the bill.

'They didn't care at all. They were charming about it,' she said smugly. 'Maybe they thought we were having a night of extravagant sex.'

We sped off with Phillip across the Mundi Mundi Plains on the dusty dirt road. The Barrier Ranges ran alongside us to the right and nothing at all, bar the horizon, was visible on the left. Phillip was a tall, craggy bloke not gifted with small talk.

He told us, 'It's quite green at the moment; we've had some rain. There's only a hundred people in a straight line between here and the west coast of Australia. Our nearest neighbours are eighteen kilometres away.'

It was clear on our arrival at the property that Phillip and Isabel, his wife, were doing it hard. Rusting equipment lay round the house. We were their only guests. It was Phillip who settled us into our large motel-style room and filled us in further.

'We've reduced our property to 40,000 acres and we've got 1500 sheep and 75 cattle. The drought has meant that we've had to turn to tourism.'

Isabel was noticeably not there to greet us. She didn't appear until after breakfast the following day, and then only to clear away. She didn't want a chat, which I found unusual for a country woman. We returned to our room.

'Do you think she's suffering from depression?' I worried.

'You're such a drama queen, Hil. If there's no visible drama, you just make it up,' said Liz.

'Coming from you, that's rich,' I responded. 'I challenge you,' I went on. 'Let's see who can get the most out of her at teatime.'

We buttonholed Isabel, and by sitting down with her and drinking a cup of tea, both of us did surprisingly well.

We learnt that Phillip looked after the farm while Isabel had completed a Masters in Tourism Management. She had been chairperson of the local Broken Hill Tourist Board until recently.

Isabel was the daughter of a magistrate and had spent her childhood in various small towns in New South Wales. She had reluctantly embraced tourism and now welcomed a diverse group of visitors: university students studying geology, ancient American tourists or eccentric 'newly old' birds like us. She had tried to follow the advice of government departments, 'consultants' and tourism head honchos and had instigated various plans to attract punters. It was hard, because she was technology-phobic and quite naïve. Her latest scheme had been to pay a man to devise a bush trail for visitors. When the time came to advertise the trail, the charlatan disappeared, leaving behind only a book of pressed plants with their Aboriginal names. 'Phillip was furious with me,' she said.

The next disaster, on an even larger scale, occurred when both Phillip and Isabel decided to pay an artist to plough up a gigantic stretch of their land and plant it in the shape of a stockman's face. The idea was to take tourists up in a helicopter to see the face etched into the bare landscape. This artist disappeared too. (Liz and I agreed that country people were far too trusting.)

Phillip and Isabel had two sons, Martin and Luke. Luke left home when his help was most needed and hotfooted it to Broken Hill, where he was working as a handyman. Isabel missed him dreadfully. Martin was still struggling with school and bearing the brunt of his parents' problems. He looked after all the machines within the house, from espresso machines to computers.

The first morning, Liz set out after breakfast, walking towards the horizon. When she returned she was full of information.

'There are two huge pools of red water—'

'Dams, you nutter.'

'With an old-fashioned windmill groaning and moaning as it pumps up the water. It's quite scary, with the desert rolling away for hundreds of miles before reaching the Flinders Ranges.'

The second day a hot wind in the early morning swirled around the property, buffeting Liz's legs as she briskly set forth again, only to be driven back to our quarters, frustrated by the wind's power. It gathered strength during the day, as the sun baked the cracked earth. I decided early on that a leisurely breakfast and chilling out with a book in the comfort of air conditioning was the only answer to the extreme heat, while Liz managed to connect to the internet by sweet-talking Isabel's son Martin into helping her. She was soon happy as a clam, chatting to her friends all over the world.

It was during our first breakfast that we realised that cooking was not Isabel's forte. There were stale packet cornflakes, cold greasy bacon with rubbery eggs and white soggy toast causing instant heartburn (memories of Darwin). Isabel had done her best to make her guests comfortable, even to the extent of importing a cappuccino machine, but the trouble was only Martin could operate it and he had already gone off to school so cappuccino coffee was a distant dream. Dinner was no better—tough chops with packet mashed potato, packet gravy and tinned peas. Ever 'Pollyanna', I vowed that it was the perfect opportunity for me to lose weight.

By four-thirty in the afternoon on the second day of our visit the wind had died down and Phillip offered to take us for a drive to see the property and enjoy the sunset. He showed us the remains of the Browning Station. The Brownings had been the first people to farm in Mundi Mundi, and had been totally self-sufficient. They'd set up in the 1850s and stayed until they were booted out by the government as squatters. The land was then carved up into smaller portions and Phillip's great-grandfather was handed one of them. We walked among the stone rubble of pigsties, stables and a dairy barn and came upon four graves outlined in pebbles. We stood silently as two scruffy emus darted past and a wallaby sat watching us, its ears twitching.

'That'll be us—dust to dust.' Liz didn't like graveyards.

I took a more sanguine view. 'I like to think that after our death our spirit, soul—call it what you will—becomes part of a giant energy grid. It would be nice to think that our end will mean a new beginning for someone somewhere, and possibly coincides with the birth of another human being or living thing. I'm not sure—I haven't a clue—but I like the thought.'

We moved on to where majestic Heysen-esque silver gums were embedded in the dried-out creek. We watched them change colour as the evening approached and Phillip pointed out a shadowy silver fox picking his way through the fallen tree trunks and then racing up the hill in search of a skinny sheep for supper. You had to be

Liz and Hil outside 'VW' (Vauxhall Walk), in 'dreary old London', just a short walk from the Thames.

Liz spends more than 300 days a year away from home. Here she is on a rare day at VW.

A rainy day on Regent Street, London—the weather, though utterly miserable, was not enough to discourage a truly avid shopper.

LEFT Our first holiday together was to Morocco. This is the view from our hotel in Fez, perched on a hillside overlooking the Medina.

ABOVE Liz and Hil at Machu Picchu— Liz has not yet succumbed to vertigo!

ABOVE In the nineteenth century hunters went on safari to kill the 'big five'—lion, rhinoceros, buffalo, leopard and elephant. We came not to kill them, but to gawp. Here we are on safari in Botswana …

RIGHT … and in the Serengeti, in Tanzania, with our guide Charlie.

ABOVE Liz tries on a costume on the Eastern Cape.

BELOW Hil riding a bike in Namibia.

ABOVE Kakadu in the wet season.

LEFT
Boys playing in
the Todd River.

ABOVE Liz and Hil about to board the Ghan.

BELOW The Ghan in its Christmas finery.

On a honey-anting expedition in the Australian outback, Hil received a massage from Indigenous elder Nura Rupert and her friend, both skilled in traditional healing.

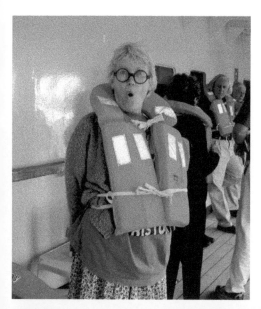

A cruise is a lifetime in miniature—you enter it friendless and aimless; you leave overwhelmed with instant intimates and a resolve to start a New Life.

Liz takes a dip at Korčula, an island off the Dalmatian coast in the Balkans.

LEFT
To say the food was dismal on
our Balkan cruise would be the
understatement of the century.

BELOW Liz and Hil in Naples—
a city high on Liz's list of RIZs
(Robber Infested Zones).

Liz's friend Norma is a brilliant cook. Her homemade Bara Brith ('speckled bread') has the power to restore weary world travellers.

ABOVE 'Iona of my heart, Iona of my love.' We made a pilgrimage to the mystical isle of St Columba, Hil hauling rather too much baggage along behind, as usual.

Riding the Intercity-Express,
Germany's very latest high-speed
answer to the Eurostar.

BELOW 'Heavens, Lizzie's in the
ball!' On Majori Beach in Riga, we
watched as two boys tried to propel
a huge transparent ball out to sea.
Liz's interest was piqued—with
near-fatal consequences.

ABOVE Music, fireworks and fountains at the famous
Peterhof Palace, outside St Petersburg.

LEFT
Scarlett
surrounded by
'scarlett' blossoms
in the Kadriorg
Palace gardens in
Tallinn, Estonia.

The shop windows in Venice are dressed so sumptuously that wandering the streets is like browsing a wonderful gallery.

In Venice, we chose rooms overlooking the canal, so Scarlett would be lulled to sleep by the gentle lapping of water. She was enchanted and hung out of the window gazing at the *gondolieri* manoeuvring their boats below.

quick with Phillip—he was so used to spotting animals that he assumed that Liz and I could manage without his help. I had to tell him that a kangaroo had to be pretty well nuzzling out of my hand for me to spot it unaided.

We sat on the top of the hill and watched the sun go down. As the shadows lengthened, taking on thin, sinister shapes, I thought about the intensity of the Aboriginal connection with the land and how brilliantly they managed to communicate this connection through art and their stories of the Dreaming. The colours in their paintings—from soft and mesmeric to dark and explosive— perfectly matched our experience on Widgery Hill.

At breakfast on our last morning Liz questioned Phillip.

'So what about wind power?'

'Yes, they're going to build a wind farm up on the range.'

Liz told me later that the wind farm would provide five per cent of New South Wales's energy requirements.

'It's curious that this remote part of Oz should be visited twice by capitalists and exploiters. And all within less than 150 years. They only found silver here in 1885. And later on lead and zinc. And now they're going to harvest the wind. What next?!'

Back in Broken Hill we had time to have a good look at the town before catching the Indian Pacific back to Sydney. The town seemed familiar now, dominated by the mountain of waste left over from the mining boom. On the mini-mountain they had built a now-rusting memorial to the miners who lost their lives. Mining conditions had been abominable until the unions became strong and were able to dictate terms to the mine owners. Perched beside the memorial was a spanking new restaurant, the pride of Broken Hill, with stunning views over the town and countryside.

Broken Hill is a gracious town enhanced by its large number of art galleries, of which Pro Hart's is the best known. Hart had some artist mates who lived around Broken Hill and they started the Brushmen of the Bush school of art, with an emphasis on super-realism. Liz loved Pro Hart's gallery, but I found it crass. There were four Rolls Royces parked next to the front door. The ostentation was mitigated by one of the cars being painted all over in Hart's trademark primitive style.

Liz thought one of the Brushmen had produced by far the best 'event' in the town. It was a huge picture, twelve by 100 metres, which took five years to paint, using over 3000 tonnes of paint, and is said to be the world's largest acrylic painting done by one artist. It includes 20,000 trees, 100,000 salt bushes and 3000 clouds. Liz said that in the mid-nineteenth century these panoramas were a popular way of representing landscape and battle scenes.

'I saw a battle scene in Wrocław just like this Broken Hill panorama. The enormous panorama creates a thrilling illusion of actually being there.'

The Broken Hill painting seemed to wrap itself around us and the 'real' foreground, which was made from actual red earth, bushes and stones, was difficult, if not impossible, to distinguish from the painting itself.

*

'I wonder what sort of lavatory culture they'll have in the train. Do you know, Phillip?'

Phillip was taking us to the station to catch the Indian Pacific to Sydney and looked startled by Liz's question.

Of course the loo was the same as the one on the Ghan—an impossible fold-away bedpan. Liz said, 'I think this crazy object is almost a metaphor for our travelling relationship—uncomfortable, but durable. Even when we're pushing up the daisies it will still be around.'

6

Package tours: cruising the Balkans and music among the Mafia

There was one thing I thought I knew about Liz—she would not entertain the idea of going on a cruise. And over our fifteen-year travels we only did one, which became known in our lexicon as the Balkan Cruise from Hell.

I was going to be in Tuscany on a cooking holiday during July one year and emailed Liz:

> Do you have any ideas for a 'hollier' in August?

She emailed back:

> What about a cruise up the Balkan coast?

I was surprised:

> You said you hate cruises.

Apparently it was her sister who had changed her mind:

> Well, Judy says the Balkan coast is all the rage these days and I'm keen to see the coast towns. She and John have been there three times. They say the only way is on a ship.

Liz added a list of 'must see' places at the end of her email. I should have smelt a rat when I found a remarkably cheap cruise on the internet, with berths still available. It was going to all the places on Liz's list.

The ship was leaving from Venice, so Liz and I were able to meet up beforehand and have a day and a half in La Serenissima before embarking. As we wandered through Venice's tiny streets, taking in a few Bellini paintings in a couple of churches and drinking actual Bellinis in St Mark's Square, we pondered what was in store for us.

'I've always had mixed feelings about the thought of being trapped on a boat with a large number of strangers, unable to get off,' I said.

'I agree. Cruises are in the same category as small islands. I also have a dread of 'cruisees'; I can do without them.' Liz shuddered at the thought.

'But it'll be the chance of a rest, with no decisions to make, no food to cook, no planes to catch and no packing and unpacking. I intend to loll by the pool listening to the water lapping and engines purring, drinking daiquiris. You can hoover up the lectures on archaeology. I want to be the complete slob. But I know I'll enjoy going ashore each day to sample the Balkans.

'It'll be so wonderful to be suspended in time at sea, dreaming away the hours and staring at the perpetual motion of the ocean. I have this fantasy that I'll be sitting on my deckchair watching the spray break over the hull while whales show off their tails and dolphins pirouette in the wake of the ship.'

'You're quite forgetting the weather,' Liz reminded me. 'It can be rough. What about the sea when it tosses you from side to side and throws you out of bed? Can you picture rushing to the rail to throw up, fervently praying you haven't been spotted by a fellow cruisee?

'And cruisees fall into two categories,' she went on. 'The young, and the forty plus. If they're young, their sole aim is to get laid by a swarthy deckhand. They haven't the remotest interest in their surroundings.'

'And what about couples our age?' I added. 'They've been bored stiff with each other for forty years and will sit silently wading through mountains of bland food and milky tea with arrowroot biscuits especially designed not to aggravate their ulcers or cause wind and farting.'

Liz warmed to the topic. 'They're desperate for a series of new chums to ease the boredom but, having lost what few social skills they might once have had, they're forced to spend an inordinate amount of time trying to prove the six degrees of separation theory.' We grinned and broke into a crazy impro.

'Where do you come from?'

'Coonabarabran,' I replied.

'You don't know my brother Brad Jones's family by any chance?'

'Jones the butcher, you mean?'

'No,' said Liz, 'they're a farming family.'

'I've got a second cousin who's married to a farmer Jones's great-niece in Coonabarabran,' I said triumphantly.

'Well, would you believe it!' said Liz. 'What a small world!'

Once this kind of cruisee had proved their six-degrees-of-separation theory, they would move on to ailments. We hoped there'd be a limit to the number of times we were expected to extol the virtues or otherwise of hip replacements, the best knee surgeon in London or the best drug for arthritis, migraine, cholesterol, indigestion, low-functioning thyroid or bunions. And if we weren't already driven to screaming point by ailments, we would surely reach it when the cruisees argued about the ship's choice of Trivial Pursuit questions and the inadequacies of the tour director. ('He's got a speech impediment—I can't understand a word he says.')

We both agreed that the choice of travelling companion was the crucial key to happy cruising. At this point we had come through enough mini-crises to discover that, while our very different personalities could have been disastrous, in fact we were increasingly able to enjoy our differences rather than grind each other into the dust! And humour was the glue. We would be hinged together, basking in our imagined superiority and amusing ourselves by creating exotic lives for our fellow cruisees. We were sure that we could liven up the mind-numbingly dull conversation that the cruisees would produce.

Our final day in Venice had augured well. We sipped coffee in the café opposite our hotel. Then we took a trip down the Grand Canal, walked round St Mark's Square, lunched at the Guggenheim Museum and finally, as a treat for me, indulged in my ultimate delight, a sprint to the museum shop for a spending spree. With no time to spare, we then sped back to the hotel to pick up our bags for the cruise. As I went to pay the bill I discovered that my wallet was missing. Nightmare. My pulse started speeding; I felt my chest constrict and my hands become cold and clammy. I feverishly upturned my bag onto the foyer floor, sending the contents skittering. On all fours, I chased my lip balm and loose change around the room. But there was no wallet. When and how it had happened neither of us had the faintest idea.

There was no time to go to the police, no time to ring anyone. I would have to do it from the ship. But no, when I arrived on board, stressed and breathless, they were not set up for credit card cancellations and the phone was out of order. (Mobile phones had not yet entered our lives.) The ship had recently been taken over by a Croatian company who were running it on a shoestring. The receptionist was blonde, Swedish and friendly enough, but hardly spoke any English. I spent the first three hours trying desperately to get access to a phone in order to stop thieves having a field day with my credit cards. I had to battle for attention against an armada of angry passengers who were already complaining about the very basic facilities they had discovered on board.

'Your sewerage system isn't working!' said one irate couple.

'There's a distinct smell of rotten eggs,' insisted another.

'If it smells bad now, what will it be like in three days when we're out at sea and nowhere near a plumber?' trumpeted a third.

Certainly the staff had no time for my stolen wallet. The blonde Swede was out of her depth. The ship was about to set sail and she hadn't a clue what to do. And it got worse. A very large American couple pushed their way to the front of the queue.

'We want a new cabin. The bed will not support us during our marital matters,' said Bradley, the husband, clearly not prepared for any compromise on such an important topic. Eunice, his wife, nodded emphatically.

A ship's bell rang loudly, the engines shuddered into life and everybody made for the deck. We sailed sedately past St Mark's Square and the slightly pink Doge's Palace. We lined the ship's side with our fellow cruisees, sighing with delight and anticipation as the perfect Venetian skyline gradually faded away into the dusk.

As night fell the most serious task on the cruising agenda reared its head and we proved to be sublimely ill prepared. We failed to find congenial people on the boat to sit with at meals. Cruisees, we observed, went about this quest in many different ways.

'I want to sit next to the most interesting person on the ship,' demanded an English lady from Sevenoaks as she stared at the *maître du bateau*'s list.

'Hide,' hissed Liz, firmly convinced that we were the most interesting people on board.

We got our comeuppance; having snottily refused to play the game, we were dumped with the also-rans in a corner of the dining room, well out of sight of civilised persons. The jewel among our fellow misfits was a tiny lady with beady black eyes. Her insistent gaze focused on each person at our table, darting from one to the next as she pecked at her seafood cocktail. She had a chalk-white painted face, toothless sunken cheeks, crimson lips, thinly painted black eyebrows and jet black hair. She dressed for dinner in a full-length lace Victorian evening gown, with a giant cameo brooch depicting two naked lovers planted in the middle of her chest. Despite severe arthritis, she wore antique silver rings on the fingers of both hands. She was so thin that I could have placed one hand round her waist. I was initially enchanted by her, but realised that conversation might prove a challenge. But it didn't take much to get her started. She told us that she worked for the company that owned the ship and had sailed on its inaugural voyage some forty years previously. Quite dotty. She must have been pushing a hundred years old, but maintained that she still did some account-ancy work for the company and would be getting off at their Dubrovnik office. 'They won't let me go,' she trilled. And having got that off her chest she promptly closed her eyes and went to sleep.

Later Liz and I argued about her.

'She's living in a total fantasy world,' said Liz.

'You always rush to judgement, Liz. There's probably a basis in truth and dementia has partially taken over.'

'You are so naïve, Hil.'

'Maybe so. But I like the idea of her sitting in splendour all by herself in Dubrovnik in a shoebox-sized office provided by the management. A reward for forty years of loyal service. "She's doing no harm," I'm sure that the office manager tells his staff. "Make sure she gets a cup of tea."'

Back in our cabin after our first evening on board Liz reminded me that we were here to see the Balkans, and not just to gossip about the cruisees. She had found out that the ship would be travelling mainly at night and that at dawn the next day we would be tying up at the quay alongside Korčula, an 'iconic' (as Liz described it) fortified Balkan town—a pimple of land jutting out into the sea with a backdrop of steep, densely wooded mountains. The ancient town of tiny, red-roofed stone houses huddled within fortress-like walls. Marco Polo was born there into a seafaring tradition that went back forever.

When we were 'released' by the first officer for the day, we decided to go for a proper walk down the coast and were amazed to see the amount of new development springing up. Holiday homes for the discerning Pom, we decided. I forgot my walking limitations, but after four kilometres sank onto a bench to admire the sea view and watch the passing parade. A man plonked himself beside us and we attempted conversation. Well, nods and smiles were the best we could do. I turned on a display of puffing and wiping my brow and made it clear that I was not looking forward to the walk back.

The man disappeared and returned with his wife. She spoke a little English, indicated a nearby car and invited us to get in. As she drove us back to the ship, she told us about her son, whom she had visited in Australia the previous year. Like so many people in

Croatia, her son had left during the 1990s and she missed him. 'Next time you visit him you must look me up,' I said, and gave her my email address. We were touched by the friendliness and generosity of these strangers, so unlike shipboard life with the cruisees.

That evening after we'd got back from the Korčula trip, Liz said that she was bored and intended to liven up the atmosphere on board.

'I came down with leprosy while on a cruise to New Guinea,' she announced to a group of cruisees, including Bradley and Eunice, as we sipped martinis at the bar before dinner. Eunice reeled back, clutching Brad's hand.

'I had visited Molokai, inspired by Father Damien in that movie, before the cruise, and the nuns gave me the task of washing bandages. That's where I caught it.' Eunice shuddered.

'By the time they were able to airlift me off the ship I'd turned blue and gone into a coma. They hospitalised me for a month and then sent me to a lepers' colony in East Timor. If it hadn't been for friends in high places I'd still be there.' The whole group stared at Liz rigid in silent horror. I was privately wondering when one of them would say 'pull the other one', but no. Liz rose.

'Please excuse me—I must rest. I still get palpitations.' And with that winning line she beat a speedy retreat to our cabin, leaving me to pick up the pieces. Eunice immediately plied me with questions about Liz's current state of health.

'Your friend is very pale. Are you sure she's not infectious?'

'She's fine. She's fine. The diagnosis was wrong.'

I wasn't sure whether Eunice believed me, but I noticed that from that day on the two of them steered a wide berth whenever they saw Liz.

By the time I joined Liz in the cabin she had found a steward and was regaling him with the tall tale. We all drank some red wine and dissolved into laughter.

Split was our next port of call. In 295 AD the megalomaniacal Roman Emperor Diocletian started building his remarkable palace there. It took ten years to build both the palace and the 26-metre high walls that enclosed it. It is spread over nine acres and the stones have been recycled over the centuries into a mass of higgledy-piggledy houses for less regal people. It is now a commercial and residential centre. The downstairs halls of the palace retain their grandeur despite the indoor stalls, which have been set up with a variety of local arts and crafts. There is an outdoor market too for fruit and vegetables, which had an especially large nut section. Much to Liz's delight she was able to replenish her pecan, macadamia and almond supply, which she kept as a buffer against the worst of the ship's food. The palace was named a World Heritage Site in 1979, as much for its Gothic and baroque buildings, which date from the Middle Ages, as for its Roman origins.

We wandered round Split's tiny alleyways, rushing to the quayside from time to time to see fishermen dangling their lines in the water and to check that our ship was still there. Ringing in our ears was the first officer's warning that if passengers were not back on board by 5 pm the ship would leave. It would wait for no one.

Split's central square was buzzing with cafés and activity. We sat sipping a coffee and chatted to an English couple at the next table. They were buying a house in Split. 'Croatia is the new "in" place. Buy now and you'll make a fortune in a few years,' they enthused. We were so engrossed in money talk with them that we lost count of time, particularly as neither of us was wearing a watch, and barely made it to the boat. I couldn't run, but Liz nobly tore on ahead, waving her arms and crying out, 'Wait, wait, Hilly's got bad legs, she's coming.' I was eyed grimly by the FO as I climbed the gangplank, puffing. We missed Diocletian's mausoleum, which had been refashioned into the town's cathedral, and had to rely on cruisees' descriptions. 'Seen one cathedral, seen them all,' seemed to be the general feeling.

The sewerage situation worsened that evening. The smell was so bad that Liz was convinced we would die of gas poisoning if we remained in our cabin for one more night. She set me up, as usual, insisting that only my overbearing manner could achieve results. Seduced by the flattery of her backhanded compliment I whirled into action and managed to gain the one remaining deck side cabin, much to the chagrin of our fellow cruisees, who were suffering just as badly as we were.

The ship raced through the night and an intense storm. The noise of the thunder, lightning and ferocious waves penetrated even our superior new cabin, but we slept at last, our noses quivering with relief, and woke to a blessed and serene silence. We had arrived at dawn at Kotor, way up a fiord, with high mountains rising on either side of the narrow strip of water.

The cruise had arranged an excursion for us from Kotor. Up, up, up the mountain we drove. The Austrian engineer who had built the road was in love with his Empress Maria and had designed it in a massive M shape, carved out of the mountains.

At the top we crossed into the tiny statelet of Montenegro, with a population of a mere 650,000. When its president recently visited China he was asked why he had not brought all his fellow citizens with him on the visit.

Cetinje is the former royal capital of Montenegro. Liz was in her element here and gave a rant about the iniquities of nineteenth-century nationalists carving up the Ottoman Empire.

'Some trumped-up Montenegrin bandit who caught the eye of the Austrian Emperor was declared King Nikola,' she declaimed, 'and all his eight daughters made magnificent marriages to European royalty. One even became the Queen of Italy. This was the king's old palace and has been made into a museum. I believe it's like a shooting lodge and filled with the impedimenta and clutter of a large nineteenth-century family.' We trudged around with Liz muttering about the 'grim photographs' and 'appalling paintings of bemedalled, uniformed old boys with those ghastly plump ladies standing beside them dolled up in great stiff frocks'.

Meals were the centrepiece of the Balkan cruise, around which everything else flowed, even the shore expeditions. They were designed to last as long as possible. On our return from Montenegro that evening the captain and his crew dressed up and paraded through the dining room behind a gloomy, out-of-tune Croatian band. The meal which followed was one of the worst and the music that played as we ate was a morbid medley of Croatian standards. Bradley, who turned out to own a waste disposal company, got bored with the music choice and insisted that the band play 'Funiculì, Funiculà' followed by a medley of tunes from *South Pacific*. The band had terrible difficulties with 'Some Enchanted Evening' and 'Bali Ha'i'. Only the lead guitarist had any idea of the tunes and finally it was left to him, with a bit of percussion to help with the beat. Eunice, Bradley's wife, was deeply frustrated when the Entertainment Director seized her arm as she mounted the stage and prevented her from joining the band. 'They're not used to passengers singing with them, you can have a turn later,' he said, guiding her back to her seat.

'You surely can, sweet pea!' Bradley was quick to back her up. Within minutes she was back on stage letting rip with a full-throated warbling version of 'I'm Gonna Wash That Man Right Outta My Hair' with the band hopelessly struggling to keep up. But Eunice was unstoppable; she sang all the verses, with accompanying hair-washing gestures, and brought the song to a ringing conclusion on a high trill. Brad rose to his feet calling out, 'You're a star, Euun!' and hollering with delight. Liz and I followed suit, bravo-ing and cheering, 'Good on you, darl!'

*

Dubrovnik is described by the brochures as the jewel of the Balkans, a walled town perched on the Adriatic sea coast. For centuries it was an independent city-state, an enclave within the Ottoman Empire, and later attached to Venice. The secret of its success was apparently its maritime trade and its supreme negotiating skills, which brought its citizens untold wealth. This translated into intricate, palatial buildings which filled the town. It is the numero uno Balkan tourist destination and I confess that unlike Liz, who loved it, I felt as if I was walking around a film set.

'It's all so perfect, so clean—there isn't a single piece of waste paper or a cigarette butt on the cobbles. I can't see a single Dubrovnikian, other than the shopkeepers.'

'That's because there aren't any. They're in the suburbs. Remember, Hil, the original city was besieged for seven months in 1991 by Serb–Montenegrin forces and heavily damaged. It had to be totally rebuilt in its fifteenth- and sixteenth-century form, but now the buildings house one long string of cafés and tourist shops.'

We climbed up to the battlements, planning to walk around the encircling walls of the city. The view there looked just as it would have from the fifteenth/sixteenth-century city, and there was a stunning view down the coast. We started walking at a brisk pace. Well, in truth I only got halfway and then plonked myself down and ate fresh figs and salami, while Liz sprinted off and completed the whole circuit.

Finally at the end of the Balkan coast there was Corfu, made famous by Lord Byron, who started a trend for the rich and famous by holidaying there in the nineteenth century. The day we docked, five other cruise boats joined us and disgorged ten thousand people into the town. It wasn't good, but by the luckiest of chances—Liz said it was because we were such experienced travellers—we found Costa, a cheery, grey-haired grizzled café owner in Lemon Square. Even though we were way outside his lunch trading hours and into siesta time he made a point of serving us olives, feta and grilled fish. He was full of anecdotes about his time in America, where his proudest memory appeared to have been teaching his son to use an ice-cream machine. Friends and members of his large family dropped in to visit him and were introduced to us with beaming smiles and many handshakes.

After Corfu, the captain turned back north up the Balkan coast for one final stop at Pula, neatly positioned in the armpit of the Adriatic, across from Venice and just down from Trieste. We sailed into it past a host of pretty islands, one of which was Tito's favourite when he ruled communist Yugoslavia. Pula is dominated by a vast Roman amphitheatre and massive fortifications associated with the erstwhile naval headquarters of the Austro-Hungarian Empire.

The old town was in the midst of being refurbished for tourists; the main square sported a 'sweet' (as Liz put it) Roman temple, some good cafés and a brand-new information office, which on the day we docked was holding a smart party to cement links with

Ireland. James Joyce, we discovered, had taught English here to naval cadets for a few months before he got fed up and moved to Trieste to write his blockbuster *Ulysses*. We cleverly managed to wangle our way into the party, got stuck into the grog and rapidly made ourselves the centre of attention. I made out that I had recently produced and directed *Exiles*, the only play Joyce wrote, and Liz announced that she had run the annual Bloomsday celebrations in Dublin. The embroidery of our stories grew more and more extravagant. Finally, brimming with alcoholic goodwill, we were guided carefully but firmly to the door by the customer relations officer.

'Irresponsibility is part of the pleasure of all art,' I called out to no one in particular.

'A man of genius makes no mistakes,' sang out Liz as she tripped down the steps. And as a postscript she called out, 'Ireland sober is Ireland stiff.'

As we floated on to a vast museum stuffed with Roman remains we congratulated ourselves on our recall of Joycean *bon mots*. Normally my heart sinks at the sight of room after room containing bits and pieces of pots and dishes but with a residual glow still warming my heart I could see that they were artfully displayed and could feel the excitement those early collectors must have felt as they unearthed treasure dating back two millennia.

We had very little Croatian money left but the woman in charge of the desk let us pay the student rate since that was all the money we had. After we had seen the museum, I naturally wanted to buy things in the shop but strangely, for a town pushing tourism hard, the museum would only take Croatian currency. It wouldn't even take Liz's credit cards. Emboldened by our first 'Irish' experience, Liz was resolute.

'We're going back to the tourist place, Hilly,' she announced. 'They need to smarten up their act.' We barged into the office, where various clerks were now clearing up after the party.

'We need to see your Head of Cultural Affairs,' said Liz. Secretaries sprang to attention and tried to halt our advance, but Liz was having none of it.

'Where is his office?' she demanded, and started down the corridor. A secretary worriedly indicated the last room on the right. 'He's very busy,' said the nervous girl, but Liz was undeterred. She marched on down and, without knocking, entered the room, with me bringing up the rear. Sitting doodling on his notepad behind an empty desk was the man who had escorted us from the party. We, and he, behaved as though we had never set eyes on one another before.

'Were you aware of the absurdity of having a positive tourist policy which does not allow purchases with credit cards in your museum?' Liz began imperiously.

'Most people who visit the museum don't have credit cards,' he replied, after a pause.

'Frankly, sir, that is no argument at all,' said Liz, banging her fist on the table. The poor wretch looked flustered and rose to his feet.

'I am afraid I must ask you to leave,' he said, coming round the desk. 'The office is closed. Please enjoy the rest of your stay in Pula and thank you for your observations.' And with that he ushered us from the room and into the hands of the secretary, who was hovering outside the door. Later, as we were walking towards the dock, she came running after us.

'Oh, hell, what now?' I groaned.

But with a beaming smile the girl thrust two free entrance tickets to the Roman amphitheatre into our hands. 'Enjoy.'

The amphitheatre was a crumbling ruin, not unlike a mouth full of decaying molars. The tourist office had done little to spruce it up. We climbed up to the back row of the gods and sat breathlessly on the curved stone seat. Far below us in the arena Liz spied a gaggle of cruisees and pointed out Brad and Eunice among them. Eunice was resplendent in a red miniskirt and pink plunging neckline. Liz started shouting out at them: 'Zombies, bores . . .' The cruisees looked up towards the noise, recognised their 'friends' Liz and Hilly from on board and waved and smiled at us.

'Behave yourself, Liz,' I said. 'You're an outrage. We've still got to get through the next two days. Come on, it's five to five. We don't want to miss the boat.'

The cruise was nearly over. On the last night the management went berserk: chefs strutted through the dining room with platters of lobster embellished with mayonnaise squiggles and decorated with fading hibiscus, followed by waiters wearing pillbox hats and red military-looking jackets, bearing above their heads dishes of ham with pineapple rings and glacé cherries. A second flotilla of waiters followed, with poached salmon swimming in creamy pink seafood sauce and rare roast beef drowning in thinly disguised blood. The *coup de théâtre* was the pudding, which was announced by the *maître du bateau* amid a roll of drums. 'We are happy to present for you tonight the signature dish of our chef, Fabio—the Dalmatian Lantern.' The cruisees clapped as an ice-cream cake—covered with browned eggwhite sculpted in weird abstract shapes and surrounded by blue flames—toured the dining room. To say the food was dismal on this cruise would be the understatement of the century.

We were on our way to Venice the next day.

During the cruise Liz had befriended a crowd of losers. Milly from Worthing, desperate to find a man to replace her dead husband; middle-aged, fey George, who sniffed and blew his nose when anyone looked at him; and a couple of old-age pensioner twins who had lived with each other all their lives and had no social skills whatsoever. I, meanwhile, had befriended Stella, the ex-wife of the chairman of a well-known film production house and distribution company. Over dinner Liz became horrified by Stella's descriptions of her ex-husband's priapic behaviour, recounted while her daughter, Hermione, sat squirming beside her. As soon as the jelly trifle pudding had been served Liz beat a hasty retreat.

'I gave up my life to look after Hermione,' said Stella, as if Hermione wasn't present. I remember looking at her daughter and seeing her blank expression. I could think of no words of comfort, so stayed silent. Stella took this as an invitation to continue. She detailed the horror of the divorce and her belief that Benjy, the loathsome husband, had been squirrelling money away in the Caymans. Hermione interjected. 'You don't know that, Mummy— you're so unfair to Daddy.' Stella couldn't handle the criticism and burst into tears. It was very embarrassing.

'Sacrifice is so unnecessary. It's an overrated pastime. Thank God it was you, Hil. I couldn't have coped when she burst into tears,' said Liz later in our cabin.

We were arriving in Venice in the late afternoon and everyone was busy making arrangements for how to spend the evening there. I had mopped Stella up and invited her and Hermione to join us for dinner. I had assumed that Liz was coming with us, but no, she had promised to show off Venice to her bunch of losers. When she heard about my arrangement, she said, 'Why can't the losers come with us, then? Why can't we all go together?'

'Look, Liz, this is real life; we're not the welfare state, where the weak are to be looked after and cosseted by the strong. You know perfectly well that the two lots won't get on. And I admit I can't deal with Stella on my own. She's a crashing Big Bore and I really do need you to leaven the evening.'

I could see we were headed for a showdown, but Liz averted it.

'OK then, Hil, I'll put my lot off and say we have no time after all.'

We kept dinner with Stella and Hermione short and I felt guilty about the losers. Liz, of course, doesn't do guilt.

The cruise had lasted six days; it seemed like an eternity.

Liz waxed eloquent on the subject of cruises as we debriefed the next morning at breakfast in St Mark's Square.

'It's a lifetime in miniature—you enter it friendless and aimless; you leave overwhelmed with instant intimates and a resolve to start a New Life. The extraordinary thing is that the hothouse atmosphere on board reduces everybody's inhibitions to a remarkable extent. There were people telling me—a total stranger—their innermost secrets in the belief that I had become their best friend and was to be trusted. What a mistake! I've never kept a secret in my life. And look at you, Hil, you had a field day. If you weren't pouring out stories of your own dramatic and emotion-filled life to anyone who would listen, you were listening to weeping divorcees and other similarly overwrought persons.'

'True. I'm completely dotty. Incidentally, Lizzie, did I tell you that the ship's office in Dubrovnik managed to cancel my credit cards and, amazingly, no transactions had taken place. What a relief.'

Liz wasn't listening. She had turned her attention to a cute waiter and was regaling him with her homespun cruise philosophy.

After Venice we hotfooted it to Naples for what turned out to be another cruise experience, although more on the heavenly side of hell than the Balkan one. There would be the same horror of being cooped up with a crowd of people, but this time the cruise was on land and, instead of calling in on towns down a coast, we would be listening to music with our fellow cruisees in churches, palaces and theatres.

Naples was high on Liz's list of RIZs (Robber Infested Zones), places not to be visited. Liz was convinced that I looked like a tourist and that this would make us an instant target for thieves and muggers. I was equally determined that Naples was a must, and came up with a good wheeze to convince Liz to visit. I had discovered the Rupert Dickens Travel Agency. Rupert ran sophisticated specialist tours. There were several to Naples, but the one that caught my eye was a festival of baroque music and I sent the details to Liz. She liked baroque music and was cajoled into agreeing to go.

Two weeks before our visit, while we were still cruising the Balkans, Italy's then prime minister, Romano Prodi, announced a reduced sentence for 27,000 prisoners, many of whom would go free. In Naples this resulted in a frenzy of killings—ten people in twelve days, we read in a two-day-old English paper in Split.

'I warned you about RIZs,' Liz said.

'A life lived in fear is a life half lived,' I responded loftily.

We were booked into the Hotel Santa Maria on the Bay of Naples. Liz had decided to travel to Naples via Rome while I flew straight from Venice. I'm a firm believer that there is no need to worry: when your number is up, it's up, so with more bravado than I could really lay claim to I emerged by myself from Naples airport and tentatively hailed a taxi.

The driver proceeded to hare at breakneck speed through dimly lit suburbs towards, I hoped, my hotel on the other side of the city. Shouting incomprehensibly down his mobile phone and gesticulating wildly, he wove his way in and out of the traffic. It wasn't long before he was tailed by four sirened police cars. One signalled my driver to stop and pulled alongside. There was a sharp exchange and I felt a sick feeling in my stomach. I was convinced I was in serious trouble, for weren't cops in Italy hand in glove with the Mafia? After what felt like an eternity, the police appeared to be satisfied with my driver's explanation and we were motioned on our way. I leant forward: 'What's going on?' The driver put his fingers to his head. 'Bad men . . . bang bang.' 'See Naples and die' suddenly seemed a distinct possibility. He continued screeching around corners as I sat frozen and silent, my heart pumping far too fast. We finally arrived at the hotel and screamed to a halt. Breathing a sigh of relief I tottered from the cab, over-tipping the driver, and fell into the arms of the porter at the Hotel Santa Maria. The ambience of the hotel was calm, welcoming me warmly with its flowers, muted lighting and chocolate mints.

When Liz arrived in our room an hour later I burbled out the story of my horror journey from the airport.

'It's your own fault, I told you Naples was a bad idea. You'd better have a restorative whiskey—you're still gibbering,' said Liz.

'*Due prosecci* would be more on the mark, I think.'

The drinks arrived borne on a silver tray by a gorgeous Neapolitan Lothario. His sultry gaze from beneath hooded lids was directed at me, I was convinced, and it cheered me up enormously.

'*Buona sera, signora, come sta?*' Nothing like practised Mediterranean charm to bolster a girl's spirits.

'*Bene grazie,*' I replied, smiling winningly.

'Eeef you need something, you ring me,' said Paolo, my new friend.

'What a dish!' I felt my spirits lift as he and his cute bottom withdrew from the room.

We repaired to the balcony facing Mount Vesuvius on the other side of the bay and drank several *prosecci*; the cold bubbles hit the spot and we relaxed. As the sun sank blood-red into the sea I felt shielded from any assassins at large in the city.

After such an unnerving start to the holiday it was hard to switch gear and concentrate on baroque music. I was curious about the Rupert Dickens approach and anxious that it meet with Liz's approval. His was no common-or-garden package tour. He catered for the A-list. A Rupert Dickens festival was organised as a private event; concert venues, musicians, orchestras and the whole program were carefully chosen to appeal to the finer sensibilities of the English upper class. If a client desired intellectual pursuits in addition to music, he or she would be accompanied individually to museums or galleries by his or her very own art historian. And if that sounded too much like hard work, the punters could opt for leisurely walks through historic Naples, always accompanied by a walker briefed to keep us to the 'safe' parts of the city, well away from assault and battery. Rupert had gone to the expense of adding security guards to his staff, employed solely to calm the uneasy.

Every morning a genial musicologist called Basil bounced into the hotel ballroom to give the exclusive two hundred a witty lecture about the music we were to hear. He was shaped like a toby jug and bald, save for a ring of hair surrounding his pate and one or two wispy stragglers protruding from his ears. 'You don't have to take notes, there won't be a test—ho, ho, ho,' Basil chortled, his tummy wobbling up and down. His captive audience smiled politely.

Clearly briefed by Dickens not to challenge or bore his clientele, Basil stuck mainly to saucy anecdotes about the goings-on of the composers, occasionally allowing his fruity baritone to burst into a phrase or two from the *cantate* we were to hear that night by way of illustration.

Rupert had taken great care with accommodation and dining as well. He chose four hotels with price tags to cater for all of us at appropriate levels of comfort and took private rooms in restaurants graded five-star, brasserie or café. This enabled the repeat Dickensians and five-star persons to stretch out in their suites on the thirty-first floor and to cluster together for meals, avoiding the riffraff, in fine dining establishments like George's where Chef Vincenzo Bacioterracino wove his magic for the discerning foodies. (We managed to penetrate George's by dint of a cleverly concocted tale from Liz.) Rupert made sure, however, that we all came together in a show of egalitarianism at L'Antica Pizzeria Da Michele for their fabled pizza marinara or margherita. I was reminded that feeding large numbers rarely produces excell-ence and I pined for the Italian home cooking of my foodie friends, Helen and Iain, with whom I have spent so many nights in fabulous Italian 'cook-ups' and whose *spaghetti alla vongole* is the best seafood pasta I have ever tasted. It certainly beat the Da Michele pizza marinara hands down.

* * * * *

Helen & Iain's Spaghetti alla Vongole

Serves 4

Ingredients

    1 corm of garlic (bulb)
    olive oil

500 g spaghetti

1.25 kg vongole (fresh clams)

1 bunch flat-leaf parsley, finely chopped

Preparation

1. Chop garlic finely into small cubes.
2. Put on hot water for the pasta.
3. Fry the garlic in the oil in a large, deep frying pan.
4. When the water is boiling, add the pasta.
5. Add the vongole to the garlic and oil (on high-ish heat) and cover with a lid. The vongole are cooked when all the shells are open.
6. When the pasta is *al dente*, drain it.
7. Mix in the garlic, oil and vongole, then add parsley and serve.

* * * * *

The 'five-starrers' used Basil's briefings to parade their expert knowledge of baroque music in front of their fellow travellers, trumping each other and Basil with increasingly obscure fragments of musical trivia. Curiously enough, it was the ladies who led the competitive stakes. They all appeared to have taken baroque music appreciation courses and voices shrilled as they corrected each other about the date that Handel arrived in Naples or the year when *La Serva Padrona* had been composed. Meanwhile, the crème de la crème of British justice and industry sat quietly, chins sunk into their chests, dreaming of their mistresses and the golf course. Liz and I began to feel distinctly out of our element in this elitist hothouse.

We were all thrown together for dinner the first evening before the concert at a cheery brasserie, with half the restaurant cordoned off for us. To my horror they had placed Liz and me on a table for eight with two businessmen, their wives and one legal couple. Clearly one of Rupert's minions had made a mistake. After introductions, Liz downed four glasses of chianti and grew expansive.

'Did you know that Gesualdo, who we are to hear tonight, murdered his wife and lover but got off because he was a prince? How about that?' Liz remarked to Arthur, a retired insurance chief executive who was seated opposite her. 'In the eighteenth century, apparently,' she went on, waving her fork dangerously near his shirt front, 'you could murder your nearest and dearest but be completely absolved if the deed was considered "honourable". What do you make of that?'

'Really, is that so?' Arthur muttered politely before Libby, his wife, interrupted, brittle with black onyx earrings and diamante décolletage. 'It's a pity his musical life was so cruelly interrupted.' Her voice sounded like a sharp metal object being drawn across a pane of glass.

'Well, I suppose there had to be some recognition of wrong-doing. However, we are fortunate that there was barely a lost moment and he continued composing happily when the trial was over,' Liz continued gaily, unaware of the gathering storm.

'I understood that he retreated to the family castle and didn't compose for four years.' Libby's voice was cold and hard.

'I think you'll find that story is a myth,' said Liz, and I kicked her under the table.

Libby glared at her. 'In any event, his private indiscretions are hardly going to affect our enjoyment of tonight's music, are they?'

The rest of the table nodded vigorously. Game to Libby—but the next moment I found myself holding my breath as an horrific scene played out in slow motion.

Liz knocked over her wine glass and the contents sloshed across the table and landed in Libby's lap. A red stain spread across her ivory silk skirt and dripped onto her matching Ferragamo shoes. 'I'm *so* sorry,' Liz gasped. Libby's smile vanished and she excused herself from the table. After a few agonising minutes she returned, wearing a grey cashmere coat.

'Darling, is everything in order now?' asked the ever-solicitous Arthur, now in damage-control mode. 'I'm sure the hotel will be able to sort it out.'

'Well, I won't be trusting Neapolitan dry-cleaners. It will have to wait until I can see Helmut,' responded Libby, casting a look of extreme distaste in Liz's direction.

'Please allow me to pay for the dry-cleaning,' said Liz, adding, 'and I will be more than happy to replace your exquisite shoes.'

Her exaggerated concern was making matters worse; she had no idea that a pair of Ferragamos would set her back the price of an Air Baltic fare to Australia.

I was intensely relieved when the meal ended and we were able to escape to the Gesualdo concert, which was held in the octagonal chapel of the Pio Monte della Misericordia on Spaccanapoli, a street in the heart of old Naples. The chapel was built around the corner from the Duomo for a charitable institution founded in 1601 by seven noblemen as a place where they could carry out acts of Christian charity, feeding and clothing people in need, nursing the sick, sheltering pilgrims and burying the dead.

This was our group's first excursion out of the hotel. The coach taking us to the chapel was frequently brought to a standstill in the narrow cobbled streets by the jostle of pedestrians. The busload became silent and small talk dried up. Libby looked nervously out of the coach window. Liz and I had taken care to make ourselves scarce at the back of the coach. The driver was forced to park some distance from the chapel. Before opening the doors a Dickens guide stood at the front of the bus and delivered words of warning.

'Make sure you hold on to your bags. You have a three-minute walk to the chapel. Please walk briskly. You were alerted before you left England that there has been a rise in violence in Naples recently and the government has even been threatening curfews. The police have informed us that several armed robberies have taken place recently in this area.' I noticed that the guide chose her words carefully. No mention of abduction or murder. 'We don't want to lose any of you,' she joked.

Her attempt at humour met with a titter at best. Libby gave a pinched smile and anxiety spread like swine flu round the coach.

Italian novelist Curzio Malaparte once said, 'Naples is the most mysterious and dangerous city in Europe. And yet it is one of the few cities of the ancient world that has survived.' But today, two-and-a-half thousand years on, we felt apprehensive as we set out on the three-minute walk to the chapel. Relief was palpable when the final Dickensian had turned the corner and climbed the steps away from the street and Rupert's guide allowed us all to proceed through an arched foyer into the modest chapel.

Any remaining fears soon evaporated as we listened to the soaring voices of the British *a cappella* group the Tallis Scholars; music always manages to lift my mood.

During the interval I noticed the famous Caravaggio painting *The Seven Works of Mercy* hanging over the altar. I couldn't believe that such a masterpiece would be hanging in the church, quite unprotected from thieves.

'Caravaggio's another one,' commented Liz loudly to no one in particular. 'Fled to Naples after murdering someone in Rome.'

'Don't bang on any more about murder, Liz,' I shushed. 'Behave yourself and tell me about the painting.'

Liz opened her trusty 1980 Frommer's and read: '*The altarpiece was painted in 1607 and shows the seven acts of mercy and the virgin being carried by two angels down into the streets of Spaccanapoli. You can see the passionate and spontaneous reactions of the people in the streets. It's a remarkable picture.*'

The following day we went exploring by ourselves. There were no sounds of police sirens or foot patrols on duty at street corners. The Neapolitans were friendly wherever we went and, surprisingly, we felt quite safe. We had a pizza arrabiata in one of the many cafés which stretched along the Piazza Bellini with its creeper-covered walls and then continued our walk through the more 'monumental' part of the city. Crossing the open Piazza Plebiscito with its dramatic colonnades we watched narcissistic young Neapolitan men doing push-ups or jogging around the perimeter in skimpy shorts.

'Too much testosterone,' remarked Liz.

'Your mind is single track—sex.'

'Not at all. It's Italian macho exhibitionism, which is quite another thing,' responded Liz.

Soon I was moaning about my aching knees so we sank into the lavish Belle Époque Caffè Gambrinus and sipped espressos as the world passed by. Liz pulled out our schedule and read with delight about our next musical event.

'You'll be pleased to hear that all those tales of murder finished when Handel arrived in Naples in 1708. Can you imagine how *fabuloso* it will be to hear the Gabrieli Consort performing Handel's dramatic cantata, *Aci, Galatea e Polifemo*, at the Royal Palace at Caserta? How exciting is that—a whole theatre exclusively for *us!*' Liz's enthusiasm was infectious.

Before the concert we had lunch in Caserta's Villa Porfidia. The gracious old mansion had seen better days. In the dining room the frescos at one corner of the ceiling had caved in, the ragged edges revealing the original Renaissance design painted beneath. The owners had attempted to distract our attention from the ceiling by piling the tables with Italian delicacies.

This was no ordinary catering. We feasted on *braciolette napoletana* (rolled veal stuffed with pine nuts and sultanas, garlic and parsley), *coniglio in agrodolce* (rabbit in sweet-and-sour sauce), *pesce spada* (swordfish), *vitello tonnato* (chilled veal in a creamy tuna sauce), *timballo* (a pasta pie with any number of fillings), *risotto alla milanese*, *carne al ragù* (stew made from lamb shoulder with pancetta, garlic and white wine) and of course Naples's own *spaghetti napoletana*, made the traditional way. There were pastas of every conceivable shape and size—*ravioli*, *fusilli*, *tagliatelli*, *rigatoni*, *trenette*, *spaghettini*, *orecchiette*, *linguini* and *penne* with every conceivable sauce, hot and cold, sweet and sour, spicy and plain.

And, though we were already straining to keep our zips zipped, it didn't end there. In came the 'puds'. First, an elderly retainer-type character limped in struggling under the weight of a vast silver salver containing a mountain of strawberries with mascarpone. Five more frail attendants followed in procession, carrying dishes piled with *torta di rabarbaro* (rhubarb tart), *semifreddo al torrone* (semifreddo with nougat), *zuccotto* (a semi-frozen dessert made with brandy, cake and ice-cream), *tiramisù con fichi* (tiramisu with figs) and *cassata*, of course. As a self-confessed foodie, I was spoilt for choice.

The family who owned the villa were clearly in financial straits and were busy trying to fill their coffers by entertaining tourists who were prepared to ignore the villa's Fawlty Towers appearance.

I wondered how they could possibly be making a profit given the variety and extravagance of the lunch. They must have hired all the local signoras to prepare their favourite dishes and sent the husbands out at dawn to pick up the day's fresh catch.

*

After lunch we wandered into the courtyard and I was particularly taken by the neat queue of Dickensian ladies in tweed skirts, jerseys, pearls and sensible walking shoes standing politely but urgently in line for the single loo, observed by a line of sneering stone-lipped Greek gods and a few moth-eaten retainers.

When the ladies' ablutions were complete we were bussed to the Royal Palace at Caserta. Built by Charles III to emulate Versailles and containing 1200 rooms, there was not much to it now—a sad, neglected building, with room after room only partially furnished and mournful looking.

But we were bound for the theatre. The two hundred faithful spread out like excited kids on a school outing and claimed forty boxes, which rose in four gold and crimson tiers around the horseshoe-shaped auditorium. Liz ran around the perimeter of the theatre, darting into box after box, calling out to me at the top of her voice, 'Hilly, can you hear me?' from the top semicircle of boxes. 'The acoustics are brilly.'

'Yes, shh! Come back here. It's about to start.'

I had spotted our 'best friend' Libby, seated nearby in steely silence.

As Liz bounded into our box she gave me a rapid précis of the opera. 'You're going to see the young lovers, Acis and Galatea, sorely tried by the evil cyclops, Polyphemus. There's no happy ending. Polyphemus kills Acis in a jealous rage and all poor ol' Galatea can do is turn Acis into a fountain. Cold comfort.'

And almost immediately the lights dimmed and the performance started—just for us. The lovers sang affectingly about their love while the cyclops grew wild with jealous fury. The music soared to the rafters. Liz listened intently and I located Basil on the other side of the theatre miming a few 'pom-titty-pom-poms' and tapping his fingers on the edge of his box. Meanwhile, three boxes away, Arthur stared attentively at the stage while Libby sat with her eyes closed, her back ramrod straight.

'How did you find it?' Liz fearlessly buttonholed Arthur at the conclusion of the performance.

'Very fine indeed,' replied Arthur, before being removed from Liz's grasp by Libby. Liz was perplexed.

'The problem is you never know when to stop,' I said, by way of explanation.

*

'Did you know that Pergolesi was also from Naples? Have you ever heard his *Stabat Mater*?' asked Liz, as we walked up the path that evening towards the Certosa di San Martino.

'Yes, I'm sure I have,' I said, in a feeble attempt to sound knowledgeable. Liz knew full well that I was lying.

'Well, that's what we're hearing tonight. It's one of the great baroque choral works,' she said, assuming the lofty manner she used when she knew more than I did, which was most of the time.

She continued with a potted history of the building.

'The Certosa di San Martino is one of the richest monuments in Naples. It was begun in the thirteenth century as a monastery and additions were made over the centuries. It's now a museum with a hodge podge of corridors, cloisters and chapels decorated in a confusion of styles. It's the most visible landmark in Naples, positioned on top of the Vomero hill which dominates the Gulf.'

'You sound like Wikipedia.'

During the interval, we wandered around the many rooms which led off the concert hall. In one we found tables groaning with food. Any minute now, guests at a wedding reception in the adjoining cloister would be descending on the grub, but my eye had alighted on plates of rum baba and *sfogliatelle*.

'Now then, Hilly, put them back,' Liz called out, in front of our entire group. Her eagle eye had spied me from the other side of the room. Sprung, I was shamed into missing out on Naples's famous flaky pastry and yeast cakes. Seething, I returned to the concert hall and concentrated my mind on the second *Stabat Mater*, this time by Scarlatti.

*

'I preferred the Scarlatti,' I said to Liz afterwards, even though, if I were honest, I thought it unlikely that I would be able to tell one from the other in a month's time.

'Definitely superior, I agree.' Liz was being chummy now. I decided charitably that she felt mean having publicly humiliated me, but I would learn over the years that it was a technique of hers to shock me into reducing my food consumption. It didn't work, but I gave her full marks for trying.

Andreas Scholl, a star among countertenors, provided the highlight of the week in the Salone delle Feste at the Capodimonte art gallery. The distinguished surroundings and rarified quality of his voice made for a unique event. The Dickensians were thrilled to have a famous name to drop into conversation at their dinner parties back in South Kensington and Hampstead. After all, he'd sung at the Last Night of the Proms.

Most mornings during our stay in Naples Liz woke early, turned her back on Vesuvius and went for a walk along the promenade towards a fishing port where the catch was temptingly displayed on stalls each day. I rose later and, in order to avoid too much walking, discovered a café not far from the hotel on the corner of a narrow cobbled street festooned with washing. There I sat, drinking *caffè latte*, people-watching and reading the daily papers. Every day there were horrifyingly graphic shots of the latest murder on the streets. One day I dragged Liz into my café to show her a picture of the Madonna, prominently displayed on one wall, her head crowned with an illuminated neon halo. It was deliciously kitsch and I was very taken with it.

'It's ghastly, Hilly.'

'You need to broaden your aesthetic, Liz,' I retorted. But sensing this argument would go nowhere, I asked Liz to tell me more about Pergolesi, since we were soon to see one of his most famous pieces performed.

'Pergolesi died young from tuberculosis. He never knew what a furore his opera, *La Serva Padrona*, started in Paris.'

'Why a furore?'

'Well,' Liz warmed to her topic, 'he introduced comedy into opera for the first time, but his opera didn't get performed until sixteen years after his death.'

A performance of this one act *opera buffa* (comic opera) took place in the theatre of the Palazzo Reale and provided the week's finale. Naples used to be an important player in Mediterranean politics and the Palazzo Reale reflected its significance. The Palazzo was one of the four residences used by the Bourbon kings of Naples during their rule of the Kingdom of Two Sicilies, from 1815–1860. It was badly damaged by fire in the nineteen-hundreds and restored and restored again after it was bombed in the Second World War, but since then it has been somewhat neglected. *La Serva Padrona*, or *The Maid Turned Mistress*, by contrast, had become very popular: European audiences were enthralled by the then revolutionary tale of a man in love with his servant.

Liz and I seemed to be the only people excited after the performance. Our two hundred sheep waited silently before being herded by Rupert's girls into the balcony area of the palace, watched by thickset and unsmiling security guards. Liz, disgusted by the dreary atmosphere, wandered off to explore the rest of the building. She was promptly pursued by two guards and manhandled back to the pen.

'What did they say?'

'I haven't a clue, they're Italian, remember? But I got even with them when they grabbed me round the waist and grasped my wrist. I remembered Miranda's mother and said loftily, "Would you kindly take your hand from about my waist or I shall report you to the management."' Miranda, you may remember, was the mutual friend who had brought Liz and me together again.

'They got the message,' Liz went on. 'Anyway, there was nothing to see. The staircase must have been magnificent in its heyday with all the gilt and mirrors, but now it's dust and gloom. Naples's glory days are well and truly over.'

The caterers had clearly been urged by Dickens's staff to serve the buffet supper speedily. It was an uneasy occasion. The presence of the guards mingling with the cast, musicians and audience was an uncomfortable reminder that Mafia killings, abductions and armed hold-ups were still a daily occurrence. 'Is everything all right?' An anxious junior Dickens guide wearing a blue pillbox hat and sensible flatties was checking that Liz had recovered after the 'episode'. I had heard her with a colleague discussing a police warning they had received earlier in the day. I got the distinct impression that the staff wanted all of us safely back in our hotels and preferably on the first available plane back to London. For nearly five days Dickens had closeted us in a world of *cantate*, opera and *prosecci*, but outside on the streets of Naples a battle was being waged, however much the Neapolitan tourist industry tried to disguise the fact.

Our one-week stay was not nearly enough. Next time we vowed we would travel under our own steam and take an apartment overlooking the Piazza Plebiscito for three months.

'We'll both have to take conversation classes and I want to learn advanced Italian cooking and settle down in the evenings salivating over cookbooks written in Italian. I might even learn to make my own pasta. And if you give me loads of praise I'll cook my way steadily through Marcella Hazan's recipe books. You will have *orecchiette* coming out of your ears.'

'Just make sure it's small portions.'

'Fair enough. That will be the perfect incentive for me to lose weight. And what fun to go with the chef to the market and learn how to choose the best artichokes and sardines in season.'

'I think I'll go to the university and take a course in fascist architecture of the Mussolini period,' said Liz.

'You're on your own there, mate.'

When the time came, we could not resist waving goodbye to Arthur and Libby as they boarded the airport coach on the last morning.

'*Ciao, ciao!*' we waved. '*Buon viaggio.*'

Libby responded with a thin, wintry smile.

'What's the bet they'll be met by their chauffeur, George, when they touch down at Heathrow?' We broke into one of our now familiar fantasies. Liz began: '"Welcome home, sir; welcome home, madam," George will say as he opens the door to the Roller and tucks them both in under a cashmere blanket. Then he'll pass Libby a thermos flask of hot chocolate—'

'And Arthur a flask of 2005 Tullamore Dew whiskey,' I interjected.

'And two mugs embossed with the family coat of arms,' said Liz.

I took up the tale. 'And as the car purrs down the M1, Libby and Arthur will gradually sink into their familiar alcoholic stupor and the terrors of Naples will recede forever.'

'Libby will heave a sigh of relief when later she briefs Helmut and hands over the offending skirt,' said Liz.

'"No problem, madam," he will murmur.'

'Libby will feel comfy back in Moreton-in-Marsh,' Liz concluded, 'and Arthur will relax, reassured that their orderly Gloucestershire lives have been restored and all is right with the world. "Stands the Church clock at ten to three?"'

'"And is there honey still for tea?" That's Rupert Brooke, isn't it, Liz?'

'Certainly is,' she replied. 'As I've often told you, Hilly, most people don't really enjoy holidays—as soon as they're out of their comfort zone, they want to go home.'

7

Staying with friends and family: searching for an elusive poetry festival in Donegal and ending up in Spain

Have chance of renting cottage in Vejer de la Fontera on Costa de la Luz. Reply within 24 hours if you're interested. Hil xxx-x

Liz's response was instant:

Yes.

I found out later that Liz had no idea where Vejer was and only guessed it was in Spain. During a phone call to her sister Judy she found out that by an extraordinary coincidence Judy and her husband John were meeting friends on the Costa de la Luz over exactly the same dates that I proposed. The two holiday destinations were only fifteen kilometres apart.

I telephoned Liz that I would arrive in London three weeks before we went to Vejer.

'Good,' she said, 'we can go to Wales to see my friends Norma and Gerry, and *Aida*, and then you can come with me to the Opera Festival in Wexford. And we'll stay with Judy and John.'

'But how will Judy feel about me descending on the family?'
I asked.

'Judy and John will like you a lot—it won't be a problem.'

No sooner had I arrived in London—and I mean the very morning I got off the plane from Australia—Liz whisked us onto a train to Cardiff to see *Aida* done by the Welsh National Opera Company at the brand-new Wales Millennium Centre in Cardiff.

I was excited to be meeting Norma, her French husband Claude, and Gerry, about whom I had heard so much over the years. We were going to stay with Norma and Claude. Friendship, I know, can't be willed into being overnight, but Liz's reminiscences, stories and gossip had helped enormously to bring her friends to life for me and with these shortcuts there was a good chance that we would be *simpatico*. The fun for all three of us would be in seeing if the individuals corresponded accurately to Liz's descriptions. Liz was keen that we should all take a trip together at some point; she was keen that I learnt the virtues of economy travel.

Norma met us at Cardiff Station and gave me a hug like a long-lost friend. We piled into her tiny car and drove through Cardiff, past the medieval castle tarted up in the nineteenth century by its owner, Lord Bute. Next door was the Civic Centre, built in flamboyant Edwardian baroque style. Cardiff had been immensely rich in those days, prospering from the massive coalmining industry in the valleys behind the city. Sadly, that massive prosperity was well and truly over, and Cardiff was struggling valiantly to find a new role.

Claude was at the door to greet us when we arrived. He was all Gallic charm, addressing me as *madame* and throwing in a '*Comment allez-vous?*' for good measure. Their semidetached house looked quite modest from outside, but inside they had done a renovation to make a vast kitchen overlooking the garden. It had a cosy farmhouse feel to it, with a large oak table down the middle. We sat around while Norma handed out tea and cake.

I had never tasted bara brith before and Norma's homemade version was very special. Bara brith is Welsh for 'speckled bread' and is made either with yeast as a bread or with self-raising flour and baking powder as a teacake. It was so popular that the Welsh emigrants who went to Argentina in the nineteenth century took it with them. It became a traditional food there and was known as *torta negra* (black cake). I enthused so heartily to Norma that she kindly gave me her recipe. All thoughts of tiredness after my long journey from Australia had evaporated.

* * * * *

Norma's Bara Brith

Ingredients

    400 g mixed dried fruit (can be seedless raisins)

    250 ml cold tea

    400 g self-raising flour

    6 tbs soft brown sugar

    1 tsp mixed spice

    1 egg

    grated peel and juice of 1 orange

    1 dessertspoon marmalade

    honey

    walnuts, for top

Preparation

1. Soak the dried fruit in the tea overnight.
2. Mix together the flour, fruit, brown sugar, mixed spice, egg, grated peel, juice and marmalade.

3. Bake in the oven at 175°C for 1 hour.
4. Remove from the oven and, when cool, melt the honey and brush over the sides and top of the cake. Sprinkle with walnuts.

* * * * *

Claude was eager to hear about my *Tap Dogs* venture and Norma about my grandchildren—she had two of her own and was over the grandmother moon.

Later Gerry arrived on her bicycle, pink-cheeked, her dark hair windswept. She was stylishly dressed and looked miles younger than all of us. She launched into a vigorous discussion with Liz about late Verdi and specifically *Aida*, the opera we were about to see. Norma is a brilliant cook and rustled up supper before we left for the opera. We started with a *cawl cennin* (a Welsh leek broth), followed by a white bean and tomato casserole and slices of Norma's homemade apple tart.

The Millennium Centre is down on the rejuvenated Cardiff Docks. The old docks fell into disuse in the middle of the last century and now the government is spending a mint encouraging the building of offices, shops, restaurants and flats. The centrepiece is the opera house, which looked to me like a beached turtle clad in grey slate. Gerry, Norma and Liz disappeared up to the gods and their £5 seats while I sat in solitary splendour in a £100 front circle seat—the only seat left when my late booking was made. It's a huge auditorium. The Welsh National Opera is one of the foremost opera companies in the world and the *Aida* production we saw that night was spectacular. Verdi had demanded no less when he wrote the opera for the opening of the Suez Canal.

The next morning Claude gave us a kerbside drop at Cardiff Airport. Liz loves travelling from small airports so she was in heaven bragging about how convenient and quick it was checking in and going through security. Skipping gleefully across the tarmac, Liz bounded on board the tiny thirty-seater plane belonging to Air Wales. It felt as if no time had passed before we were disembarking in Dublin. We didn't even have time to order a second drink.

Liz told me that she had been going to the Wexford Opera Festival with Judy and John, her Irish vet husband, ever since they had moved to Enniscorthy twenty-five years ago.

'Do you really go every year?' I asked Liz incredulously.

'Yes, every year,' she said. 'Only by regular attendance, like regular bowels, can you appreciate the quirks and development of the artistic director.'

When the festival was over we would take off and see where fancy led us.

I have felt a huge affinity with Ireland ever since going to the Dingle Peninsula with friends many years ago, when I fell in love with the red fuchsia hedgerows which line all the small country roads. We had driven down to the farthest south-west point of the island past wind-blasted stony fields; it felt mystical, as if we were about to witness a benign end to the world. On that trip, too, I had the chance to absorb the humour and the storytelling brilliance of the Irish.

On another trip I had taken Dein Perry's show *Tap Dogs* to Dublin. Our performance followed in the wake of *Riverdance*, the worldwide hit Irish dance show. The Irish were amazed to see clodhopping beefy Australian blokes tapping up a storm. It was an uneasy segue from the incomparable lightness and dexterity of the Irish dancers to the workboots of the lads from the steelworks of Newcastle, New South Wales.

I love Irish literature and theatre and it was exciting to discover that Colm Tóibín, a writer I had discovered at a recent Sydney Writers' Festival, came from Enniscorthy and had set many of his novels there.

So it was with great enthusiasm that Liz and I rented a runabout car for our trip to Judy and John's home in Enniscorthy, County Wexford. It's a dull drive if you're on the main road, but we put on a CD and got in the mood with U2 and Bono. We stopped in Gorey on the way down, where I diverted Liz with one of my favourite travelling pastimes, reading out the Court Circular from the London *Times* newspaper. It is playtime for the fantasist and much better than 'I spy with my little eye'. I lamented the disappearance of Sarah, the Honourable Lady Cottesloe, who was attending the Princess Royal and appeared to have been abducted or abandoned in Botswana. Certainly there was no sign of her in the Circular when the Royal Party returned to London. 'Where is she, Liz?' And what happened to Angus Ashleigh Belcher, Equerry to Prince Edward? One day he was the aide-de-camp accompanying HRH to a tea plantation in India as personal aide-de-camp, the next he was gone, replaced with no explanation by the Honourable Rupert Boggis Rolfe. 'Had he indulged in conduct unbecoming, Liz?'

The two-and-a-half hours flew by. Enniscorthy lies on the banks of the River Slaney and is overlooked by the site of the famous Battle of Vinegar Hill, the battle that marked a turning point in the Irish Rebellion of 1798 and represented the last attempt by the Irish rebels to defend ground against the British military. I became heated when I heard stories of the British Army's slaughter of the Irish rebels. I was convinced that I must have Irish ancestors, but was never able to come up with any.

Towards the end of the journey we travelled through the greenest of green countryside and, as we drove in through the gates of Aughnagally House, I knew I'd arrived in heaven. Here was the perfect creeper-clad house sheltered by tall beech trees. We sailed into the backyard and a labrador bounded towards us, happily barking out greetings; Judy and John appeared, smiling and warmly taking over my mountain of luggage.

We were ushered into the kitchen and then settled in the conservatory among a profusion of geraniums, cacti and a couple of vines, all speaking at once.

Then it was out into the fields to see John's two white horses, one so old that Methuselah would have been a stripling beside him. John had hunted him until the day he fell off and broke his shoulder. 'Never again,' he vowed. We walked through a copse of silver birch trees which John had planted ten years previously and which were now twice our height.

Judy showed off her vegetables: lettuce, beans, peas, parsley— she grew them all—she even had an asparagus bed. There were lashings of fruit trees and beds of raspberry canes, currant bushes and strawberry plants, but her pride and joy was a 'growing' room—a converted stable especially devoted to exotic plants. Liz told me that Judy had slipped into motherhood and domesticity with ease, but that she was also fearlessly engaged in local politics. She had fought tooth and nail to get equal membership for women at the local golf club. The fight had raised hackles among the deeply conservative, small town population.

'I've always been amazed by Judy's well-grounded moral certainty,' said Liz. 'I have so few morals myself and even those I have are easily blown away by the arguments of persuasive people.'

We had arrived the evening before the opening of the festival and Judy and John were giving a dinner for their house guests and a few local friends. John said with fiendish delight, 'They've been chosen with you two in mind.'

We gathered around the dinner table and I was introduced to the group. There was Peter, a gynaecologist down from Dublin, wearing an expensive pink shirt unbuttoned at the neck, who lost no time in asking me, 'What is your narrative quest, Hilary?'

I wasn't going to be silenced by this smart-arse remark and replied swiftly, 'Oh, you know, the usual—love, fame and fortune.'

Peter continued unabashed, 'And if I may be so bold, how many gentleman admirers have you had?'

'Goodness, what a question! I've no idea, I'm a lover not a mathematician.' That fixed him.

Judy produced a gorgeous meal. I had asked for an Irish stew and Judy, a Welsh woman, produced her Welsh/Irish version—a beauty—together with traditional Irish *champ* (a potato and parsnip puree) and oodles of vegetables straight from the garden. She had also made an Irish soup with a chicken base for the non-meat-eaters: it had a fabulous name, *skink*, and was not the slithery lizard I had conjured up. My nostrils relaxed in relief as an aroma of fresh vegetables and herbs rose from the pot. I particularly enjoyed the delicacy of this dish, a contrast to the more robust flavours to which I am usually attracted.

* * * * *

Skink

Serves 4

Ingredients

    4 sticks of celery, trimmed and finely diced

    6 cos-type lettuce leaves, rinsed and chopped

    ½ cup green peas

4 spring onions, trimmed and chopped

1 dessertspoon fresh chopped chives

bouquet garni

1 litre chicken stock

100 ml double cream

1 egg yolk

salt and pepper, to taste

chopped parsley, to serve

Preparation

1. Place the vegetables, herbs, seasoning and stock into a saucepan and bring to the boil.
2. Cover and simmer for ½ hour or until the vegetables are tender.
3. Remove the bouquet garni.
4. Blend the cream and egg yolk and add them to the soup.
5. Heat without boiling.
6. Add salt and pepper to taste.
7. Serve with a light sprinkling of parsley.

* * * * *

The wine flowed and the conversation and laughter rose. After dinner, John put on the CD player and we danced until far into the night.

The next day we were hung-over but people kept popping in.

'Oh lord, here comes Hector,' said Judy looking through the window. 'He was recently diagnosed with throat cancer and now apparently he's been told that he's got a diverticulum as well. What on earth shall we say to him?'

'We'll ask him if his diverticulum has taken his mind off his cancer,' said John laconically. Somehow John and Judy managed to see Hector warmly on his way without offending him, explaining that we still had to get ready for the evening.

All the house guests were busy putting on their glad rags for the evening event. Everyone wears full evening dress for the Wexford Festival. Wexford is a small seaside town with a long quay and a tiny theatre where for a few weeks a year three little-known operas are pulled out of mothballs and given spanking new productions. Opera buffs come from all over the world and the town is filled with music; the pubs are full of music lovers and the hotels and streets bulge with locals and opera lovers mingling happily. John drove us to Wexford, where we drank champagne and tottered over the cobbled stones to the theatre. I can't say that I enjoyed the opera itself and was not surprised that it was rarely produced. Afterwards we repaired to one of the local pubs, where members of the opera orchestra and cast relaxed and regaled us with salacious stories about their conductors and directors.

Judy and John were enthusiastic hosts. The next day we settled down to more delicious meals in the kitchen in front of the Aga— I have a particular memory of Judy's beetroot chutney—and we passed the time telling each other jokes and stories.

Judy and John competed keenly for the title of best storyteller and I remember them battling it out with two corkers. Judy started off, 'Noel Gleeson, an old time vet in Killarney, used to go out on calls in the morning and would not return home until the evening. So whatever farm he was in at lunchtime, the woman of the house would offer him his 'dinner'. The dinner was invariably bacon and cabbage, this being the height of culinary sophistication at the time in County Kerry. Noel liked a bit of mustard with his bacon and cabbage. He knew that mustard would be beyond the resources of most of the farmhouses he would be visiting, so he always carried a small pot of ready-mixed Colman's mustard with him. One day he was sitting alone at the table waiting for the meal to start. The plates were already laid out so he took out his pot and put a dab of mustard on the side of his plate. Just at this moment the woman of the house walked in with the pot of potatoes. She stopped dead when she saw his plate. Reaching over his shoulder, she took the plate and gave it a quick rub of her apron before putting it back down in front of him. 'Ach,' she said, 'them bloody hens. I can't keep them out of the place.'

We all fell about laughing and John rapidly set out to trump Judy's tale.

'There was a character called Gereen "Suck" Mahony living in Tralee when I was working there. Gereen suffered from a speech impediment and called his little house Bunratty. Not, as you might expect, after the Great Castle of Bunratty in County Limerick but because there was nothin' but rats around the place.' John warmed to his story. 'Do you want to hear how Gereen came by his nickname? Well, his mother was a market woman who sold fish in the town. In those days the market women wore shawls and blankets over their shoulders. Little Gereen, a hardy lad of four or so, had not been weaned from the breast by his mother and as she was sitting selling fish he would creep under her shawl and help himself. One day he was doing just this when one of the other women in the market rounded on Mrs Mahony saying, 'Really, Mrs, it's time you weaned that young fella. He's too much for you. You should think of your own health.' Gereen, enraged by this interference and fearful that his milk supply might be brought to an end, came out from under the shawl and said to the good neighbour, 'Why don't you mind your own fucking business,' and resumed sucking.

There was more rolling about at the table, but after a hand count Judy was pronounced winner of the night's contest.

Locals continued to drop in for a glimpse of the new arrival from Australia, only to find themselves subjected to close scrutiny by Liz and myself. Then, when they had departed, we would pour another drink and get Judy to tell us the minute details of their lives.

The following day we said a fond farewell to Judy and John and spoke excitedly about meeting up with them again in a week's time at Vejer. Bursting with joie de vivre I fired up the rented car, accelerated and drove straight into their front gate! J and J waved the incident aside. I was mortified and in a lather of apology. 'Not to worry,' they chorused. The rain started pouring down and John urged caution on the roads. We took off again without a whiff of a plan.

Liz was getting a cold. A sick Liz is not a pretty sight. I drove for about an hour through rain, heavy mist, poor visibility and heavy sniffing.

'I don't want to go any further,' said Liz grumpily. I pushed on, ignoring her, and eventually found a crumbling mansion beside a lake which Lonely Planet said provided bed and breakfast. We decided to give it a try for the night as Liz's condition was deteriorating fast. She warned me, 'When I'm sick I behave very badly. I'm like an animal; I want to crawl away. I become gloomy and pessimistic and the last thing I want is a solution—I'm just *in* it and can't think about the future. I just want an end to it.'

Great, I thought but did not say.

It continued to pour with rain; the lake in front of the mansion was overflowing and creeping towards the front courtyard. Ivy gripped the building so hard that the walls seemed to crumble and disintegrate before my eyes. And the rising damp formed pustules on the internal walls. The overflow from the rusting gutters cascaded in a river of water down to the windowsills, finding its way through cracks in the frames onto the floor inside. A decorative potty had been thoughtfully left to catch the drops. Not the day for a walk. Instead, I spent the evening scouring my Lonely Planet guide for an abbey or castle of historical interest nearby. I also had a look at the pictures in the house and was particularly struck by a framed sepia photograph on the stairs of nine naked youths diving off and frolicking around in a rowing boat.

'What on earth's going on here?' I asked Liz, in an attempt to divert her.

'A homosexual secret society or a paedophile's picnic,' she sniffed, and retired to bed immediately after dinner with whiskey, lemon and honey.

I found a castle within easy driving distance to tempt Liz into action. It was now a question of when she would decide that she had spent enough time on her back. Fortunately for me, she gets bored rapidly and the following morning at breakfast I could see that my suggestion of moving on to Kilkenny Castle was preferable to 'being stuck in this hole'.

I remember virtually nothing about our visit to Kilkenny Castle. Kilkenny is instead etched in my brain as the place where I lost yet another possession, this time the keys to the hire car. Again I had to depend, like Blanche Dubois, 'on the kindness of strangers'. This time the stranger was a round, watery pink-cheeked matron working in the castle gift shop who chased me puffing down the path to the castle exit in the pouring rain, arms outstretched, keys clinking. 'You dropped these,' she said, beaming. I hugged her in gratitude and felt very foolish. 'Thank you so much. I can imagine the panic I would have felt when I discovered "no keys" at the door of the car. You've saved my bacon—thank you, thank you, thank you—' I sounded like a cracked record.

I acquired my pattern of losing things when I was eight. I can trace it back very simply to my stepmother, who bawled me out repeatedly about my frequent loss of the door key. She would even berate me *before* I lost it.

'I don't know why I bother to give you another key, you'll only lose it. This must be the fourth one. Has it occurred to you that they cost money? Have you considered that there are now thieves out there in possession of our front door key? Does it cross your mind that we could be burgled as a result of your carelessness? Do you realise that theft isn't the end of the story? If we are burgled the incident may be reported in the press and your father will face an unwelcome invasion of his privacy—and all because of your stupidity.' Well, after I had heard that speech repeated routinely over the years I became incapable of looking after any key that came into my hands, together with many other precious possessions.

I had explained all this to Liz. At the end of my rant, Liz looked at me quizzically. 'I can see that my Welsh mother and your stepmother come from the same place. Exactly the same midget concerns dominated my youth. You'd like to think those aspiring middle classes would have more important verities than lost keys to instil into impressionable minds.'

A wave of relief passed through me. It was nice to feel that Liz understood my demented behaviour.

We stayed in Kilkenny that night and ate comfort food: rump steak and sticky date pudding. And drank a large amount of red wine.

*

Next day Liz's cold was getting better and I suggested that we should try and get to the Isles of Aran, which were a romantic holiday fantasy of mine.

'Yes, good idea. They are essential viewing for all you Irish devotees. It was on the Aran Islands a hundred or so years ago that the whole modern Irish love-in started. Synge, Yeats and that crowd went bananas when they went there and discovered the Pure Irish Person, who they distilled into print and paintings. And it's still being celebrated today by the likes of you. But first,' she said, reverting to practicalities, 'we'd better find out where the ferry goes from.'

We drove along the Galway coast, where Liz asked three people for directions. She was, not surprisingly, given three conflicting answers and we found ourselves finally taking a punt on a tiny inlet with one other lone traveller. A doll's house ticket office with no one in it looked as if it was about to be blown away. It was a grim, grey morning and the waters were churning and rough. We could see an island in the distance but no ferry. After a long wait Liz spied a black speck in the distance coming towards us. Success at last! But no. Just as we were jumping up and down and congratulating ourselves on our sleuthing, the bobbing boat turned around and disappeared out of sight. It was so Irish, the caprice of it all. So final. I supposed we were meant to go another day.

But we decided to press on to Donegal. After all, we had to find Gortahork, where Liz was to take part in their International Poetry Festival. Sad to say, I remember little of the long journey there except Liz asking me what side of the road we drove on in Australia.

'The same as here,' I replied.

'Funny,' she said. 'You've just driven round a roundabout the wrong way.'

Eventually we found ourselves perched on a cliff on a tiny part of Donegal's spectacular 300-kilometre coastline. We marvelled at the run of headlands, promontories and peninsulas which stretched out to the right and left of us. Even though the sun shone that day, there was breeze enough from the Atlantic Ocean to whisk up the waves into a frenzied froth as they hit the rocks beneath us. From time immemorial, severe gales have lashed this north-western part of Ireland. Tiny fields lie scattered between stubborn rocks; they'd produced barely enough food to support the despairing families who had lived there. For centuries the area had been poverty-stricken, but now prosperity had come to Donegal. Ugly modern boxes were springing up everywhere—holiday houses for the Irish middle class.

That night we drove inland towards the mountains and found ourselves in Glenties, a charming one-street town where every building was either a hotel or a pub. We stayed in the Highland Hotel. The owner was an artist whose paintings hung along all the corridors and private rooms. Meryl Streep had stayed there in 1998 for the opening of the film *Dancing at Lughnasa*, in which she had starred, her visit marked by a brass plaque on the door, MERYL STREEP SLEPT HERE, but the locals were reluctant to talk about her now. It was old hat.

A fiddle festival was in progress in the town so we went from pub to pub listening to the contestants, who in many cases had difficulty being heard above the noise of shouted conversations. There must have been a thousand people in the crowded pubs that night; the hotels and pubs were jam-packed; there was hardly a soul out on the streets.

We had to find Gortahork: Liz had written a poem and hoped to win the festival's 5000 euro prize. As we drove along I insisted that Liz rehearse reading the poem out loud. 'You're bound to be asked,' I said. Liz launched forth:

'Time in his precise moronic
Way asked Life why she was always
Getting in his way.
He wanted to know
Why Life needed so much of him . . .'

At this point I interrupted Liz's flow. 'That's enough,' I said rudely. 'Is it meant to be a joke? ... We're here. I think we've arrived in glorious Gortahork, home of poets. Look out for a café, I'm famished.'

'I'm just coming to the best bit,' said Liz crossly.

'Later,' I said as I got out of the car.

Gortahork, like Glenties, was a one-street town nestling between the hills and a landlocked bay with a few fishing smacks bobbing at anchor in it. There was only one hotel in the town. There was no one to be seen in the streets; we couldn't even find a café for lunch and everyone denied knowledge of the poetry festival, even though it was billed to start that day. It was curious that we had noticed leaflets and posters for the festival in villages a considerable distance from Gortahork but as we got closer there were none to be seen—certainly none in the town which was meant to be hosting the event.

We eventually found a young girl who pointed us towards Maggie Dan's Tea Rooms, Beauty and Pizza Parlour. We crossed the road and walked in through an open door to a scene of complete chaos. We could just make out three large cardboard boxes stuffed with publicity material for the festival on the floor. We started rooting around until a man emerged from behind piles of crates in a far corner. He was on the phone. He waved us away with his spare hand and shouted out, 'Come back at eight,' not very convincingly. We didn't, as by then we had settled into comfortable Arnold's Hotel at Dunfanaghy some twenty miles up the coast.

At dinner we sampled two more Irish dishes; I plumped for a 'Dublin coddle'—a ham, sausage, potato and onion casserole; the quintessential comfort food and a great name—while Liz settled for a steak and Guinness pie. After dinner I leafed through a 1794 edition of the *Encyclopaedia Britannica* which to my surprise I found in the well-stocked bookshelves in the hotel lounge. Liz, meanwhile, was reading out her poem to an admiring audience of oldies. At the end of her recitation I was staggered to hear her tell the audience that she had won first prize for it at the Gortahork Festival down the road. I shuddered as I imagined the door flying open at any moment; the rightful winner of the poetry competition would come striding in, denouncing Liz as a fraud and a trickster. 'You should be drummed out of town,' the winner would scream, pointing an incriminating finger in Liz's direction. Liz would stand frozen, her mouth opening and shutting like a stranded codfish, and I would have to escort her wordless from the room.

The next morning Liz took a breezy walk along Sheephaven Beach, which was conveniently situated across the road from the hotel. Later she joined me for a hearty breakfast—'the works', as she called the Full Irish. There was no mention of the previous evening. We then set off to stay with Johnnie and Fiona, Liz's friends of forty years, with whom she had been spending a lot of time now she was retired.

We drove through the stark and imposing Derryveagh Mountains, which form a backdrop to Donegal's windswept landscape, and into Glenveagh National Park, where golden eagles have recently been reintroduced.

'Sadly the 244 tenants who were so cruelly evicted from the town in 1861 cannot be brought back. They were moved to make way for Glenveagh Castle, a huge pile of bloated magnificence,' said Liz.

Nearby was the strangely named Poisoned Glen.

Liz told me the story of the evil Cyclops Balor being slain by the Celtic god Lugh. The Cyclops's single eye fell out and poisoned the ground. Later in the pub in the nearest village, Ardara, the publican told us the true story. He said, 'The Irish word for poison, *neimhe* (pronounced niv-uh), has the same spelling as the word for Heaven, apart from one letter in its spelling, *neamh* (pronounced nyow-uh). The glen used to be called the Heavenly Glen by locals, as it was to them as they imagined Heaven would be. An English map man made a mistake with the translation and "poisoned" the name of one of Ireland's most beautiful places forever.' The publican shook his head gravely.

As we drove away from the mountains, I was surprised when Liz interrupted one of my paeans of praise for Ireland.

'Those mountains are magnificent,' I was saying. 'We'll have to go back some time.'

'For god's sake, Hilly, give Ireland a rest.'

'But I thought you loved it too,' I blurted out. 'You spend enough time here.'

'I do like Ireland; but not in the tourist way that you seem to.'

I was stung; the wasp in Liz was at it again. But at least this time Liz could see I was upset by her reply.

'You see, Hil, you must realise that Johnnie and Fiona will just keel over, vomit in the sink and more than likely boot you out of the house if you carry on like that.'

'I can't imagine them doing that. Why?'

I looked around at her as I was navigating a sharp corner, and nearly landed us in the ditch.

'I'd have to give you a treatise on Irish history to explain, and I'm not in the mood,' she replied.

'I'm surprised you don't want to sort me out.'

Liz looked uncomfortable.

'Do you see how the countryside has changed, Hilly?' she said, changing the subject after a few minutes of silence between us.

'Well, it's still pretty gorgeous and green,' I replied.

'Yes, but it's much, much flatter; in fact, there's hardly a hill in sight. This is the Midlands. You won't see many tourists here. The Lonely Planet guidebook said: *The best thing about its three main towns is leaving them.*'

'Turn right; left here, right again.' Liz was now focused on giving me clear instructions as we sped down tiny high-hedged country lanes and finally turned through a gate and up a muddy avenue. We wove past grey stone outbuildings, stabling, hay barns and assorted cottages before drawing up outside a huge house which looked benignly over acres of gently rolling grassland studded with horses, trees and cattle.

'Wow,' I murmured, 'no tourist brochure could do justice to this view.'

Liz jumped out and rushed up the steps, opened the huge door and yelled. I got out and followed her.

'There's nobody here,' she said. 'Typical.' We walked through an immense hall, the walls decorated with Japanese swords and cutlasses, to the back of the house and into a vast kitchen. Two huge dogs, tails wagging feverishly, set upon us. Bruce was a brown wolfhound and Cordelia, a black-spotted Dalmatian. They jumped all over us, their slobbering heads caressing our chins. It was a great welcome.

'You go and look at the house and see if anyone's around,' said Liz. I wandered down the corridor and discovered a number of vast, high-ceilinged rooms. They looked, at first sight, a little dilapidated but on further inspection the sofas, chairs, glass, silverware and curtains, while worn by age, were beautifully cared for. The silver shone and the glass glinted. I went back into the kitchen. Liz was sitting in a chair stroking Cordelia, who was seated by her side. 'I've put the kettle on.'

'Good-oh,' I replied. 'I've found a lovely sofa. I think I'll curl up there and have a rest.'

Half an hour later Liz woke me up to say that Johnnie had got back and was asking who 'the farrowing sow' was in the drawing room.

'He doesn't like the drawing room being used, as he sees it, unnecessarily. Just for guests,' she said.

I got up rapidly and followed Liz back into the kitchen. There was no sign of Johnnie or anybody else. Liz opened the fridge door. It was almost empty and you could see the back of it clearly— something I hadn't observed in my own fridge since I bought it!

'Now you see why I bought food this morning in Donegal. We'd be supper-less if we'd relied on Fiona,' said Liz.

Johnnie, an elegant, elderly gentleman, reminded me of a secretary bird with long spindly legs as he bounded into the kitchen. He was charm and enthusiasm personified and made me feel most welcome. Had Liz made up the farrowing sow bit? I couldn't credit him with such gratuitous crudity.

Johnnie gathered me up and took me on a tour of the property. First of all we inspected the walled garden. He opened the gate and we walked down a magical tunnel of beech hedge. He spoke of the garden as it must have been over half a century ago, when his mother oversaw a dozen gardeners who produced fruit, vegetables and flowers, enough for a household of twenty people. It had changed a lot since then. Weeds and undergrowth were quite obviously winning against valiant efforts to keep them at bay; a few plants, fruit trees and shrubs were making a desperate effort to survive.

We walked through fields of white Charolais cattle and a scattering of potential racehorses. The woods and front avenue were pointed out to me, with their varieties of fine trees. Johnnie told me with pride how he had developed and nurtured his livestock and arboriculture. Thomas Mann said that 'genius, energy and life show themselves most freely in old age', and Johnnie was certainly living proof of that. Here he was at eighty years old waxing lyrical about some of the enthusiasms that had filled his life.

Back at the house, in the kitchen, I finally met Fiona, Johnnie's beautiful younger wife. The kitchen table was covered in glasses, bottles and ashtrays. She and Liz had already got stuck into the alcohol, even though it was only teatime, and cigarette smoke hung heavily over the sleeping dogs, who lay spread-eagled on their enormous mattresses. Fiona ran the household impeccably, preserving the well-worn household furnishings and using her spotless cooking utensils to produce delicious, mouth-watering dinners for Johnnie's guests.

'Thanks for bringing dinner, that's a treat,' she said. 'Have a drink.'

She poured me a huge gin and tonic, Liz a gigantic whiskey and herself a triple vodka. Johnnie had disappeared.

'I bought some potatoes and beans. Why don't you peel them, Hil,' said Liz, 'and we can grill the steak.'

Liz and Fiona were settling down to a 'catch-up'. The dogs began circling and Fiona and Liz suddenly collapsed into uncontrollable laughter. *They're cheap drunks*, I thought.

Later, when I came to put the steaks on the grill, to my horror I discovered there was only one and realised that the other three had been manoeuvred off the table by the long, curvaceous tongues of Bruce and Cordelia, and then wolfed. Liz and Fiona had watched this happening.

'Why didn't you stop them, you maddies?' I asked.

'They were already half-eaten by the time we spotted the blood dripping onto the linoleum,' said Liz.

'Don't worry,' said Fiona, 'Johnnie wouldn't have allowed us to eat the steak anyway. It's a Fast Day. I'll make an omelette for us all.'

As I rolled about uncomfortably on a sixty-year-old, lumpy horsehair mattress that night, I realised that I was decidedly hungry. Since Fiona allowed the dogs carte blanche in the house and didn't believe in over-stocking the fridge, it was pointless for me to get up and go fossicking. I would only discover plates spotlessly cleaned by the dogs' slavering tongues and, in all probability, an empty fridge. I would have to control myself.

The next morning I woke to horsy noises in the yard and Johnnie's voice shouting in exasperation. I looked out of the window and saw a good-looking young man loading up a horse box with a couple of horses. Johnnie was scampering around gesticulating and issuing advice.

Breakfast was skimpy. Fiona and Liz were nowhere to be seen and Johnnie was tetchy and absent, both at the same time. I felt redundant.

The phone went mid-morning and all hell broke loose. David, the good-looking man, had taken the wrong horses to Tattersalls for sale. Johnnie exploded. 'That silly ass David is a complete fool!' and sped off in his car to Dublin. The house became still and silent.

Eventually Liz and Fiona returned, with no explanation as to where they had been. 'We must leave now,' said Fiona.

'Where are we going?' I asked.

'The Cliffs,' said Liz. 'Get your luggage together, Hilly. You just have to keep on your toes with Johnnie and Fiona. They rarely apologise and never explain.'

*

Two hours later we turned right and faced the blue expanse of Dublin Bay, with the Wicklow Mountains beyond; the city itself crouched along the bay's shore. I drove tentatively down a long, stony avenue, through a tree-sheltered, rocky lane with a stream alongside and finally semicircled a small paddock to draw up in front of a pebble dashed house which looked like a Dickensian institution.

Liz and I walked around the back and entered the kitchen, where two excited dogs a quarter of the size of the ones at Glencara greeted us with unrestrained yaps of delight. Liz immediately took one of them for a walk. I wandered through the house, which was a rabbit warren of rooms leading off a central corridor. Most were beautifully maintained, with all surfaces crammed with treasures. The rooms resembled the ones at Glencara, but had faded gently with the passing of years. I opened one door into a room in total darkness, where I dimly made out—once my eyes had become accustomed to the dark—piles of paper on every surface, including the floor. The bed was covered, as were two cupboards, a desk and all the chairs. I jumped in alarm as a voice, cackling with laughter behind me, squawked, 'Goodbye, goodbye, goodbye . . . bye.' Through the gloom I made out a white parrot standing in a partially covered cage in one corner of the room.

'Ah,' said Johnnie, smiling wickedly as he appeared from the garden behind me, 'Coco has your number.'

Liz bounced up. 'We're off to get fish. Come and see Howth, Hilly.'

So off we went in Fiona's small car, the three of us with the two dogs, up over the hill with its spectacular views out to sea and down the other side, through a tiny, tumbling gaggle of houses, part resort, part working fishing village.

Two piers curved around to protect an array of yachts and a dozen or so fishing boats. These supplied the shops and restaurants ranged along one of the piers. I marvelled at the fresher-than-fresh fish, and the variety on display.

Fiona went straight to Nicky's Plaice, which was packed to the gunnels with keen customers. The hubbub was huge, but even above it I could hear and see Fiona being warmly greeted by the keen-as-mustard staff, dressed in their white overalls and white wellies. She got the pick of the freshest fish on offer—she had decided on a fish pie for the dinner party that night. Johnnie had invited an eclectic group of people.

When we returned to The Cliffs Johnnie proceeded to brief me on each and every one of them after lunch. But already I was floundering—his vivid descriptions came thick and fast: the German count, the defrocked priest, the neighbours, the art historian.

Liz sailed into the room and said, 'Johnnie, Hilly won't remember a thing you've said,' and then left abruptly.

'Liz is *insortable*,' Johnnie called out with an impeccable French accent. 'She's quite impossible, nothing less than a freelance fraud—you know she never reads a book, only the reviews.' And in the same breath he continued with his thumbnail sketch of a horse whisperer I'd be meeting later.

We all gathered at seven o'clock for drinks in the drawing room. The guests stood around talking animatedly. 'This reminds me of the cocktail parties my parents used to give. Except that Johnnie's guests are more relaxed and interesting,' I reflected. I heard one of the female guests ask Johnnie what Liz did. Johnnie began to explain and was quickly shushed by the woman.

'I will ask her myself,' she said. 'Liz, what kind of work do you do?'

Liz was ready. 'I'm a love activist,' she replied.

Johnnie overheard the reply and shot Liz a withering look.

The dinner was impeccable, fully laid out on the highly polished dining room table with the full array of sparkling cutlery, glasses and napery. There were candles flickering in shining silver candelabra and everybody was in fine form, chatting and laughing. Fiona was dazzlingly efficient; she appeared equally at ease in both the role of 'lady of the house' and 'chef', serving three courses, clearing away, washing up and putting the crockery and cutlery back in the cupboards and drawers all before we had finished the meal. The kitchen looked as though nothing had happened there all day.

I sat next to a neighbour who leant back and accidentally brushed against the curtains—there was a tearing sound—they had been there since Johnnie's parents had put them up just after they were married. The sunlight and time had rotted them into strips, which hung artfully but were now exposed by my companion. 'What should I do?' she said sotto voce to her sister, who was seated next to her on the other side. 'Don't worry,' reassured her sister. 'No one will notice. This look is so in fashion—it's called shabby chic.' I fervently hoped Fiona hadn't heard or observed the episode.

The next morning Johnnie came into my bedroom in an old-fashioned nightshirt with a cup of tea sweetened with honey. He sat on my bed and rattled on about the party, and was eager to know what I'd thought about everybody.

Later at breakfast in the kitchen, the German count, who had stayed overnight, came in, clicked his heels and whipped my hand to his lips before I could swallow my mouthful of muesli.

Liz and I agreed that it was time to leave. After all, we were due in Vejer the next day. I had found a flight from Dublin to Seville, where we hired a car and drove south.

*

Vejer de la Fontera is 100 kilometres from Gibraltar, 50 kilometres south of Cádiz and 10 kilometres from the Atlantic Ocean, where the waves beat down on the Spanish coastline, south of Portugal. It's a hilltop village with magnificent views, including the lights of Tangier, away in North Africa. J and J were staying not far away on the coast near Barbate.

Our house was in the old part of Vejer, a tiny stone cottage with an internal courtyard cut into the rock. The owners had preserved many of the original features—the sink was an old olive crusher. The owners had rather ominously left a fourteen-page 'introduction' to the house (the 'rules & regs.') over which I pored after discovering that the lavatory was malfunctioning, the sink blocked and all the taps dripping badly. Finally I found a reference to Teresa and her husband, Antonio, who 'looked after the house' but were—and here the document resorted to capital letters—NOT SERVANTS OR HIRED HELP. I was over the road in a shot to introduce myself and ask for help, but as neither of them spoke a word of English I had the greatest difficulty in explaining our problem in a way that would be sure not to offend their sensibilities. Reluctantly they came across to look at the offending facilities. 'Could you tell me where I can find a plumber?' I attempted to ask in schoolgirl Spanish, creating an uneasy pause as I looked up the word for 'plumber' in my phrasebook. They stood silently while I went through this pantomime, then replied in a flurry of Spanish, none of which I understood, shook our hands and departed. I hadn't a clue whether they were going to help us or not.

'Let's go and check out J and J's set-up,' said Liz. 'There's no point in hanging around here. We'll just have to hope that Antonio has taken pity on us and has a friend who's a plumber.'

J and J were staying in a new bungalow on the Costa de la Luz. Their local beach was a nudist one for old hippies and local families. I felt too fat for nudity, but Liz and John were starkers in a flash and jumping in over the waves. Refreshed from the Atlantic, we sunbathed and later went to Barbate to check out the fish market. All manner of fresh fish lay sprawled on icy slabs just begging me to turn them into a fish soup, which I had promised J and J I would give them when they came to dinner with us. We breathed a sigh of relief on our return to Vejer. The loo flushed, the sink had been unblocked and the taps were dry. I raced over the road to thank Antonio and give him the money for his plumber, but they were out.

The following day it started to rain. There is nothing to do in Vejer in the rain. Once you have seen the church and the square and walked around the walls, that's it. It was as if everyone had gone into hibernation. No one on the streets, just a few old boys drinking in the bar. Even the shops had given up and closed. I took advantage of a day off to lie in bed and read a book while Liz walked eight times round the village. That night after a couple of tapas at the pub we went to bed early. But when we woke up the following morning—disaster. Our tiny dining room was ankle deep in water.

Oh God, the plumbing had failed again! We mopped up as best we could but the water kept pouring in and Antonio and Teresa were nowhere to be found. When we opened the front door brandishing mops and brushes to sweep the water out of the house and into the gutter, excited neighbours gathered at the doorway, beckoning us into their houses. We thought, *How kind, they're offering coffee and a rest from our labours.* We graciously accepted and sank into armchairs. But no, we were in for a rude shock. It emerged that we were all in the same boat. The neighbours explained that the rain that had fallen in the night had seeped through the rock and into all the houses on the high side of the road. There appeared to be nothing that we could do—just stick it out. The rain continued all day and the flood in our house rose further.

The promised fish soup had to be abandoned and we decided to take J and J to dinner in the village square. Over dinner I quizzed Judy about Liz's childhood. She was mostly discreet but did mention a sweet story about Liz wearing her father's tie to school when he was away at war and getting into trouble because she wasn't wearing school uniform.

The rain finally stopped and we had two days left, which gave us time to whiz into Cádiz for a quick squiz. But as soon as we arrived there, it started pouring again.

'Let's at least find a delicatessen and buy some "deliciousnesses" for lunch, even if we have to picnic in the car,' I said.

We found a deli bursting with unusual and inviting antipasti, marinated vegetables and freshly baked bread. The tapas were laid out in a glassed-in counter, among them Serrano ham (Ibérico, the best and most expensive, taking pride of place), freshly cooked sardines, pickled onions and cauliflower. Just as we were about to leave, clutching our assorted packages, I caught sight of a television suspended high above the counter. Following the anxious gaze of the old woman who had served us, I looked at the pictures on the screen: sinister shots of soldiers in full combat uniform, wearing gasmasks, darting through the streets, crouching behind parked cars and leaning stiffly against walls, their AK-47s primed. The voice-over was in Spanish.

'What on earth is going on?' I asked Liz.

'I haven't a clue, but it doesn't look good.'

'I hope to God there hasn't been a terrorist attack in Seville—or is it something to do with germ warfare? Lizzie, find someone who speaks English.'

She grabbed the next customer and pointed at the screen. 'What's going on?' Fortunately he spoke a little English. 'Army exercise,' he said.

'Thank you, *señor*, thank you, *gracias*,' said Liz.

'*De nada*,' he replied and shook her hand formally.

'*¡Qué alivio!*' I added. (What a relief!)

'*De nada*,' he replied again, shaking my hand warmly, and the old woman beamed in agreement.

The day before we were supposed to be leaving Vejer, in my eagerness to navigate the tiny laneways I managed to hit a wall and destroy a crucial wing rear mirror. It was a Sunday and there wasn't an open garage to be found, but John and the friends they were travelling with came to our rescue and attached the mirror with string and rope—quite how, I had no idea. It looked very precarious.

'What's happening in the world?' Liz asked John. 'We saw part of an alarming television news program in Cádiz yesterday.'

'I heard they're doing some counterterrorism manoeuvres in Madrid,' said John.

'That's a relief,' I said. 'We thought we were going to be stranded. It will be quite enough dealing with getting the car back to Seville.'

I was very nervous as I drove back on the freeway, cars zooming past me at 200 kilometres an hour. Magically, I wasn't pulled up by the police and even more magically, our insurance policy covered the rear mirror. We flew back to London, very happy campers.

8

Exotic stories and island reveries

Liz was staying with me in Sydney for a month or so. Over the years her visits had gradually been growing longer and I was delighted; it was fun to have her staying with me over Christmas, and in January we both looked forward to the Sydney Festival. We were not on the move and so able to relax and enjoy reminiscing about our travels.

Liz was also avoiding the English winter and setting me an excellent example by plunging into the pool every day and swimming forty or so lengths. She would place a hard, round seed which had fallen from a tree on the tiles every time she reached the end of the pool. In this way she kept count; it was obsessively methodical. And I was soon copying her slavishly and there were two neat piles of seeds at the end of the pool. Occasionally a visiting cat or rabbit would knock the seeds into the pool and we would be forced to start again.

One evening, as we were chatting over camomile tea before bed, I asked her, 'Tell me, Lizzie, what's the most exotic experience you've ever had?'

'Honestly, Hil, what a dotty question. How long is a piece of string? Do you mean exotic eroticism or erotic exoticism?'

'No, just plain exotic, if that's not a contradiction.'

'Well, if you insist, I'd say it was a picnic in Baluchistan with four hundred tribesmen and their tribal chief. I wrote an article for the *Karachi Evening Star* at the time. I'll send it to you. Now tell me yours. As you brought up the topic, you obviously have one in mind.'

I couldn't wait to launch into my story. 'I had been on an extraordinary journey to find the leading lady for a feature film I was hoping to produce with the late Sydney artist Patrick Hockey. Patrick was funny, stylish and very naughty and we became friends. He told me that he had written a screenplay with the actress Diane Cilento. I was very taken with the haunting, original story which had been brought to Diane by the actor George Mikell. The film centred on a Mysterious Woman in Black who placed a red rose on Rudolph Valentino's grave every year.

'The key to the film's successful financing was the casting of the mysterious Madame X, the enigmatic leading lady. We came up with two contenders—Diane was keen on Gloria Swanson; Patrick and I favoured Jeanne Moreau. I was a young green producer—it was only my second venture into the pitfalls of production and I was daunted by the challenge of meeting either of these iconic figures, let alone signing one of them up. Diane, through her connections in Hollywood, put me in touch with Gloria Swanson's agents. I learnt that she lived part of the time in a "Longevity Centre" in Los Angeles—which immediately conjured up images of ghostly figures from silent movies, with skin of transparent mother-of-pearl. I imagined the old girls gliding along the garden path on their Zimmer frames, trying to avoid the gaping darkness of a swimming pool shaped like the Black Sea, waiting to swallow them up if they fell in.'

'Great image,' commented Liz.

Truthfully, I thought that Gloria was too old for the part, I told her. Our leading lady still had to be *séduisante*. Gloria was so much the stuff of legend that I was surprised to find she was still alive—and in fact it can't have been many years before her death in 1983. I wondered whether she would be interested in travelling halfway across the world to work on a low-budget movie. But the thought of actually getting to meet a screen icon, the star of *Sunset Boulevard* and lover of Rudolph Valentino and Joseph Kennedy, was very alluring and would call upon all my acting skills to play the part of the producer.

Miss Swanson liked the screenplay, so I used my credit card and flew to Los Angeles. I felt excitement tempered by nervousness as I caught a taxi to her country home, seventy-five kilometres from LA. It turned out to be a modest home, not the Hollywood mansion I expected. Miss Swanson looked ageless. She was tiny, elegant and walked as if she was balancing a book on her head. A couple of elderly carers looked after her. They had set up a projector and screen in her drawing room and proceeded to run slides of Circular Quay and the Opera House.

'Where is your studio?' asked Miss Swanson.

I entered into the spirit of the occasion, unable to bring myself to reveal that I only had a dingy one room office in downtown Woolloomooloo.

'Over there,' I said, airily waving to a point off the screen. (Liz grinned at this point in my story.) We chatted about the financing of the picture for a few more minutes and I promised to be in touch when I got back to Sydney.

In the taxi back to town I felt dazed by this surreal experience. Even though she had expressed interest in my film, I felt sure that she wouldn't want the hassle of making such a long journey. But it did occur to me that she might be a bit strapped for cash.

The meeting made me surer than ever that Jeanne Moreau was the answer. Jeanne was not only a consummate actress—she was a film director in her own right. My challenge was to place the script in her hands. Sometimes you get lucky, and this was one such occasion. An American friend had written a musical with a French composer. The composer happened to be the musical director of a television special that Jeanne was recording in Paris, and he offered to give our script to Moreau.

'I love your screenplay,' wrote Jeanne. 'I will be in London on Thursday. Do join me for tea at the Ritz.'

'I'd be delighted,' I replied, as though London was a bus ride away. Out came the credit card again to pay for my flight; to economise I caught the bus to the Ritz from my B&B in Paddington.

Jeanne was seated in a lofty salon, with a very cute, very young French actor in tow. We ate cucumber sandwiches and I invited her to Australia to meet Diane and to approve the casting of her leading man, an actor called Tyler Coppin. A month later, in my airless office in Woolloomooloo, I put on the videotape of his audition. She looked at it for fifteen seconds.

'He is fine,' she said. As we left my office she agreed to play Madame X.

'How brillio, Hilly,' said Liz.

'It certainly was,' I agreed. I had been beside myself with relief, and my excitement brimmed over when two months later Jeanne invited me to stay at her farmhouse in the hills behind Cannes. I was wound up like a clock and desperate to finalise the deal. My story was reaching its climax.

I was picked up at the station by Florence and Regis, an aged couple who looked after Jeanne and the property. When we arrived Jeanne greeted me warmly; she appeared carefree and tranquil. She led the way to the garden terrace where we ate hors d'oeuvres—olives from her orchard, baguettes and a local goat's cheese—and drank chilled Pouilly-Fuissé. It was a dream. I sat listening to the noisy cicadas as Jeanne prepared lunch— local fish caught that morning which she filleted herself with an array of different knives. Florence lightly grilled the fish while Regis tottered into view bearing freshly picked herbs. Jeanne whipped up a light dressing. '*Alors, mange, cherie.*' She had a husky, sexy voice. For dessert she plucked aromatic mauve blossoms from a tree nearby and Florence dipped them in the most delicate of batters before lightly frying them. It was a theatrical performance.

I did her proud when she returned to Sydney to meet the investors and work with Diane. There was a queue of admirers already in love with her who sat at her feet while we sailed round Sydney Harbour, Jeanne captivating in dark glasses and flowing scarves, drinking champagne. She bewitched *le tout* Sydney and had my investors salivating, hanging off her every word.

'How exciting,' said Liz.

Jeanne had capped off the generosity of her visit by selecting one of her own designer label dresses from the wardrobe and pressing it into my hands.

'No, no, too much,' I demurred.

'*C'est rien,*' she said smiling.

After Jeanne departed, Diane dropped a bombshell: she needed another quarter of a million pounds in the budget. I knew an increase in the budget would kill the project. Diane was to direct, and the investors said they would not invest a penny more in an art film with an inexperienced director.

'So I let the project go,' I finished.

Liz consoled me. 'That must have been so disappointing, Hilly. I'm sure you would have made a fine picture.'

'But I've got golden memories of pursuing the two leading ladies, and maybe it was better that it ended as it began, as an extraordinary adventure. Speaking of fantasies, did I ever tell you about my romantic island holiday with my filmmaker boyfriend at the time, Jack?'

Liz yawned, but I pressed on.

'Just before Christmas one year Jack rang me. "Hil, find your passport. We're going to Rhodes." He was like that, he loved spontaneous adventure. He had no money but, hey, what's an American Express card for? We touched down on Rhodes and headed for Lindos, a small village with whiter-than-white houses clinging to the hillside against a vivid blue sky. We found a tiny room in the village next to the bakery, with a bed and little else. During the day we basked in the sun, ate olives, fresh fish and Greek salad and drank carafes of the local white wine. Between sips I gazed at the sun-soaked blue bay, with its fishing boats bobbing about, and melted with happiness.'

I brought out some photographs of the trip.

'Who's that?' asked Liz.

'Me.'

'How amazing, you're slim.'

'On one outing I climbed onto a donkey who immediately had a shit and then wanted to lie down. His owner gave him a whack and the poor wheezing beast delivered me to the top of the hill, honking loudly, while Jack puffed up on foot. He was too heavy for a donkey. Once at the top I posed for Jack among the bleached columns, hoping I looked like a bronzed magazine model. The days passed in a bubble of bliss and I didn't want to leave. Guilt alone drove me back to Sydney. I was already in pre-production for my film *Heatwave*, and it was a bad time for the producer to take a holiday.'

Liz jolted awake. 'Excuse me, I must have fallen asleep. You know I don't like small islands. Big islands I don't mind: Crete, Sicily, Ireland—even Britain I can cope with,' she said. 'It's those small ones I dislike, where after a few days you know everyone and everything about the place.'

'But I like that,' I replied. 'It's easy to meet the local Lotharios in the bar and make friends on the beach. In my youth I used to fantasise about hot sex in the midnight surf under a full moon.'

'Surely once the excitement goes off the boil a small island becomes a prison?'

'Well, I suppose it's true that ecstasy is fleeting. When the first fragrance of frangipani has faded, the trots arrive and sunburn has fried you to crackling, it's hard to maintain exotic fantasies. After a week has gone by, I want to read a book.'

'I've had one fantasy about a small island,' said Liz. 'I'd like to live on one facing west over the Atlantic for a year and watch the setting of the sun.'

'And what would you do the rest of the day?' I enquired. Liz looked at me dismissively, but I continued undeterred.

'Actually, my first island boyfriend started off as a romantic dream. I met him on the beach of a small island off Thailand. He had blonde curly hair, a great body and I found him irresistible. But there was a catch. In my desire to play the part of the perfect surfie-chick girlfriend, I found myself sitting alone on the beach for hours while he rode the waves with his mates. When he hired a motorbike and took off round the island at lunatic speed with the boys, I was hurt that I wasn't invited.'

Hours passed, I told Liz, and I became convinced that he had crashed. But, no—finally the door burst open and in he limped, a gash on his thigh.

'What happened?' I cried.

'We were nearly gored by a bull. We were shit lucky that there was a gate.'

'Did you fall off?'

'Sort of,' he replied grudgingly.

Nurse Hill leapt into action, all sympathy as she helped her hero onto the bed, gently (but I confess, lustfully) replacing his board shorts with a fine love-in-the-mist blue cotton sarong and applying Betadine to the wound. 'Have a Panadol and see if you can rest,' I said, leaving the iced water by the bed, closing the shutters and padding out of the room. I resisted the desire to say, 'I think you'll live,' but when I returned later to check, he gave an immediate groan.

'Hils, you'd better call the doctor. I think it's turned septic.'

'There isn't a doctor on the island.'

'Well, get the local medicine man—anyone!' he wailed. I turned to go.

'But don't you go away, doll, I need you.' He smiled winningly.

Now for the first time I understood my psychologist friend Nell's warning: 'Beware, Hil, he's an only child.'

A big yawn from Liz, but I couldn't resist continuing. 'My love of islands isn't only about men, though. I love crumbled seashells scrunching and swooshing as waves break and recede on the shore;

rich pink bougainvillea against white walls; the taste of pawpaw and limes straight from the tree. What better?'

Liz explained that her island experiences—in contrast to mine—had been tough and raw and almost always cold and bleak.

'I used to spend a week every year camping on Skye with my friends Peter and Sian. We used to camp in a field behind a large sandy beach, right under the shadow of the Cuillin range. The mountains towered above us. The weather was always fickle and the peaks and the mountains responded to the mood. Sometimes they were black and forbidding. Occasionally after a shower of rain the sun would shine briefly and the peaks would sparkle and glint in the blue sky. And the winds were a nightmare on Skye; in fact, they weren't just winds—they were fully fledged Atlantic gales that swept in unannounced and devastated our camping site within an hour.

'The camping party was divided into two groups,' she continued, 'the climbers and the base camp. One year, Peter decided that half of the party should climb one of the more accessible peaks, walk over the rugged pass and down the other side to Loch Coruisk. Sian's group would motor thirty miles to a small harbour and hire a boat to take them to the Bad Step, which was the access to the loch from the sea. The two parties would meet up, have a picnic and then all take the boat back.

'I was in the climbers' group. I remember so vividly as I approached the top of the mountain, the dizzying heights brought on my vertigo big time. When I foolishly looked down on the loch thousands of feet below I felt overwhelmed by feelings of dread and inadequacy and the sensation that I had no right to be there. The feelings reached a fever pitch when we met up with the others and set out a vast picnic on the shores of the lake. I didn't say a word but luckily my silence was interpreted by the others as a left-over from vertigo.

'We always camped in June, when the days were at their longest. The evenings stretched until three in the morning and even then it didn't get really dark. Those were magical times, sitting in the camp site after a meal of haggis and neeps, drinking whiskey, watching the light slowly disappear over the Cuillins. In the distance the muffled roar of the ocean. We used to walk down to the beach to hear Peter playing his bagpipes and see the moon rise. Nobody talked much; there was no need to.'

Liz made Skye sound very compelling, but I was really keen to visit Mull and Iona. My friend, Jodi, had told me that Iona was the most spiritual and tranquil place she had ever visited. Liz kindly fell in with my ideas the next time I was in London. We went first to the Edinburgh Film Festival and saw thirteen films in four days, by which time Liz was more than ready to escape the claustrophobic cinema scene. We arrived in Glasgow from Edinburgh in plenty of time to catch the train to Oban, where we would take a ferry to Mull. The train showed up on the indicator board on three different panels, but there were no platform numbers. Liz opened fire.

'Do you see Colleen up there?' she said, pointing to the murky window of a first floor office. 'Her computer qualifications made her ideal for the job of punching in platform numbers on that giant indicator board. But what we didn't realise was that Colleen was a conceptual artist with a creative streak lurking inside her and she got a curious frisson as she watched the chaos on the platform when the numbers failed to show up. She spun out the agony as long as she dared. She particularly adored watching the Highland Bunch, a motley group of walkers, knapsacked and tweed-skirted old ladies and check-capped old men, as they tore down the platform like grapeshot from a blunderbuss.'

When our number finally came up Liz took off at a sprint while I puffed behind her. 'Colleen will be giving the thumbs up to Angus,' said Liz when I caught up. 'Angus is Colleen's mate on the platforms, in charge of carriage formation.' This day we were convinced that he took particular delight in having only two of the carriages going to Oban while the other five would go to Fort William when the train divided at Crianlarich. Angus knew full well that many more people were going to Oban and that they would be packed in like sardines. As the train drew out of the station he grinned as he saw the crush in the first two carriages compared with the sepulchral calm of the last five. We were sure he crowed, 'Serve 'em right!' to Colleen.

We glided along beside the River Clyde and Loch Lomond and then rose, gaining ground among the heather, bare rock and grey skies. Liz's eyes were glued to the view, but I dozed off. She kept trying to rouse me by pinching my arm and shouting out, 'There's a sea eagle!' or 'Look at that flying sporran!' but all I did was humph. I was finally roused from my torpor when Liz called out, 'We've reached Dalmally and the widow of the Campbell of Breadalbane is leaving the train. Look over there, that's Prince Charles's gillie helping her off.' The woman in the seat opposite sprang to attention. She and I were fooled again.

Oban was hell: there was nil signage. Where was the ferry to Mull, and how was I going to manage my luggage? People were unhelpful, saying that everybody travelled light in the Highlands, and particularly to the islands.

I eventually huffed and puffed my way to the ferry and hauled myself and my luggage on board. I bought a bar of chocolate at the cafeteria while Liz went up to the top deck. The sea was quite calm as we plied our way along the Sound of Mull. It was a grey day but the ferry was large and comfy. Liz called to me from the stairs, 'Why don't you join me on the top deck?'

'I'm perfectly happy reading the newspaper,' I replied. 'Just leave me be—the view is not spectacular.'

'You can eat and read the newspaper anywhere,' said Liz.

We arrived on Mull to find a bus waiting for us. Liz loved public transport—that it existed at all was a ceaseless cause of wonderment to her—but I was of the opinion that public transport was what I paid my taxes for: I was entitled to an efficient bus service.

We arrived in the main street of Tobermory, which was a delicate crescent of multicoloured houses fringing a sheltered bay. Nearby there was a jolly stall selling fish and chips. Liz would have been satisfied with an al fresco supper on the quayside, watching the world of Tobermory promenading in the evening sunshine, but not me. I wanted to try Café Fish at the end of the bay, which one of the guidebooks had said was excellent. I asked the people at the fish and chips stall whether they would look after our bags while we went off to eat. In Sydney a shopkeeper would have told me to rack off but here on Mull they kindly roped off our bags in their rubbish bin area and kept their thoughts, if they had any, to themselves.

So we walked along Tobermory's crescent to the far end, where part of a little-used ferry terminal had been partially converted into the Café Fish. Here we had a gorgeous meal. I had the seafood platter, which was so enormous even I had difficulty finishing it off. There was lobster and crab, langoustine hiding behind the lemon wedges and parsley, scallops, and prawns the size of yabbies, mussels and clams and even cockles and whelks. I was amazed.

And they delivered two different kinds of seafood sauce. The sun was setting over a twinkling sea and every so often Liz would dash out onto the balcony to check its progress. Above and behind Fish she had seen a sad sight: a neglected, decaying Victorian building with its name in large white capitals pinned to a rusty fence—The West Highlands Hotel. She told me that this was where people used to stay overnight before they set forth on the all-day ferry journey to the Outer Hebrides; now most visitors flew to the Outer Hebrides by plane and the remainder travelled by ferry from Oban to Lochboisdale, South Uist.

Liz wished we were staying at the West Highlands, although it looked as though it was no longer open. The accommodation I had booked was a few miles outside Tobermory at Glengorm Castle. I asked the waitress if she could possibly ring us a taxi. It's a small world in Mull; our waitress told us that she had a day job in the shop at Glengorm.

We drove across a bleak moor and eventually rolled up to the doors of the castle—a great, gaunt building perched on a hill. There were no brightly-coloured flowerbeds nestling against its stern walls to soften the scene. It stood ill at ease, half a mile from the sea that pounded into dark and ugly coves. Marian and Graham, the owners, greeted us warmly and showed us our rooms. We dumped our bags and while it was still light walked over close-cropped grass towards the glistening sea. It was magical—just us, lots of sheep, a few highland cattle and eight thousand kilometres of ocean.

We watched until the sun went down and then returned to the house, where we explored the rest of the castle, ending up in the library, where our hosts had displayed twenty-five different brands of whiskey, which they encouraged us to sample and record in the visitors' book provided. The Inishowen whiskey Liz decided had 'a full, smoky start'. She became very taken with the Dallas Dhu and started identifying all the ingredients: from fresh apples, cinnamon and citrus to a Bakewell tart! 'That can't be true,' I said, but after sampling it myself I thought perhaps she was right. She finished off, 'As Humphrey Bogart said on his deathbed, "I should never have changed from Scotch to Martinis."' Liz wished we had bought takeaway fish and chips from the stall in Tobermory instead of wasting valuable whiskey time in Café Fish.'

Staying with us at Glengorm Castle were Linda and Mike, a retired American couple from Milwaukee. Mike was a clean-cut right-wing evangelist from the Evangelical United Brethren Church. Linda was his shadow. This was their first world trip, which they had started with their church group but then extended in order to visit the homes of Mike's ancestors. Linda had inherited some money from her mother and this had enabled the couple to broaden their travel plans. In all, they were going to be away for six months. Linda was completely out of her comfort zone. Mike made all the arrangements but was thick as a brick and at a loss away from his church group. Neither of them knew what to do or how to make new friends, so they were delighted to make our acquaintance and Mike was very happy to get stuck into the whiskey with us.

They were novices at the travel game, ripe fruit ready to fall into our laps if we played our cards right. The next day we were going to the ferry terminal for Iona, and we knew we had two excruciating bus rides ahead of us. I had wanted to hire a car so that we could wander wherever the whim took us. Liz had put her foot down, still enthralled by the rudimentary bus system, but she secretly wanted to see the famed white sands of Calgary Bay, which was not on the bus route. If we buttered up Linda and Mike we could easily manoeuvre them into driving us via the bay to the ferry terminal. We both toyed with the idea: was it worth spending a day entertaining them in return for a comfy lift and sightseeing? We decided that the lift was not worth the boredom of their company. And of course there was the added horror that Mike and Linda would get stuck in a bog, get out a bible and insist we get down on our knees and start praying.

The next morning, despite a blistering wind, Liz walked along the edge of the cliff beside the sea. The landscape was morose and magnificent by turns. Life here was tough. We talked a little about our hosts, Marian and Graham, who were doing their best to make a living from the sheep and highland cattle that roamed across their infertile land. They were now letting out a few bedrooms, which they'd recently done up to luxury standard, but had left their own ornaments and furniture in the rooms for the homely touch. Liz said, 'They should have left the horsehair mattresses, that would have completed the picture.'

'They're trying to attract the well-heeled American tourist, and I hardly think horsehair fits the picture,' I countered. 'Poor old Linda would get an asthma attack and Mike's hayfever would break into a volley of sneezes followed by a trumpet of nose-blowing.'

They had also converted their outbuildings into an art gallery, a pottery and a lunch place, as a means of making money. There was a message on the wall saying they were cutting down on portion sizes because so many people were leaving food, with an added proviso that locals could still have a bigger portion at no extra cost if they asked. We found Marian working on the grounds, heavily pruning the rhododendron bushes which bordered the drive up the hill. She stopped to show us her walled garden, which she had regenerated with masses of neatly growing organic vegetables.

We were worried about Marian and Graham; their smiling faces only just concealed the stress of scraping a living together. True, the place was a bit rundown but I really liked that they had kept it cosy, with their dog curled up asleep at the front door like an old rug. They were a friendly couple and Graham was clearly deeply attached to the land, talking at length about the generations of his family who had farmed it. There was a wall of family snaps going back three generations in the loo, which said it all.

After bidding them farewell, and giving Mike and Linda the slip, we managed to catch the bus and found our way onto the ferry to Iona, hauling my baggage on board. The crossing was grey and choppy, but didn't take long.

*

'You must go to Iona. It's a mystical island,' my friend Jodi had told me more than once, and I always trusted her judgement. She had handed me St Columba's poem to get me in the mood. I spoke its words aloud now as we chugged across the sea:

> 'Iona of my heart,
> Iona of my love,
> Instead of monks' voices
> Shall be the lowing of cows.
> But ere the world shall come to an end
> Iona shall be as it was.'

Liz was less than impressed and muttered dismissively about some saint coming from Ireland 1400 years ago to carve a few Celtic crosses and convert the locals to Christianity. 'Nothing of that now remains,' she said. 'The Vikings came three hundred years later and sacked the lot so that what's there now is a recent construct.' She moaned at the inauthenticity of it all. 'Anyway,

I've listened to the weather forecast. It's going to rain all week,' she added gloomily.

I decided to ignore this downer and pointed out our accommodation as we docked, a cheery pub on the quay which had recently been turned into a hotel. I was reminded of the Cornish cottages of my youth, old fishermen sitting on lobster pots smoking their pipes and kids impatiently reeling in empty fishing lines. A few 'spiritual' tourists smiled at us as we stepped off the ferry and I found myself smiling back until one gigantic smile seemed to weave its way up the path, meeting the smiling locals congregated to greet the boat.

'This is heady stuff, Liz. Go on, give the spiritual a chance.'

'I'll leave that to you.'

Liz finds that laidback hospitality often comes together with organic produce, and in the case of the two cheery hotels on the island, both had large vegetable gardens full of genuine organic produce stinking of sheep manure, which they lovingly served at meal times—the produce, not the manure!

'No school dinners here, thank God,' said Liz, as she glimpsed the vegie garden at the Argyll, where we were staying.

The hotel had two tiny lounges with unreadable books, roaring fires and subsiding sofas. We dropped our bags in our room under the roof and headed off in the direction of the abbey, which lay a fair distance away across fields of munching sheep. Beyond the abbey was the path to the rugged seashore at the northern end of the island. The stones, sand and seaweed here were dry and bleached. The wind exposed every tiny piece of unprotected flesh and nipped our ankles. I was plunged again into memories of Cornwall—stony paths bordered by tamarisk down to the beach; Grandpa Gill with his walrus moustache sitting at the kitchen table holding a pasty in bent arthritic fingers. I remembered the hidden rockpools full of crabs and little fish washed in on the tide, sea anemones clutching the sides of the rock and cowrie shells lining the bottom.

We found cowrie shells on Iona, and pink and grey rocks. One large rock looked like the creamy thigh of a reclining Henry Moore nude. Pure white gulls wheeled high above our heads, nothing like the scruffy, chip-pecking upstarts squawking around the picnic tables of Bondi Beach. These birds were sinewy and wild, swirling around the ruins, preoccupied with finding food. I noticed that they kept away from one corner of the ruined nunnery near the abbey; it had been lovingly turned into a sheltered flower garden of lavender and roses by the local ladies' gardening auxiliary.

By late afternoon we were getting cold so returned to our hotel for a pre-dinner whiskey. Liz had settled into one of the uncomfortable lounges to rest and was deep in a book when Naomi, a pallid guest and would-be new friend, entered the room, desperate to pounce on the first person she encountered. She was longing to share her stories of St Columba and the events of her day-long pilgrimage around the island.

'Did you know that St Columba was over forty when he came to Iona to found his monastery? And that he lived here for thirty years?' she said breathlessly to Liz.

'I thought he rowed to Iona from Ireland because he was bored with writing the Book of Kells,' said Liz.

'Oh, no,' said Naomi. 'He was building his monastery. And he had to survive dark days when northerners attacked and killed seventy of his monks. But the Community had such a healthy spirit that it survived for a thousand years.'

'Fancy that,' said Liz.

'He could forecast the weather, you know, and had many mystical qualities.' Naomi was warming to her topic. 'One night he was sitting by the fire in the monastery when he saw one of his novices reading a book. He said, "Be careful. That book you're studying is going to fall into a bowl of water." The young man looked confused, tucked the book under his arm and got up to do some chore in the monastery, forgetting what St Columba had said. As he crossed the courtyard he slipped and the book fell into a pail of rainwater. Isn't that miraculous?' said Naomi, her eyes wide with wonder. 'And another time Columba exorcised a devil who was trapped in a pail and kept spilling the milk in its effort to escape.'

'Well, Naomi, I found evidence of St Columba myself this morning,' said Liz mischievously. 'I can show you some crab claws fastened to a cave entrance, a footprint caught in prehistoric mud and a cleft in an ancient tree. All very strange.'

'Please, would you? Tomorrow would be wonderful,' said Naomi, eyes glistening in anticipation of fresh discoveries. She glanced at her watch. 'Oh, gosh, I'll be late,' and with that she left Liz to her book and scampered off to an early service in the abbey.

We ate a delightful dinner of homemade fish pie and bread and butter pudding. Being a Pom by birth, I am a staunch supporter of the fish pie, but it is hard to find a good one and I was thrilled to discover something so special on the tiny Scottish island of Iona. Maybe it's all the 'love' on the island. I persuaded the chef at the hotel to tell me his ingredients and then adapted it to suit my own taste and our local fish supply when I returned to Sydney.

* * * * *

Ionian Fish Pie

Serves 4

Ingredients

1 kg potatoes

50 g butter

splash of milk

500 ml fish stock

100 ml white wine

small bunch of parsley

350 g white fish fillets or salmon fillets

350 g smoked white fish

200 g small peeled prawns

50 g butter

plain flour

200 ml double cream

2 anchovies, finely chopped

handful of white breadcrumbs

Optional extras

2 hard-boiled eggs, halved

1 tsp capers

Preparation

1. Preheat the oven to 180°C. Peel the potatoes and cut into evenly sized chunks. Put in a large pan, cover with cold water, add a generous pinch of salt, and bring to the boil. Simmer for about 20 minutes, until tender. Drain, and allow to sit in the colander for a few minutes, then mash until smooth, and beat in the butter and a splash of milk. Season well and set aside.

2. Put the fish stock, wine and parsley stalks into a large pan, and bring to a simmer. Add the fish, and simmer for five minutes,

then lift out with a slotted spoon, remove skin if any, and cut into large chunks. Discard the parsley stalks.

3. Melt the butter in a medium pan over a lowish heat, and then stir in the flour. Cook, stirring, for a couple of minutes, being careful not to let it brown. Gradually stir in the stock. Bring to the boil, then simmer for about 20 minutes.

4. Take sauce off heat, stir in double cream, parsley leaves and anchovies and season. Add fish and prawns and toss to coat.

5. Put the seafood and sauce into a baking dish and top with the mashed potato. Bake for 15 minutes, then sprinkle over the breadcrumbs and bake for a further 10 minutes, until the top is golden.

6. Top each portion with half a hard-boiled egg, sprinkle with capers and serve.

* * * * *

After swallowing a short black coffee to keep us awake, we followed Naomi to the church. The locals had beaten us to it and were stumping up the aisle in their wellington boots, placing their buckets, spades, watering cans and brooms on the altar to be blessed. This was a weekly ritual.

At the end of the service as we went through the door I saw a notice which summed up my impressions of Iona so far. It read: CAUTION. WATCH YOUR STEP. BABY BIRDS ON THE FLOOR.

There was an innocent kindness there that I found disarming.

Liz was off at dawn the next day for her habitual early morning walk. I decided to try a spot of meditation at the water's edge near the hotel and was pleased when I found it quite easy to reach a state of 'mindfulness'. *Iona must already be working its magic*, I thought. After a while I sauntered off to find the post office, a shoebox with barely enough room for the stock, let alone the postmistress Gwen and a vast local called Gladys. Gladys was in full swing, regaling Gwen with the latest dramas to which she had been subjected by her mean-spirited family. 'They're all no-hopers, eating me out of house and home. Not one of them contributes a cent towards board.' *Nothing very spiritual about her*, I mused. Gladys's stories grew more lurid as she gathered steam. I cleared my throat in the hope that she would pause long enough to let me buy some stamps. But Gladys wasn't giving any ground. She eyed me crossly and wagged her finger.

'There's no such thing as time on Iona,' she cautioned and resumed the list of her family's misdeeds. Chastened, I left the shoebox.

Iona was a small island by Liz's definition so we were bound to see Gladys again, and lo and behold we did, that very afternoon. We were heading for the southern end of the island when she cycled past. She was crouched over the handlebars of her bike, struggling against the fierce wind. Her legs, like red tree trunks, emerged from rough home-knitted socks as her feet strained at the pedals. Her eyes were glittering with wind-whipped tears and she seemed not to recognise the person she had ticked off that morning in the post office, instead giving us both a friendly greeting.

'Windy day.'

'Too right,' I replied, with relief. Once she had disappeared out of sight we couldn't help laughing.

'How does the bike hold her up? She's enormous.'

'Pot calling the kettle black, Hilly,' said Liz. 'Maybe St Columba's got her in hand.'

A tall, lanky man hove into view and spotted us giggling.

'You're a cheerful pair,' he said. He seemed in need of a chat. 'My name's James. Have a peanut.' He proffered a paper bag and launched into the reasons why he had come to Iona.

'I need to exorcise my inner demons before I can seek salvation for my soul,' he said. A shadow passed over his taut, angular face. I nodded, empathically I hoped.

His mother was staying in the village, collecting jam recipes from the hotel cooks. After Iona they were off to Findhorn, 'a spiritual community, ecovillage and international centre for holistic education' in Moray County, in the north-east of Scotland. James told us that Findhorn was known for its gigantic vegetables, grown with the help of 'nature spirits'.

'What's a nature spirit, James?' I asked.

'A spirit which evolves with nature—like fairies.'

'Have you actually *seen* a fairy?' I asked, my eyes widening.

'I could show you a book with photographs, if you're interested?' said James, glowing.

'Too much for me, James, I'm afraid.'

'Too much like popular mythology,' added Liz.

Our response to James's beliefs clearly disturbed and dismayed him and he ceased offering us peanuts, blew his nose and moved on.

We were soon to leave Iona and I needed more time to myself. Leaving Liz to her own devices, I walked to a hill near the ruined priory and sat on a rock ledge, listening to the sound of the sea and the sheep tugging at the scrub for their breakfast. I thought how peaceful our brief holiday on Iona had been. My reverie was interrupted by Liz, who had followed me. She had something she wanted to get off her chest.

'You've got to forget all this island rubbish, Hilly,' she said, plonking herself down by my side. 'All your nonsense about the beauty of hollyhocks peering over garden fences, nannas knitting beanies and endless photographs of stupid sheep. It's a complete fantasy. The locals aren't quaint islanders—they eat fast food and drink themselves to death in a cement brick social club down by the harbour. And the beanies come from China. All the under-twenties leave Iona just as soon as they've saved the ferry fare to the mainland. Come and see the club for yourself.'

She took me to the Martyr's Bay café and sure enough there wasn't an organic product in sight. Everything was prepacked, processed and past its use-by date.

'This is the real Iona,' said Liz, as we stood at the counter waiting to be served. I leant across and asked the sour-looking waitress how often she went to Oban.

'You mind your business and I'll mind mine,' she replied.

That'll teach me, I thought. But I wasn't going to allow Liz to ruin my belief in the spiritual aspect of Iona and the people's innate goodness. I was convinced that there were many craftspeople on the island—with or without strong religious beliefs—who had carved out a living and kept the craft traditions alive, and who were happy to live on the island. Nor could she take away the intense feeling of peace I had experienced as I sat ruminating with the munching sheep early that morning.

On the morning of our departure, I was trying to decipher the four ferry tickets I had bought on the day we arrived. They all said 'return' and all were dated with the day we arrived. Liz's suspicions about island life came to the surface. 'These tickets are useless,' she said, and we resigned ourselves to paying for the return journey. The girl at the ticket office looked surprised and said, 'You came over with us, didn't you?'

The incomprehensible tickets suddenly emerged as passports to an island where nobody was expected to stay. The ferry people had caught the goodwill fever of visitors and were loath to charge again. Liz's lifetime dislike of small islands was severely jolted.

9

Liz takes charge: trains, art and exhaustion in Europe

At the beginning of June one year I emailed Liz:

> Over to you, Lizzie.

Not without some misgiving, I admit. I had surprised myself: I was actually letting go of the job of organising our next holiday. Liz was going to be in charge. I had been busy with house renovations and had emailed Liz several times for her input on our upcoming holiday but the most comprehensive reply I had received was:

> Don't worry. I have lots of ideas. Just come. Lizzest

And, strangely, I found myself falling in with her Lack of a Definite Plan (LDP).

When I arrived in London, Liz was raring to go. Her latest interest was the CAS—the Contemporary Art Scene. I knew she'd been to the Kassel trade show and the Venice Biennale the year before, but now she was keen to pursue the CAS further afield to the Berlin Biennale and the Basel Art Fair.

Liz decided that we would go by train for both eco and aesthetic reasons—hardly for financial ones, because the fares were far more expensive than flying. Liz wanted us to experience the great plains of central Europe from our train window. Better than clouds from a plane window over a relief map of unidentifiable land. I was feeling a little uneasy not being in charge and there was definitely an LDP, but I warmed to Liz's enthusiasm, especially when she said that we would 'get the culture over first' and then move down to Italy for a series of four 'scenic jaunts'.

We set off in the morning from Eurostar's spanking new terminal in the updated St Pancras Station. We sped through Kent shrouded in thick mist, changed at Brussels and ate an organic *pain au chocolat* in a secret ecological café hidden within the station which Liz had discovered on a previous visit to the Belgian capital. Then she led the way to our platform.

'Now, Hilly, how about this delicious ICE train!' said Liz, pointing at the gleaming Intercity-Express. 'It's Germany's very latest high-speed answer to the Eurostar.'

'Very smart,' I replied, as she went about selecting the perfect carriage for us, spreading out luggage and coats to discourage anyone from entering our private quarters. The train departed spankingly on time and was soon whizzing through the country.

Liz forgot we had to change trains at Cologne until the last moment. It was all very well for her. She jollily hared up and down stairs between platforms while I followed, dragging my two suitcases, umbrella and handbag and cursing my aching replacement knees. No sign of a trolley.

'Come on, Hilly, don't dawdle,' called Liz from the top of one long flight of stairs. 'We'll miss the connection.'

'I'm going as fast as I can.'

'Good. You need the exercise. It's your own fault bringing all this ridiculous luggage.'

I sent a loud expletive in Liz's direction as I noted no sign of a lift or escalator. By the time I reached the top, Liz had sped off down the platform, past an endless line of first-class carriages and restaurant cars. By the time I arrived at the second-class carriage she had even had time to buy an English newspaper and an espresso.

'You're ignoring the heartland of Europe,' said Liz, after we'd been speeding along for an hour or so. I'd been having a little doze.

'I am underwhelmed,' I replied, opening my eyes and staring blankly out the window, although I did notice windmills, of which I am particularly fond, littering the landscape.

But trains are marvellous places to catch up on chat, far better than planes or cars. I was interested to know how Liz managed to continue roaming around the world staying with friends.

'I think they're beginning to get fed up with me,' she said. 'They say things like, "When are you going to settle down, Liz?", "Get a job", "Stop being irresponsible", "Stay in one spot for a year".'

Friends are unpredictable, we decided: one minute supportive, nurturing and loving and the next critical and dishing out unsolicited advice. As they get older most become more preoccupied with their own lives. Mainly, I supposed, because of the increased effort of keeping their 'show on the road'.

Berlin was nearly upon us and as evening fell we arrived at the vast new central station. We spent an eternity trying to find the way out; there were so many levels, connected by a maze of lifts and escalators and not a single sign indicating how to leave the place. It was a mystery. When I asked a local, they directed me to the lavatory.

We found our way eventually to our hotel in the eastern part of the city, the trendy Prenzlauer Berg area, with more restaurants and cafés per square mile than Sydney's Crown Street or Islington's Upper Street. It was a small boutique hotel with each room decorated in a different style—Chinese, Japanese, English country—in a leafy street with exercisers, bikers and dog-walkers. Luckily, Liz took pity on the state of my knees when we set out to find somewhere for dinner. We walked only a short distance and decided on a café where Bill Clinton had famously eaten, and where reputedly many 'pollies' ate. I made the wrong choice: a limply breaded Wiener schnitzel, sauerkraut and overcooked white asparagus smeared with thick, glutinous hollandaise sauce and accompanied by soggy roast potatoes. 'Well, what did you expect?' said Liz. 'It's a German school dinner.'

Upon reflection, when had I ever eaten good German food?—never. I disliked sauerkraut before I came to Germany, I thought, so why should I like it now? And I have never been tempted for a second by the endless varieties of *Wurst* on offer. I gag at the sight of *Bockwurst, Bratwurst, Knackwurst* and *Weisswurst*—and worst of all *Blutwurst*, the blood sausage which you are obliged to eat cold or fried like black pudding. Revolting. Liz had been more sensible. She had plumped for a pizza with a crisp, no-nonsense thick bottom and minimal cheese and tomato on top.

We looked around the café but there were no politicians to be seen. Well, Mrs Merkel was the only one we would have recognised anyway. Liz was intrigued by a long-bearded man with a monk-like fringe of grey hair wearing a wide-brimmed black felt hat, who called the waiter by extending his arm full length and snapping his fingers. Much to my embarrassment Liz decided that this was the way to get things done in Germany and proceeded to imitate his pantomime as she summoned our waitress. 'You are incorrigible,' I said, cringing. But Liz was delighted by her floorshow and continued extending her arm and snapping her fingers whenever she wanted anything—on planes, trains, even buses. Fortunately we tended not to sit together on our travels because Liz always wanted the window and I often wanted the aisle for ready access to the loo. So if she started up her routine I pretended I didn't know her.

It was my first visit to Germany. I had always kept away from the country, having grown up in the shadow of the Second World War, during which my stepmother, Margery, would flinch at the mere mention of anything German-related. It had taken me sixty years to shake off my reluctance.

The next day we got going by midday and were relaxing over a long coffee on the Unter den Linden. We were trying to kid ourselves that this was the Champs-Élysées of Berlin. Suddenly from behind me I heard an unmistakable voice.

'Why, hello there! What are you guys doing in Berlin?'

It was Mike, of Mike and Linda from Mull! Why is it that you meet the most unlikely people over and over again when travelling?

'What should we see?' asked Linda. They clearly hadn't a clue and were desperate for company and suggestions.

Liz and I eyed each other and went into immediate extrication alert. The task was clear: 'How-do-we-get-away-without-offending-M-and-L?'

Liz tried dazzling them with history.

'When Frederick III proclaimed himself King in Prussia in 1701, Germany was treated like a nouveau riche upstart by "real" countries like France, Britain and Russia. So that's why you must see all the buildings built in Berlin at that time. Frederick was determined to show those "real" countries that German architectural design was as good, if not better, than any other.'

255

Mike and Linda listened, expressionless. This tack didn't seem to be working, but the two of them perked up when Liz rattled off a list of the must-see buildings, adding, 'and the best place to begin is round the corner in the Gendarmenmarkt', pointing to it on the map. 'Hil and I were there yesterday,' she added quickly. She extended her arm and snapped her fingers at the waitress for our bill. I did my best to cover this unfortunate display by helping them to order a large meal of sausage and sauerkraut, hoping that it would keep them occupied while we scarpered.

Linda and Mike were still stuffing their faces with sausage as we waved them a hasty farewell and scooted across the street. Liz attracted the attention of a passing tourist bus using the extended-arm-snapping-fingers technique and we leapt on board. The driver looked annoyed.

'We're only meant to pick up people at the designated stops,' he grumbled, as we barged past him. I could see Linda and Mike preparing to cross the street in pursuit.

'You'd better move,' I said, irritating the driver further, 'or you'll arrive late at the next stop.'

The driver glowered at me, quite rightly, as he started the engine. But it worked and Mike and Linda were left looking after us plaintively from the footpath.

'The Brandenburg Gate's not a patch on the Arc de Triomphe, more of a Marble Arch,' commented Liz as we whizzed by.

Our bus had an amusing East German guide called Hans, who referred to Mrs Merkel's Chancellery as 'the tumble dryer'. He went too far with the Tiergarten, which he said was bigger and better than Hyde Park. 'Nonsense,' said Liz, 'it's not half as attractive.' Hans smiled delightedly; he liked a bit of comeback and kept on provoking us.

Liz asked him what it had been like being a Berliner living through the twentieth century in a country that had alienated the world so completely.

'It was hell,' Hans said. Liz reflected that her grandparents, parents and she had spanned the last century and, apart from a great-uncle being killed in the First World War, they had suffered no real tragedies brought about by public events. Hans expanded his story, telling us that his family had suffered horribly—many deaths in both the First and Second World Wars. He also suffered severe humiliation when it was discovered that several members of his family had been high-up Nazis, and their children had grown up and transferred seamlessly onto the payroll of the notorious East German secret police, the Stasi.

At the Potsdamer Platz and the Sony Centre we got off and I was very taken by the glass interior, which provided a number of opportunities for 'art' photographs playing with the reflections thrown up by the glass walls. While we were having coffee, I reminded Liz, 'Have you forgotten about the Biennale?' Liz looked a little abashed. She had asked the hotel the previous evening and they had given her a few indecipherable pages from the web. 'All too hard,' she said.

We got on the tourist bus again. I wanted to see the Jewish Museum, which proved to be a sad, claustrophobic place, particularly after the conversation with Hans. Liz didn't fancy anything depressing and decided to go to the Berlin Contemporary Art Museum, which she found closed despite the opening hours on the door indicating that it should have been open. We were both beginning to get a real feeling of frustration and I wondered whether, sixty years on, I was still in the lingering grip of my stepmother's hatred of the German people.

The next day Liz's friend 'Maria Luisa, Princesse de Croy' arrived from Geneva. 'Where on earth did you meet a princess?' I asked.

'In society,' Liz replied enigmatically, then relented. 'In Irish society, to be precise. They are great friends of Johnnie and Fiona.'

Liz had telephoned her from London to see if we could stay with her and commute to Basel for the art fair. 'Impossible to commute but I will come and join you and book us all into a hotel in Basel. Then you can come to dinner with Emmanuel and I in Bern and then please come and stay with us in Geneva.' Maria Luisa had travelled all night and joined us for breakfast. She was a tiny person with huge eyes the colour of blueberries and long, shiny dark hair. She seemed consumed by indecision about every aspect of her life. She told us about visiting East Germany in communist times, and how her communist parents and friends thought it was paradise to move through Checkpoint Charlie to East Berlin.

The three of us were all keen to see the famous Pergamon Museum, which is focused on the ancient world and has exhibits including the blue Ishtar Gate and the Procession Street of the City of Babylon, built in the sixth century BC in the reign of King Nebuchadnezzar. Of course, it was closed for renovation on the day we went. We were, however, mollified by seeing a reconstruction of the second century BC Pergamon Altar—a huge, full-size temple building that needed a full room to itself and had twenty-seven steps from the museum floor up to the colonnade. It had an astonishing frieze depicting in detail the battle between the Olympian gods and the Titans.

We also missed out on the four-storey facade of the gate to the ancient city of Milet, and the facade of an eighth century Arabian palace, also under restoration. Apparently restoration of the whole museum is going on until 2015.

'Why is it,' said Liz, 'that when you go to museums or galleries in Europe one of two things happens: either the particular item you want to see is in a room which is closed for renovation, or the whole building is closed because it is always closed on the day you have chosen to visit.'

Our style was cramped still more that morning by the King of Spain, who had beaten us to the Adlon Kempinski Hotel for lunch. Security informed us that we could not enter until the king had left.

Enlivened by Maria Luisa's arrival, we made yet another determined effort to track down the Biennale. Liz did some sleuthing and learnt that there was a selection to be seen in the Neue Nationalgalerie, so we hotfooted it there, Maria Luisa and Liz setting a cracking pace. My knees gave out by the time we arrived at the gallery and I sank onto the nearest bench.

Liz charged off without me to look around, but she was back soon. 'The Neue Nationalgalerie is just a great big glass box and for the Biennale they've filled it with structures, concepts, bundles of wire, piles of pots and a few weird paintings,' said Liz. 'In other words a jumble of insensate nonsense, which they call the CAS, the Contemporary Art Scene! It's so ambiguous and self-serving. Why can't they be more political and challenging?' Maria Luisa and I nodded in agreement.

Downstairs, looking at the expressionists, I was ambushed by a security guard. He embodied everything I loathed about rules and regs. 'You must not carry this,' he said, poking my chest and grabbing my jumper, which I had slung over my arm. 'You must wrap this round your shoulders or waist.'

'Why? It's too hot in here,' I said. He took no notice and began prodding my shopping bags.

'What are these?'

'Books. From your shop.'

'They must be left in the cloakroom.'

I felt a bubble of anger about to burst, but Maria Luisa wisely dragged me off.

I was badly in need of diversion after this onslaught of bureaucratic rubbish so we made for the famous KaDeWe department store, where the restaurant and food hall, all under a glass roof, were way larger than Harvey Nichols and the choice of food unending. We had lunch. The princess chose lobster; I had pasta with an elaborate sauce containing seven kinds of mushroom, cooked in front of me; and Liz had brains in aspic.

Over coffee Liz told the waitress that she was so pleased to meet Mrs KaDeWe and how delightful it was to find that the family took such a hands-on approach to service. To our surprise, 'Mrs KaDeWe' spoke perfect English, was thrilled with Liz's fantasy, and entered into it with a long story about her disastrous, but now defunct, marriage to Mr K. 'He was a gambler with a mistress, whom he paraded in front of me in the store. He didn't give me money so I ran up huge clothes bills. And,' she added, 'I get a good feed here.' Liz and I laughed, while the princess looked confused. 'Why don't you divorce him?' I asked, entering into this world of make-believe, but Mrs K suddenly snapped out of the fantasy and handed us the bill. I looked around and saw a supervising type eyeing her.

The next day we were off by train in pursuit of Liz's temple of contemporary art—the Basel Art Fair. The princess had booked a hotel twenty-five kilometres from Basel because every hotel in town was full. The hotel was not up to the princess's standards and she was consumed with guilt and apologies. Liz made a point of saying that when she travelled with her Welsh friends they stayed in hostels and this hotel was a paradise compared with double bunks and communal washing.

Art Basel was all and more than Liz had hoped for. Three hundred or so booths displaying, and sometimes selling, 'top' contemporary art—whatever that is. The atmosphere was super-cool, uber-rich and utter heaven as far as Liz was concerned. She darted from booth to booth, casting her practised artistic eye over the non-daring/daring, non-challenging/challenging paintings that were hanging like sacrificial offerings to lure the wealthy into spontaneous purchase.

So temple-like were the proceedings, so solemn the atmosphere, that when I asked an official whether they sold ice-cream at the food bars my question was met with rude guffaws by Liz. Maria Luisa was too polite.

Unexpectedly, I got my own back when I spotted in the program that Tracey Moffatt was launching her new book. I had known Tracey when she was a young filmmaker twenty-five years ago. She now has an international reputation and lives in New York, and I had lost touch with her. I dragged Liz and the princess along to the launch for fun, and to my surprise Tracey recognised me in the audience. She waved and called out, 'What are you doing here?', and without waiting for an answer pointed at me and shouted out for all to hear, 'She's a famous agent—a legend in her lifetime!' I was mortified, very aware of my ill-assembled bloomer pants, double-extra T-shirt and navy blue Crocs.

The day after the fair the princess took us to Bern, where we met her princely husband, Emmanuel, and their princely son Leopold. They suggested going for dinner at the Schöngrün restaurant, many-starred and attached to the Klee museum designed by the celebrated architect Renzo Piano.

At dinner I asked the princess about her childhood. She told me that she had been born in Colombia and brought up in Bogotá. Her father was in politics and her mother a headmistress who at one time had asked Liz to teach at her school. Maria Luisa went to University in Salamanca, where she met Emmanuel.

The following day we drove to Sauverny, where Maria Luisa lived with her husband, two sons, one of Leopold's friends and three dogs. Liz called it 'boyland'. The princess acted as the chief executive of her family. Her mobile phone was always primed, fielding calls from them as she orchestrated pick-ups and departures, maintained the social calendar and soothed their brows when troubled. It was a full-time job. Maria Luisa said ruefully that there was hardly time to visit her psychiatrist for support and a few tips.

We had a great time in boyland. Emmanuel was a superb cook and we visited their local market, where he carefully selected succulent vegies and fruit. He was well known to the stall-holders and got special attention. We didn't want to leave Sauverny and on departure day there was an on-off strike of train staff. The strike fed the princess's natural indecisiveness and we felt as though we were in a tumble dryer—were-we-weren't-we-going? Sadly, we finally left for Paris, the princess to the last carrying my bag and tearfully seeing us off.

We stayed in the Marais district of Paris in an atypical minimalistic modern hotel. It was entirely inappropriate for old bats like Liz and me. The other clients were young, chic and on business. But it was near the Pompidou Centre and we were off there as soon as we had booked in.

Before we looked at the pictures, Liz insisted we take a look at the restaurant on the top floor, which she had heard had spectacular views. It was a mad decision. Somehow she had forgotten her demon vertigo. We would have been better off in the café on the ground floor. There was no way she could ride the glass-covered escalator slung outside the building. It would have to be the lift. But how was she to overcome the glass wall on one side? Only by clinging to the other side. Liz had also forgotten that when we reached the top she had to walk along a glass-covered corridor with fearful views to the ground far below. With piteous whimpers, she just made it. When we came to leave the restaurant her terror mounted again. I hadn't helped matters by stressing out when I discovered that I had lost my camera. Again. Luckily somebody had picked it up and handed it in, but it was a distracting half hour. Meanwhile, all courage had left Liz and she confided to one of the attendants that she had severe vertigo. He listened sympathetically. 'You are not the first, *madame*,' he said and promptly called the *pompiers*. Two firemen appeared. They escorted us to the back of the building and into a vast lift which could have taken four elephants. They stood impassively either side of Liz as both she and the lift shuddered their way down to ground level.

We had another 'lift' experience at Sainte-Chapelle, a soaring, magical, fourteenth-century building hidden away within the vast nineteenth-century Palais de Justice, home to many of France's principal legal institutions. We were visiting Sainte-Chapelle for an evening concert, but were late. We had found it impossible to flag down a taxi in Paris, even with Liz's extended-arm-snapping-finger technique, and arrived late.

'The concert has begun; you cannot enter,' we were told at the entrance.

'*Quel dommage!*' we cried and looked so crestfallen that a young student attendant took pity and propelled us towards a huge flight of stairs.

'*Attendez, monsieur!*' Liz called out, her eyes widening in horror. '*Quel grand escalier!* What a big staircase!' Liz's French was flowing. '*Mon ami* with her *jambes malades* (sick legs) will never make it!'

The efficient young man stopped mid-stride, took my hand and led us both to a wood-panelled lift. 'The judges use this,' he said, as the lift slowly heaved itself up to a colonnaded corridor where a few lawyerly types were still clutching their briefs and recapping the progress of the day's cases. We were now on the same level as the entrance to Sainte-Chapelle, but unfortunately the iron doors were firmly locked. Our saviour, undaunted, was a man with a mission. He left us with the chatting lawyers and darted out of sight. Minutes later he was on the other side of the door and we heard the sound of a large key as he opened the door very gently and ushered us into the Vivaldi-filled, ethereal air of Sainte-Chapelle. '*Monsieur, vous êtes bien gentil, merci beaucoup,*' I whispered. 'Thank you, you are very kind.'

'*Adieu,*' he said in reply, smiled and disappeared.

*

Liz had strong opinions about Paris. 'It's such a well-controlled city; it's so unedgy, and it can look horribly neglected.' She had led me to the Palais Royale. 'This should be a terrific place. It's incredibly elegant—the eighteenth century buildings surrounding this tree-filled, ornamental garden—but it's sadly down at heel.'

'I don't agree at all. I really like it here; it doesn't matter that it's a little rundown.' We were standing in the middle of the gardens and I was enjoying some people-watching.

Liz also introduced me to the Batobus, a recent innovation which roamed along the Seine from one Parisian sight to another. We took it from the Hôtel de Ville to the Louvre and then on to the Eiffel Tower. At the Eiffel Tower we almost missed Bob and Bobbie beetling towards us.

'I can't believe it. You guys. We can't go on meeting like this!' shrieked Bobbie. 'Where have you been? What have you been doing since Africa?'

We exchanged feverish notes about our respective trips and I suggested that they come with us on the Batobus so that we could continue catching up.

'It's a great way to see Paris,' Liz added. Bob and Bobbie were different from Linda and Mike, fun and sturdily independent, and when we arrived at the Quai d'Orsay they hugged us fondly and sped off to the museum. 'See you in Moldavia!' called Bob.

Liz said that there was no need for us to visit the Musée d'Orsay as it was being shut down soon for renovations (surprise, surprise) and all the best stuff was being shipped to Canberra. So we got off instead at the rue Bonaparte and had a cup of tea at the Café de Flore, famous for its intellectual clientele, on the corner of boulevard Saint-Germain and the rue Saint-Benoît. It is said that Jean-Paul Sartre and Simone de Beauvoir used to meet there and discuss their philosophy of existentialism over a drink.

Restored by a cup of tea, Liz was ready for serious culture so she frogmarched me to the Grande Palais to see contemporary artist Richard Serra's six iron slabs towering above us under a delicate greenhouse roof. Liz struck up a conversation with Emil, an intense scholar who had studied philosophy under Derrida; his discourse was littered with postmodernisms. I thought 'roasted' must be one of them—'These roasted slabs speak to us directly, they flag our anxieties with their subliminal transversality.' He rattled on, 'It's the alienation and reification of the spaces in between the roasted slabs . . .' I wondered if he meant 'rusted'—it seemed to make more sense, as they appeared to be rusty.

No sooner had we absorbed Serra than Liz led us next door to the blockbuster Marie Antoinette exhibition. I'd loved the film and swallowed the line that here was an intelligent woman trapped in the impenetrable boyland of Versailles. She made the best of it by shopping for extravagant clothes and wigs while waiting patiently for her husband to ascend the throne. The museum had built an exhibit to reproduce the moonlight soirees which Marie Antoinette gave to counter the interminable boredom of her life. Through a dim haze we saw the moon shine, and heard birds twitter and a string ensemble playing gavottes.

Nearby was a row of dreary portraits of her as Empress which she regularly sent to her doting mother in Austria. Most were sent back—not pretty enough. 'There's no pleasing an absent mother,' said Liz.

*

Liz and I had breakfast each day at a small café opposite the hotel. It was the ideal spot for coffee, croissants and people-watching, including the levee of two old tramps who used the wall opposite us as their loo.

'We'll go to the Louvre today,' announced Liz. My heart sank. I'd been dreading going to that huge, overcrowded giant of a place, which I'd seen many times on previous trips.

'It's free today—first Sunday in the month,' said Liz.

'But won't it be even more crowded?' I said weakly.

'It will, but not where we'll be going.'

She was right—there was a vile queue to get in but after that we went to the cool, empty Marais Court, where the exquisite marble sculptures from Louis XIV's garden at Marly were beautifully displayed. Next door were the equally empty Assyrian galleries, where stone lions stared down at us over the centuries.

It was inevitable that Liz's enthusiasm would get the better of her as she dragged me down endless corridors of eighteenth- and nineteenth-century landscape paintings into the Salon des Bronzes where a Cy Twombly blue ceiling with golden and pale blue discuses appeared to float above Greek and Roman statuettes. With mounting excitement, she told me to shut my eyes. 'Okay, you can open them now'—and there in front of me was a collection of paintings bequeathed to the Louvre by a nineteenth-century Princesse de Croy. Her father's money had persuaded the then penniless prince to fall in love with her. The paintings were deadly dull, gloomy, Victorian-style things and I stood bemused. Liz saw my lack of enthusiasm and said, 'Sorry, Hilly, I didn't explain. You see, years ago I was completely lost wandering around these laby- rinthine galleries when suddenly I came across this room with the friendly de Croy name on it. It was like finding an oasis in a desert.'

I smiled weakly.

That evening I was truly exhausted and to cap it all Liz had chosen a vegetarian restaurant she had discovered on one of her early morning walks. We ate dismal food in a dismal setting— France and veganism are about as far apart as the North and South Poles. We mulled over our holiday so far.

'It's been a huge success,' opined Liz.

'Certainly has,' I said. 'I've learnt so much and enjoyed the culture enormously. You organised it brilliantly but, honestly Liz, the spontaneity . . .'

'Oh, you mean this sort of thing?' Liz gestured at the restaurant. 'That's travelling, Hil—taking the rough with the smooth. Experiencing all of life's rich tapestry.'

Again I hesitated.

'I'm not certain that at our age and with so little time left we shouldn't be trying to eliminate as much of the rough as possible,' I replied. 'I could have done with a perfect tarte tatin or crème brûlée to round off the Paris experience . . .' I tailed off.

Liz thought about this as she toyed with her tofu.

'Yes, I suppose a bit more planning could help. But I have learnt, Hilly, quite a lot from your carefully planned holidays. Mine used to be a lot more chaotic before I met you. And another thing,' she added, 'you won't believe this, but I'm also actually noticing more about my companion's disposition. I realise you're exhausted,' she went on. (*You're not wrong!* I thought.) 'I hope it wasn't too much. You see, I wanted to pack the culture into this leg of the trip because I knew in Italy we'd be more relaxed, just soaking up the scenery.'

Next day we returned by Eurostar to London to prepare for our Italian trip.

As Liz had observed in Paris, I was exhausted from our recent exertions. Happily, I recalled a conversation I had had one evening in Sauverny with the prince and princess, when they spoke glowingly about a German clinic on Lake Constanz that the family had visited to lose weight. The Buchinger method, they told us, was based on fasting. As Emmanuel put the final touches to his cream of asparagus soup, his béarnaise sauce and the full-cream homemade raspberry ice-cream, he assured me that they had all lost copious kilos. *Not for long*, I thought but did not say.

The great selling point for me was that the clinic took a holistic approach to health, blending western medicine with natural herbal remedies. I would get healthy and lose weight. On the spur of the moment I rang Buchinger and said to Liz, 'I'm going to go there for ten days—that's the minimum they'll accept. Will you come too?'

'Absolutely not. You know I'd go mad with boredom. Not my thing at all. I'll meet you afterwards.'

When I arrived at Buchinger it looked to me, from the street, like a suburban Sydney private hospital until the nurse showed me to my room, which overlooked the dazzling blue Lake Constanz. I breathed a sigh of relief.

The clinic was run splendidly, with a cornucopia of doctors and nurses, nutritionists, masseurs, psychoanalysts, exercise freaks and public relations personnel all designed to help us towards 'a new way of living'. You're here to 'feed your soul', they kept telling us. They were very encouraging, firm but always cheerful. 'Try some finger painting, or go to cooking class and make a muesli bar.' Not that the Arab clientele appeared to take much notice of the regime. I was told that they frequently sent out for hamburgers, much to the distress of the management, who were forced to tolerate these falls from grace because they needed their custom to keep the operation going.

Every patient had their own nurse. Mine was called Helga and I became devoted to her. She greeted me every morning, unfailingly interested in my blood pressure, whether I had slept well or badly, whether my bowels were open or closed, and she took copious notes. She pressed cold packs, hot packs and any number of creams, pills, lotions and beverages—hot and cold—into my hands during my stay.

Breakfast at Buchinger consisted of a different choice of juice every day, a herbal infusion and a heaped tablespoon of stewed kelp, and this routine continued all day. In between I swam, walked, had massages and went to the book club, where I met Ilana.

Ilana was Israeli, very large and in need of a friend. She drained my supply of empathy within an hour. 'Eleven years ago I was diagnosed with meningitis and required a brain operation. I nearly died. I was only thirty-two and spent a year in a coma. And then three years in a wheelchair. I had been a really successful insurance broker and was just about to sign a new contract when I got sick. They didn't have to pay me a cent of insurance because I hadn't signed the contract.' She fished a photograph of a beautiful, slim woman out of her wallet.

'I have to lose forty-seven kilos and will stay at Buchinger as long as it takes.'

Ilana saw me later in the day and once again took up her story. 'My husband probably committed suicide. He was a bum. He had other women. He failed in his business and then drove into a train.'

My head was whirling. How could so much have happened to one person? I thought, *What would Liz say?* and I knew the answer—'Don't be ridiculous, Hilly, it's lies. She's a fantasist.' But I believed Ilana, I don't know why.

On Sunday nights Buchinger organised concerts. A folk orchestra from Belarus, dressed in embroidered ethnic garb, visited while I was there. They played a medley from *Doctor Zhivago*, numerous waltzes by Johann Strauss, and tunes from *Carmen*. It wasn't until the tenor sang a morbidly sad song and I caught the name 'Chernobyl' that I realised how desolate these musicians were, so far from their homeland.

It was the nutritionist at Buchinger who really put me on the spot. I had tried to talk about my love of food, of entertaining my friends around a table groaning with home cooking, but she would have none of it. 'Hilary, you are in the grip of an addiction.' It was baldly put, and accurate, but I wasn't ready for it. I stopped going to see her, but salved my conscience by buying her recipe book for a healthy life.

To escape the consuming Buchinger schedule I gave myself a one-day excursion and caught the ferry across the lake to explore Constanz itself. We chugged across the tranquil blue water on a perfect summer day with a flotilla of every conceivable brightly-coloured sailing boat imaginable scattered chirpily around us. I skirted the enticing fragrance of the freshly baked croissants in the Constanz patisserie shops and, dehydrated by the heat, settled down in a little park with two gulls. With not even a crumb between us, still and silent, we spent a peaceful time staring at the fish in the water below. Then I unwillingly rose to rejoin my ferry and my gull friends flew off to seek a fish dinner.

I emailed Liz:

> You would love Lake Constanz and Constanz itself.
> You could still come. H xxx-x

Liz replied by return:

> No way. How much weight have you lost? Lizzest

When it came time for me to go, Helga's eyes misted over and we embraced warmly. 'Ah, Mees Linstead. I shall miss you. I hope it goes well for you. Vair gut. Good bye, Mees Linstead, bye, bye, bye . . .'

After ten days I had lost a few kilos, felt much healthier and was looking forward to meeting Liz in Tuscany at a cottage in Cennina, which I had swapped for my holiday house on the Central Coast.

Cennina turned out to be the quintessential Tuscan hilltop village, no more than a scattering of stone dwellings dominated by a partly restored twelfth-century castle. My friends' house was arranged around a central courtyard with a fig tree, herbs, lavender, roses, chattering birds and buzzing insects and a view down the valley past vines and olive groves. It felt like a fantasy every morning to wake up, throw open the windows and stare out at the sun-drenched grape vines and hear the cocks crowing in the valley below.

One morning I was meditating happily when I heard a very faint squawking sound coming from the back garden. I went down the stairs and opened the back door. The sound was coming from a pottery urn on the flagged path. I had my suspicions and didn't fancy facing the crisis on my own so called Liz, who had just returned from her walk and was making toast and coffee in the kitchen. We gingerly upturned the urn and out fell a dead mother bird and one barely alive, half-naked chick. It was a rude awakening to the reality of country life. We stood around helplessly until I thought to call out to the next-door neighbour, who came over and kindly put the chick out of its misery, after which we did the easy bit and gave mother and daughter a decent burial together under a crimson rose bush.

'Hilly, did you know that this place is alive with vipers?' said Liz one day as we sat on the terrace eating our lunch of bread, parmigiano-reggiano, olives and pancetta. As with her irrational fear of heights, Liz was petrified of snakes. On her early morning walk, Liz had met Enrico, the local gossip, who had told her all she wanted to know and more about village life. 'Ave you zeen zee vipers?' he had asked her. It took a while before I realised that her confidante in the village was referring not to vipers but to

VIPs. The most distinguished VIP was Count Osvaldo Righi, a charming man who owned Cennina's castle and half the village, and was a friend of the people in whose house we were staying. The connection was slim, but we decided to introduce ourselves.

The count was a ceramicist and glassblower and had a vast studio in the castle. As he showed us his work I remarked that his studio would provide a marvellous space for a performance of some kind. 'Indeed,' he replied, 'in the summer months I hold exhibitions and concerts. I had a party a week ago and brought a musical trio from Siena to provide entertainment for my guests.' Later Liz and I were looking through a china shop in a neighbouring village and, as the store owner was wrapping the pot I had bought in newspaper, I noticed a picture of Queen Beatrix of the Netherlands on the page, with a caption about Cennina. Why? What was Queen B doing in Cennina? I read on down the page until I worked out that she had attended a concert given by the count. So there really were VIPs in Cennina.

Every day Liz came back from her walk with a fresh rant. She was enraged that ordinary village life was being pushed out by rich poms with second homes. She said the church was deserted and quite neglected; a sad reminder of the once proud days when Tuscans' 'love of home' was termed *campanilismo*, which derived from the sound of the local church bell in the campanile, or belltower.

Our week in Cennina flew past, and on our last day we went to the local market and assembled a feast for our final night there. We started with antipasti, followed by *pasta aglio, olio e peperoncino* with *insalata verde*, then *panna cotta* I had made the night before and pecorino and fresh *fichi* (figs), all accompanied by lashings of the local red, Brunello di Montalcino. It was the perfect meal.

We relaxed happily afterwards, staring at the moon and the starry night.

The following day Liz and I departed for Porto Ercole, fifty kilometres north of Rome. We were going to stay at Il Pellicano, a resort about which a friend of Liz's had waxed lyrical.

I thought I needed a rest after the rigours of Buchinger. Liz was mildly curious to find out where and how the Italian haute bourgeoisie spend their holidays, but also very dubious, muttering that it was bound to be a characterless 'designer resort', and she was right. It had been crafted to make its guests feel as if they were in a bubble a zillion miles away from reality. And there were no Italians at all, just tourists from England, France and Germany.

'When people ring you on the switchboard, they ask if you would prefer them to say that you are not here,' I told Liz after I had checked us both in.

'Privacy and getting-away-from-it-all has become such a preoccupation in this hedonistic world, it's bordering on narcissism,' Liz replied tartly. 'I don't think I'll be able to handle a week here,' she added.

Il Pellicano was a series of chalets in a shallow valley curving upwards from the sea and was surrounded by tall fir trees. Each chalet had a balcony giving onto the gardens and the sea view. The rooms were furnished in pale blue and antique-washed wood. The dining room had tree-framed views all around. There was no way you could possibly be aware that any other life existed outside the resort, so all-embracing and womb-like was the atmosphere. I spent a lot of time asleep; Liz paced around like a trapped panther.

We noticed at dinner that Ruth, a well-known British journalist, was finding it next to impossible to relax as well. She had bright red hair swept up on top of her head and held in place with two Japanese combs. Her voice was loud and insistent, her eyes swivelling around constantly to see who was coming or going, while her older companion, Mike, quite happily laughed at her louche jokes and refilled her glass.

The next day at the edge of the swimming pool, lounging topless, Ruth confided to Liz that she was searching for her 'authentic self'. Liz was marginally interested in her very modern complaint. That morning she had been reading that there was no need to search for a single coherent sense of one's own identity: it was perfectly OK to have many selves and to call up the most appropriate one for a particular occasion. Liz explained this idea to Ruth, adding that this was exactly what she had done all her life and that she found it an ideal way to live.

Much to Liz's surprise, Ruth became agitated.

'What an absurd idea,' she said, twitching. 'Such an approach spells chaos, and I've got enough of that as it is.'

Fortunately Mike arrived at this point.

'Come on, darling,' he said, 'you're meant to be relaxing, not getting into arguments.' He looked at Liz accusingly. 'Denying the need for self-cohesion is not a useful activity,' he said pointedly, as he led Ruth away.

On the other hand, Brigadier and Mrs Fanshawe Smith had a bit too much self-cohesion. They quickly got themselves into a rigid routine. An early morning swim; breakfast on their balcony at seven-thirty; a game of tennis; a pre-lunch swim; and so it went on. And if they happened to meet you they were full of amiable chat, making trivia seem like intimacy.

Il Pellicano provided nothing authentically Italian—we could have been on the moon—so we cut short our stay and left after four days. Liz had reached boiling point and I wondered what had possessed me to imagine that I needed a rest after Buchinger. The regime might have been hard but there was ample time for rest between juices. It was a huge relief to board a slow train for Rome.

At one of the many stations, a carriage door was unaccountably locked so a departing passenger could not leave the train. She called and shouted but got no response; the driver and guard failed to notice or attend to her dilemma. The train departed, the cries intensified and in the end the whole compartment had joined in. I tried to find the emergency cord while Liz darted up the train to locate the guard. It wasn't until the next station that the guard managed to unlock the door and release the woman onto the plat-form. She ran after him up the platform to the head of the train and tore into him with a stream of expletives. He mounted one step and stood motionless, staring fixedly past her. After a moment he lifted his hand and signalled the train driver to move off. As the train gathered pace the woman became incandescent with rage and screamed abuse at him from an empty platform. In an instant we knew that the gilded cage of Il Pellicano was no more and we were firmly back in 'real' Italy.

Liz decided unilaterally that as we didn't have much time left we would make straight for the Amalfi Coast, south of Naples. Both of us were familiar with the great cities of Rome and Florence. So it was a fast train to Naples and another slow one to Sorrento, where we holed up in a once-grand hotel now given over to economy tourists. They crowded into the streets and thronged around the markets buying cheap goods which we imagined must have fallen off a thousand trucks labouring across Europe's gigantic motorways. When I dithered over whether to buy an exceedingly cheap pair of sandshoes from an overflowing stall, Dora and Bruce from Wolverhampton said, 'Go on, buy them. We bought some last year and they're still going strong.' It was just the encouragement I needed.

Liz and I continued our walk down a huge number of stairs to the harbour below the town.

'I suppose this is what you would romantically call "real" life,' said Liz caustically. 'It's just a seedy old fishing village with a few dirty boats back from an all-night catch. And guess what? Those tired old toxic fish will be served up tonight in the cafés on the harbour front.'

'Sadly, I agree with you,' I said.

We caught the bus to Positano, along the sinuous cliff road with the blue, blue sea stretching away on our right-hand side and high, high rocks towering above us on the left. Wherever it was possible, houses and hotels clung to whatever ledge or promontory was available. I had unknowingly booked us into a hotel outside Positano which was jammed into the cliff side, our room only accessible by inclinator. Liz was terrified; vertigo struck again. Our room was perched on a ledge with a steep drop down to lemon groves and vineyards and, beyond that, to Positano itself and the sea. Liz remained cowering inside, only emerging at night to see moonlight dancing on the water.

She was very glad when we caught the bus on to Ravello, high up beyond the precipitous cliff living.

'Ravello's got an indefinable "it's all over now" feeling, redolent of the fin de siècle,' Liz mused, as we sat in the village square drinking Campari orange.

The visitors to Ravello both past and present were a little more *recherché* than our friends Dora and Bruce from Wolverhampton. There was Greta Garbo, D.H. Lawrence, Jackie Kennedy and, of course, Gore Vidal, who had a house tucked into the cliff a little way below and to one side of the town. We craned over the balustrade to peer at his house and imagined him reading the obituaries in the daily papers, relieved to find the names of his friends—as he said in his memoirs—because it would prevent the guilt he felt for not getting in touch with them.

We had lunch at the Palazzo Sasso, a hotel overlooking the bay. Liz spent the time searching for glitterati while I chatted to our waiter and found out that his sister cleaned the rooms at our pensione, the Villa Amore. The Villa Amore had exactly the same view as the Palazzo Sasso, but was a fraction of the price. The Villa Amore was run by two old sisters who sat outside the front door knitting scarfs which trailed down their skirts into a heap on the floor.

We managed to get tickets for the Georgian Quartet, who were giving an outdoor concert at the Villa Rufolo. The concert was part of a long season of chamber music concerts which were held every year from March to November at the villa. No wonder Wagner said that the gardens of the villa, with their backdrop of sea and sky, were the inspiration for *Parsifal*. On the evening of the concert it grew chilly so I asked the sisters whether we could possibly borrow two wraps of any kind. They immediately produced two of their multicoloured knitted shawls, which suited us perfectly. While the majority of the audience sat goosebumped in sleeveless dresses, we sat smugly warm as toast.

We had come to hear one of Mozart's string quartets and were enchanted by this group of virtuosic musicians. They seemed to embroider the musical themes; they called, echoed and repeated, their technical precision and musicality lifting us into the sky on waves of overlapping sound. Then, as the light gently departed, the slow movement began: it was as if an invisible force had fused the violins, viola and cello with the rays of the setting sun. All the elements came together and we, the audience, became part of a collective euphoria. It was an all-encompassing experience, leaving Liz and me breathless.

Every morning we would have breakfast in the village square, watching the Ravellians wake up. Liz remembered that she had spent her sixtieth birthday in Ravello and it was here that she had decided to produce a small book of fifty travel articles she had written for the *Karachi Evening Star*. She told me how much she had adored seeing them in print and wondered if her years of anonymity in the Civil Service had contributed to the pleasure she derived from seeing her work in print.

'I actually wrote the introduction sitting in this café,' she said happily. She had sent copies to all her relations, friends and acquaintances and told me that she was disappointed that she had had very little response. I asked her whether she felt hurt by the lack of response.

'Not so much hurt as mystified that people hadn't even bothered to write, ring or email to say thank you, although one person had written, "Where are the pictures? You know, photos of the places you've been to?" I was staggered! Weren't my excellent words sufficient to conjure up a sense of place?!'

I didn't comment at the time but later suggested to her that some people are not very imaginative and need a lot of help.

We both adored Ravello. We went for a walk in the gardens of the Villa Cimbrone, passing the villa itself, which in 1904 became the property of an English lord, Ernest William Beckett. With the assistance of a Ravellian tailor (strange to say!), Beckett constructed a building which was a remarkable mix of styles and epochs and different ethnicities. And he added antique treasures and souvenirs from his journeys. The result was an eccentric and amazing creation. The gardens were chock-a-block full of statues, temples, fountains and grottos, the pièce de resistance being the Belvedere of Infinity, which was a long terrace overlooking the water, with a series of stone sculpted heads positioned on a chest-high wall with the heads pointing inwards at us tourists rather than having a look at the view, which Gore Vidal described as 'the most beautiful in the world'.

Our final destination was Lecce, on the heel of Italy's boot. We had a long train journey and decided to chance lunch in the dining car. We were just settling down to our Puglian minestrone when Liz realised that she had left her bag on the seat in the carriage. She was about to dart back when the guard appeared and walked down the restaurant car calling out, '*Nessuno ha perso la loro borsetta?*' (Has anyone lost their bag?) Liz rose to her feet, grabbed his hand and the bag and planted a kiss on his cheek. '*Grazie, grazie, molto gentile,*' she cried. He looked delighted and said that he had caught a man trying to pinch it. '*Che horrore!*' Liz continued, but was not quite so happy when he said that she would have to make a statement to the police in Lecce.

'What a bore, half the day will be gone,' she complained.

'Never mind,' I said. 'Eat your minestrone, it's good.' Somehow Italians always get it right with peasant food. The whole journey seemed to pass in a trice with the drama to liven it up.

Lecce was a gloriously eccentric town, known as 'Apulia's Baroque Pearl'. Three hundred years ago it was earthquaked out of existence but was rapidly rebuilt in the most chaotic baroque style. Local craftsmen must have gone mad sculpting three or four curlicues where one would have sufficed. And all in a soft, honey-coloured stone.

The evening we arrived we noticed that everyone was out on the cobbled streets, ambling in the same direction.

'Let's see where they're going.'

'Definitely.'

We followed, and heard the sound of a tenor voice floating down the street in our direction. Before long we came to the large town square, which had been partly cordoned off and was packed with Leccians. The tenor sang three of my favourite arias in quick succession: 'Nessun Dorma', followed by 'Che Gelida Manina', topping it off with 'Celeste Aida', with the local orchestra playing full throttle. 'That's an exceptional voice,' I remarked to Liz, and was desperate to find out his name. I waited until the end of the concert and then scooted around the square and found the singer seated behind the improvised stage. When I got close up I realised that he was blind.

'*Farebbe è possibile per me avere il suo autografo per mie nipoti, per favore signore?*' I asked. (Would you be kind enough to give me your autograph for my granddaughters?)

'*Certamente con il piacere,*' he said, and wrote down their names carefully on my scruffy piece of paper before signing his own name.

I could just make it out—*Andrea Bocelli*. 'I bet you he becomes famous,' I said to Liz as we drifted back to our hotel basking in the soft night air.

10

And Scarlett makes three

I was down at the hydrotherapy pool in Waverley, working out. To alleviate the boredom of multiple pliés I chatted to a chirpy fellow granny with curly white locks and ruby red lipstick. Upon hearing that I was off to Venice with my fifteen-year-old granddaughter, Scarlett, she sighed deeply and said, 'Tell Scarlett to light a candle in the church on the Island of Torcello. That will guarantee that she will return one day.'

'Now, Mary, you're here to exercise, not chatter,' interrupted Glen, our instructor, as he stood surveying his bevy of antiques attempting to halt the inevitable march of time.

Mary dutifully resumed squinting at her exercise card and executed a few sprightly bicycle movements. But she could not resist returning to Venice for long.

'Make sure you explore when the day-trippers have departed and the light is soft and balmy,' she said. 'Sit in the Giardini and watch the sun set.' I felt goosebumps just listening to her.

It is not every day that a grandmother has the opportunity to take her granddaughter away on an overseas holiday. I felt the weight of awesome responsibility, not only to look after Scarlett but also to make sure she had a truly memorable experience and returned home keen to travel again in the future under her own steam. I was a bit worried that I might not have enough energy to keep up with her so I asked Liz if she would like to come with us and she sweetly agreed. I knew that Scarlett would gain from Liz's energy and knowledge of history, politics and art. Scarlett was also a great walker, as was Liz, and they already knew each other from previous years when Liz had stayed with me in Sydney. Scarlett was intrigued by Liz's eccentricity and Liz had often told me that Scarlett was a 'special person'.

I was a little concerned about Liz's and my propensity for disgraceful behaviour when we were on holliers. I feared that Duncan, my son, might have been somewhat nervous about letting his beloved daughter loose with two old reprobates—indeed she might, herself, have been somewhat apprehensive about the trip. Scarlett was a serious, sophisticated person and she might well be worried that Liz and I would BO and BB—'Break Out and Behave Badly'—as Liz put it. 'It's all part of life's rich pageant,' I said, with more bravura than I perhaps felt.

On departure day I left Possum, my beloved waif dog, at home in the care of my dearest friend, Ed. He was devoted to her and had often looked after her when I was away. I gave Possum a cuddle. 'I'll be back in two months,' I told her, holding back tears. 'Please don't die while I'm away.' Poss was sixteen years old and had been sick for some time. I begged Ed to take special care of her, and himself.

At the airport I was moved to see my son Duncan, not usually given to public displays of emotion, with tears in his eyes as he said goodbye to Scarlett, hugging her close. 'I shall miss you,' I heard him mutter as he buried his head in her hair. The two of us were given such a loving send-off. The whole family was there: Duncan;

his joyous wife, Juliette; Paris, their wild beauty, aged thirteen; and three-year-old Django, with his halo of golden locks, cupping his hand and calling 'Ciao' as I had taught him. They had even brought Roxy, the family dog. I hastened to the security door anxious to cut short any angst Scarlett might be feeling from extended goodbyes.

We boarded the plane and inched our way down the aisle, squishing into our seats. Scarlett clutched my hand when we began taxiing down the runway. Once airborne she chose to read and sleep while I settled for a bloody mary and three formulaic American genre movies. We were well and truly off on our adventure.

We arrived at Frankfurt airport at 6 am. Scarlett located the British Airways lounge, tucked away at the end of the concourse. I wasn't sure that as Qantas passengers we would be allowed in, but as there wasn't anyone on the reception desk at such an early hour we were able to wander in casually and take up residence, commandeering a large corner of the lounge. We had first choice of breakfast, consuming ham, salami, cheese, croissants, fruit, juice and coffee, and made use of the freshly cleaned loos.

I purloined the English newspapers to hoover up the latest news on the royals. I have an insatiable appetite for royal trivia, but their antics appeared to be at their nadir, leaving me gobsmacked.

'Guess what, Scar, have you read about Fergie's latest attempt to make a quid? She's been caught on tape arranging an exclusive meeting for a sheik with her ex-husband Andrew—quite unbe-knownst to him, mind you—in return for an enormous fee. Trust a red-haired commoner to chuck good behaviour into the dustbin. I remember the Queen's coronation and how fantastical it was to see the newly crowned Queen of England and Prince Philip clip-clopping down the Mall in their golden horse-drawn carriage. That was a fairytale procession.'

'Were you really there, Ga?'

'Certainly was. Seated in the pouring rain in the Mall. So the last thing I want to see now is their offspring descend into a cesspit of vulgarity.' I gathered steam. 'It's the humbug and hypocrisy I can't stand. Somehow only the poor old Queen manages to stay dignified, and even she's a sad figure, padding round Buckingham Palace in the middle of the night turning off the lights, whether for reasons of energy conservation or parsimony I'm not sure. And then the poor soul has to wake up and find she's sharing the end of her bed with an intruder rather than a corgi or the Duke of E. Meanwhile, her dreary, chinless son, Charles, waits in the wings for a shot at kingship with chisel-chinned Camilla. And, to add insult to injury, brainless son Harry, dressed up as a Nazi for somebody's fancy dress party, has been seen lurching drunkenly out of a nightclub into the receiving arms of the paparazzi. Charles should let him go off to the front line in Afghanistan again: it's where he wants to be —serving queen and country. Bugger the innocent bystanders. No wonder I wanted to escape that lunacy all those years ago!'

Scarlett looked at me amazed.

'Well, Ga, you certainly feel strongly.'

'Yes, I do. I can't stand the class system—it was one of the main reasons I left England. The royals make great trivia, but other than the Queen, they can't be taken seriously.'

We continued crunching our croissants cheerily and the five hour stop-over flew by, marked by eating, dozing, and frequent visits to the spanking-clean amenities. Scarlett and I had always managed to remain companionably silent, something I can't do with many people.

My literary agent friend Mark met us at Heathrow and whisked us off by car to Somerset. Scarlett told him she had always dreamed of living in a cottage, 'nestled among rolling hills and flower fields', and suddenly her dream was becoming reality. Scarlett couldn't believe the postcard perfect villages with their hollyhocks, thatched roofs and picket fences. She marvelled at the winding country lanes with room for only one car to pass, and gates opening onto cornfields lined with ragged robin, meadow-sweet and hawthorn.

We stayed with Mark and Mindy, his wife, at their home, complete with swimming pool, the largest Aga cooker in the world, vegie garden and fruit trees. Mark and Mindy have four children, including my goddaughter Eleanor, who is the same age as Scarlett. I hoped they would get on and that Eleanor would be able to ease Scarlett into life on the other side of the world. I need not have worried; within minutes they were chatting away as though they had been bosom friends since kindergarten.

As Scarlett unpacked her clothes that evening she discovered a letter with a message from all the family. 'What's wrong?' I asked when I went in later to say goodnight. She was standing beside the bed silently, tears pouring down her cheeks, and held out the note:

> Dear Scarlett,
> We miss u already & are thinking of you every minute of the day. Have fun!!! Send lots of postcards at every chance!!!
> We (I) love you, Paris xoxox
>
> WE LOVE U

Darlink Scarletti,
I'll be thinking of you always & all the joy & adventures
you'll be having. Be brave, enjoy & live!!!
'Sleep with angels' every night. Don't forget I'm in
your heart, so always with you xo
Mum and Dad

When you are missing us we are missing u xox
Roxy

Paris: Do u love Scarlett?
Django: Yes, and a tool and a hammer & a nail and a
saw (grrrr)—sawing motion.

Scarlett was very happy to receive the letter. She adores her family and is very much a homebody. But it had been a huge day, she was overtired, and the loving messages tipped her into homesickness. Later that night she padded into my bedroom to ask if she could spend the night with me. I gave her a cuddle and after that she was able to fall asleep. I suggested next day that she ring home and afterwards she told me she was so pleased to hear her family's voices, even though they were 17 000 kilometres away.

We spent the following day in Bath, where Mindy and I had to prise Eleanor and Scarlett away from the 'awesome' clothes shops in order to have a swim in the Roman baths. How inappropriate and gaudy the mothers looked in their lime-green floral bikinis, propelling their dogpaddling four-year-olds up and down the steaming pool, disdainfully observed by naked stone men standing like sentinels by the side of the ancient baths.

That evening we sat on rickety scaffolding for Eleanor's school play—a sylvan production of *A Midsummer Night's Dream*, set in the tranquil monks' gardens of Downside Roman Catholic School. It was the perfect setting, the lovers gambolling about and falling asleep on the grass while the fairies perched on branches of the sycamore trees above. And then the excitement of seeing Mistress Eleanor Peaseblossom descend the branches of her tree to scratch Bottom's donkey ear while he honked in ecstasy.

From the sublime to the ridiculous, or the ridiculous to the sublime. Next day Mark took Eleanor and Scarlett for a special treat to the premiere of the latest Harry Potter film. When they returned home that afternoon the two girls gabbled excitedly that they had seen Ron Weasley IN THE FLESH in front of the cinema.

Our stay with the Lucas family was all too brief, I thought sadly as we boarded the train to London.

*

Scarlett already knew that Liz spent more than 300 days a year away from her home and I had warned her that we might have to go shopping for food as soon as we arrived at Liz's tiny house in Vauxhall Walk. Liz does not often think about her stomach. But I was wrong this time. Waiting for us on her dining table, invitingly displayed, was 'an artwork of food' (as Scarlett put it). Cherry tomatoes surrounded by dates, sultanas and nuts, delicious dark rye bread and a ripe camembert. 'You've certainly done Scarlett proud,' I commented to Liz. 'I'll remember this feast when next I come on my own!'

I had planned our trip carefully: first of all the Baltic states of Latvia and Estonia, and then on to St Petersburg. The climax of the trip was to be a soft and beautiful landing in Venice.

Scarlett had decided to keep a journal, which she showed me the day we left London for Latvia:

> On the morning of our departure for Riga, the start of our real adventure, Liz took me for a walk around London, showing me all the major sights. VW, as Liz called her house, was a short walk from the Thames and from there, diagonally opposite, I could see Big Ben. She was proud taking me around her city, which she knew like the back of her hand. Although she complained about "dreary old London", I knew she loved it all the same.

> 'I really had no idea what to expect of a trip with Ga, although I knew it would have to be brilliant. With two such worldly and eccentric people it would be something I would remember. I did not want to know where we were going, I suppose I wanted to make it more of a fairy tale. But as time went on and take-off became more of a reality I was intrigued and wanted to do my research before I went. So when Ga announced that the three musketeers would venture to Latvia, Estonia (places I had never heard of), St Petersburg and best of all, Venice (the sound of that name alone was like honey to my ears), I was beside myself with excitement.

I mentioned to Liz that I was somewhat daunted by Scarlett's description of us as 'worldly and eccentric'.

'Lizzie, you'll have to fill that description for both of us—I think my job will be straight woman to your maddie.'

Liz and I started well despite 'Ga's ridiculous amount of luggage', as Scarlett wrote in her journal. We were on our best behaviour at the beginning of the four-country hollier.

'Old' Riga made a perfect beginning for the first leg of the trip: it was relaxed and had been 'themed for tourism', as Liz put it. Our hotel had a rooftop restaurant, from which we peered down at the medieval buildings clustered below. We explored the cobbled streets of the city, passing wooden houses that delighted Scarlett.

'They're all squished up together like a pancake stack on its side,' she said.

On our first evening we spotted a poster for a concert featuring Gregorian chants and decided to get a feel for the town by walking to St Peter's church, where it was to be held. It would be more fun to see the town at night than go to bed early. Once we were seated in the church, gently lit by candlelight, the chanters moved slowly around us, their robes swishing and the boy sopranos calling to the basses from one end of the nave to the other. A pure sound. We felt the calm envelop us. On the way back to the hotel we crossed the old town square, where a live band of old timers was rocking 'n' rolling in the No Problem Café. It was still light at 10.30 pm.

Next day we looked at the gaunt, Gothic cathedral and listened to an organ concert of rousing Bach and Vivaldi topped off with the majestic toccata from Charles-Marie Widor's Fifth Organ Symphony. All this lasted a mere half an hour. The Rigans had obviously decided that we tourists had a short attention span: an old priest told us that they programmed four half-hour recitals a day to show off the organ. 'It's the Biggest in the Baltic,' he said, bursting with pride, 'and that goes for the cathedral too. Biggest in the Baltic, and the steeple of St Peter's is the Tallest in the Baltic.'

'And,' we chorused happily, 'Riga is the Biggest city in the Baltic.'

As we explored Riga in more depth Liz found more and more fine Art Nouveau buildings and Scarlett responded to her excitement. 'The main architect of all these buildings was a man called Eisenstein, the father of the film man,' Liz told her, making the unlikely assumption that Scarlett would be as familiar with the architect's son as she would be with Beyoncé.

We were staying just off the main square near the No Problem Café. It sounded Australian, but the waitresses employed there were backpacking Swedes with long legs and short skirts. The café had a resident band and produced a variety of pizzas, but that was about as far as it went.

Scarlett remarked on how music seemed to fill every corner of Riga: first Latvian music in our taxi into town, then the band, then the buskers, particularly students who played flute, violin, oboe and even trombone surprisingly well. She hoped the musicians playing in front of the cathedral were encouraging the artist she spotted in the ubiquitous paint-spattered smock, who had set up his easel near the portico. Near him sat an ancient woman who took up her position daily from 7 am to 7 pm, her hands clasped in prayerful entreaty. An old man had taken up a position beside her; his wolfhound puppy lay panting at his feet, covered with fleas and with sores on its legs. Scarlett poured some of her water into the dog's empty bowl and the old man smiled his thanks. Scarlett made certain that we never passed beggars by on the other side of the street.

Liz located a strange teashop. In the basement there were comfy sofas and beds on which Rigan youth lay about. Liz sat and chatted away to them and I noted how polite they were, since they clearly couldn't understand a word she said. I ordered tea upstairs. The three of us perched decorously, stiff-backed on spindly chairs, cups poised, fingers crooked around delicate handles: we could easily have been distant relatives of the British royal family, who were depicted taking tea in a photographic reproduction on the café wall. 'The original is in the National Portrait Gallery,' said Liz.

Back at the hotel, I lay like a whale in the bath, recovering from the day's exertions, while Scarlett brought her journal up to date and Liz went out again to explore. She returned in some excitement.

'I've found the perfect place for our dinner. It's a medieval-themed basement restaurant with wooden tables and chairs and lashings of helmets, armour and swords hanging from stone walls.' I looked doubtfully in Scarlett's direction. 'There's oodles of venison, roast boar, steaming jugs of mead and jugged hare. You'll love it.'

'Go on, Ga, let's try it,' said Scarlett.

This time it was I who BO'd and BB'd. I got stuck into two large glasses of the local rough red and soon leant across the table to speak to the people next to us—a tiny Thai lady in her forties smooging with a tall, blonde Dutch man in his twenties.

'I'm Hilary. How did you two get together?' I said to the woman. 'You're a surprising duo.'

Scarlett cringed. I was already tipsy.

'Why do you think that?' said the woman, smiling. She held out her hand. 'My name's Chit-dee and this is Anton. Do you think I'm too old for him?'

'Well!' I wasn't prepared for such a quick comeback and stumbled, catching sight of Scarlett's horrified expression.

She had turned beetroot, acutely embarrassed by her grand-mother's impertinent intrusion into the couple's evening.

'It's always hard to tell people's ages—' I paused in the nick of time. Fortunately Chit-dee and Anton were highly sophisticated and played along.

'We met at a party,' said Anton.

'We were both suffering from broken hearts, so we spent a lot of time consoling each other,' added Chit-dee.

'Oh, so you were both on the rebound. Were either of you married?' I asked, completely ignoring Scarlett's discomfort.

'No, I was single,' explained Anton. 'But Chit-dee used to be married, and was going through a difficult divorce.'

'We won't go there,' said Chit-dee.

'It may have been on the rebound,' said Anton, quickly changing the direction of the conversation, 'but we've been together for four years now and I'm as madly in love with her today as the day we met.'

Fortunately, just at that moment our food arrived. Liz's hunter sausages turned out to be tepid frankfurters and I'd made the mistake of ordering sweetbreads, which I remembered from my childhood as being delicious, and served in a creamy white sauce. These bore no resemblance to my memories. I was served an oily mess with too much onion. Best forgotten. Scarlett had taken the safe and sensible way out, a mixed salad.

'The trouble with these old communist countries is that they have consultants planning the menu,' said Liz, 'but fail to take into account the fact that the chefs have no idea how to cook the recipes. We certainly won't bother with the puddings. Let's get the bill.'

While we were waiting I put the helmet from one of the suits of armour on my head and lowered the visor, imagining that I was amusing my new friends. Chit-dee and Anton laughed politely at my antics but Liz wasn't impressed—this was her territory. Scarlett removed the helmet and propelled me towards the door. Waving cheerily to Chit-dee and Anton, I called out loudly, 'Lovely to meet you. See you again soon.' When we got outside, Scarlett hissed in exasperation, 'Ga, that was really embarrassing.'

Fair enough, I thought, as the cold night air hit me and I started to sober up.

We visited Riga's central market the next day, housed in five recycled zeppelin hangars on the edge of the old town. Good produce was very limited; the vegetables and fruit on sale were pitiful, both in quality and variety. Old ladies sold tiny little piles of blueberries—presumably they had picked them that morning and brought them from their cottage gardens. We dispatched Scarlett to find a decent espresso. She found a number of stalls advertising 'proper coffee' but sadly very few of the stall owners had a clue how to use the coffee machines. They preferred to use hot water from a kettle and dribble it over Nescafé.

'I'd really like to find the beach sometime today,' said Scarlett, who'd consulted the map and seen that it was not far away. 'Apparently there's a weekend holiday resort made famous by the tsars, who visited it often in the nineteenth century.' Scarlett had been doing her homework.

We walked to the station and took a train. Not having a clue where to get out, we plumped for a station called Majori. 'Why don't they say "Majori Beach" in English, to help confused tourists?' said Scarlett.

It was Sunday and we found a pedestrianised main street thronged with weekenders. The village was pumping. Rigans, dressed in best casual, were promenading with their families, looking at the stalls groaning with food, clothes and knick-knacks. We stopped at a restaurant nestling under the trees. Scarlett boldly ordered 'Plaice Kiev'. I kept her company and looked disparagingly at Liz's choice of the cheapest thing on the menu—smoked herring, black bread and potatoes. Of course, our dish was revolting and Liz's a fine example of Rigan simplicity.

We reached the beach and Liz and Scarlett took off for a walk while I sat on the sand and watched in alarm as two boys tried to propel a huge blue transparent ball, in which they appeared to be trapped, out to sea. They looked like two rats drowning, trying frantically to claw their way out of the ball, but I noticed that none of the picnickers seemed concerned.

When Liz and Scarlett returned I pointed out to sea at the big blue ball. 'I suppose it's some kind of game, but at first I was convinced they were drowning—it looked terrifying.'

Liz's interest was piqued and she went off to check it out.

'I hope the boys don't mind her interfering,' I remarked to Scarlett as she plonked herself down beside me.

'I wouldn't worry, Liz will get bored before long.'

'You're getting a handle on Liz very quickly, Scar.'

'I wish we could have picnics like this in Sydney—there's always too much wind at Bondi,' said Scarlett.

Not long after, we heard faint cries coming from the sea. I looked over to where I had seen the boys inside the giant ball; a breeze had sprung up and the ball was moving rapidly out to sea. Three hulking youths swam in close pursuit.

'Heavens, Lizzie's in the ball!'

Scarlett and I ran to the water's edge just in time to see one of the boys disappear inside the ball. We watched as he emerged at the opening, a flailing Liz held firmly in his arms. The others propelled them and the ball back to the shore. With one gigantic effort, two of the boys heaved Liz out and onto the shore. She lay on the sand with her eyes closed, breathing rapidly. We hovered around while she recovered; I thanked the boys and Scarlett helped Liz to her feet.

'I don't know what the fuss was all about,' said Liz later. 'I was perfectly alright. It was great fun.' Scarlett and I exchanged a look.

No more was said and Liz was soon onto a new topic. As we left the beach she said, 'The tsars loved to summer on this stretch of coast. The daughter of one of them married Queen Victoria's son, the Duke of Edinburgh. I noticed a street named after him on our walk. What do you make of the houses, Scarlett? Quite Chekhovian, those wooden *dachas*, don't you think? A bit of a worry that half of them have *Pardod* written on a signpost at the front gate.'

'What does *Pardod* mean?' asked Scarlett.

'It has to be "For Sale",' Liz said. 'Times are tough. But I notice far fewer signs attached to houses with an Art Nouveau design. Not surprising, really. If you managed to buy or rent one of those houses, you'd hold on to it, wouldn't you? I love the nonchalant flamboyance of the Art Nouveau buildings, don't you, Scarlett?'

'Definitely,' replied Scarlett. 'I'm not sure what you mean, but it sounds good!'

*

Back in Riga the next day we visited the Occupation Museum, where we all found the darkness of Latvian history disturbing. Scarlett had never had to contend in any immediate way with war and Latvia opened up an upsetting new world for her. Liz was obsessed with the 'tragic sad world of Balkan politics' in the twentieth century. We went through a series of cheerless rooms with agonising pictures of war wounded and reconstructions of what it must have been like to suffer through the country's numerous occupations. Liz tried to explain.

'The Russians under the tsars ruled Latvia until 1917, when the country got its independence for twenty years. Then it was overrun briefly by the Soviets in 1940. After a year, Germany—or rather the Nazis, as the museum calls them—sent the Russians packing until after the war, when the Russians returned and ruled until 1991, when the state of Latvia re-emerged free once more.

'Whose side would you be on through all this?' Liz went on. 'Indeed, which side were the historians and the makers of this museum on? Would your family or friends collaborate with whoever was ruling the country at a particular time?' Liz didn't pause for an answer, and Scarlett was left more confused than ever.

On our last evening in Riga we ate at a western-style restaurant called Garlic before returning to No Problem for green tea, jazz and dancing. A young American student approached Scarlett.

'I'm Joe. Would you like to dance?'

'Love to. I'm Scarlett.'

And with that they took to the floor, jiving and jitterbugging. Scarlett loved to dance; the two of them were very good and danced up a storm. Liz soon joined them in a freeform frenzy, to the delight of the band. It was a pity that we were leaving next day. Joe and Scarlett were having fun.

We took a coach from Riga to Estonia's capital, Tallinn. We passed forests of pine trees, lakes, a scattering of villages, and herons in nests high up on telegraph poles.

'Have you noticed the bus shelters, Scarlett?' said Liz. 'They're less robust in Estonia. Positively rickety. Whereas in Latvia they were good solid structures. Can you tell a country by its bus shelters, I wonder?'

Tallinn proved to be more 'bijou' than Riga. We settled in to the Merchant's House hotel, which distinguished itself by serving vodka in glasses made of ice. The hotel was just around the corner from the huge cobbled square, where the buildings were freshly painted in attractive shades of pastel. I felt as if I had been set down in the middle of a set for a Disney children's movie. The old town above the square was dominated by the vast Alexander Nevsky Cathedral, which crowns Toompea hill. The cathedral was built during the Russification of the late nineteenth century. The communist Estonians hated it and wanted to pull it down but never had the money to carry the plan through, so the building fell into disrepair. Finally, when the country gained freedom from the Soviet Union, the cathedral was restored meticulously. Religion had been an underground activity under Soviet rule, but now it was out in the open and very popular. The cathedral also appealed to the tourists, who are the lifeblood of Estonia's emerging democracy.

Lizzie loves the tsars, and Peter the Great in particular, and couldn't wait to show us the palace he built for his Lithuanian peasant mistress, Catherine, in the Kadriorg gardens.

'You see, Scarlett, Peter westernised Russia in a single generation,' said Liz. 'Without him we would not have had Tchaikovsky, Rimsky-Korsakov, Dostoyevsky, Tolstoy and all those giants of nineteenth-century Russia.'

'It's interesting, though, that the same man could be violent, ruthless and impetuous,' I said. 'He was a restless man, constantly searching for new challenges. He learnt carpentry and absorbed all that mathematicians could teach him and then he studied the best way to train soldiers. You forget, Lizzie, that Peter also taught his soldiers how to torture his enemies and insubordinates by giving them 500 lashes with a birch rod, or by removing their nails and cutting off their ears. He formed a small army made up of his servants and used to play war games with them, firing live ammunition.'

Liz looked surprised by my sudden burst of erudition. 'I glanced at my history books before we came and got briefly interested in Peter the Great,' I explained.

Peter employed the Italian architect Niccolo Michetti to design the palace, park and a small temporary summer residence, and later involved him in building the famous Peterhof Palace outside St Petersburg. Kadriorg Palace was now in poor repair and shabby; the gardens contained dull shrubs, and the surrounding hedges were in need of a good clipping, but we still got a taste for the elegance of Russian tsardom.

After nosing around I managed to find an oasis, a few flowerbeds full of brilliant rose bushes. A perfect opportunity for a few quick portraits of Scarlett surrounded by 'scarlett' blossoms.

Nearby we found Kumu, a spanking new art gallery with a fine collection of contemporary and interactive Estonian art on the top floors. There was a room full of hundreds of old speakers in all shapes and sizes, through which the sound of waves came crashing; there was a futuristic graffiti guy telling us why he had posted graffiti of his name all over the town; and there was a film story of an artist trying to get a yellow pipe into the Venice Biennale. It was a lively collection which could well have been exported to the Museum of Contemporary Art in Sydney. The second floor was devoted to nineteenth-century Estonian art, and the first floor to Soviet Estonian art.

'Scarlett, look at those pictures of dreadful old Soviet social realism,' said Liz. Scarlett looked bewildered. 'Peasants and factory workers with cheery expressions and pink cheeks pretending they're happy in their "paradise" work places. I suppose it's quite brave of them to display this art publicly, given the banality and repressiveness of that regime.'

'But Liz,' I said, 'look at the three-storeyed wall of finely sculpted heads of noblemen and women—it's not all banal.' Scarlett nodded her agreement. Liz sniffed and moved on.

That night we ate at a basement restaurant which had been decorated like an old Estonian dining room; we were assured that the food would be authentic. Liz was brave and tucked into herrings and wild boar, which she described loudly in textbook Liz terms as an 'Estonian school dinner'. She asked for Russian vodka, which offended the waitress.

After dinner we climbed the Toompea hill and gazed at glorious views of the countryside and the turrets of Tallinn glinting below in the late evening sun.

The next day we took a taxi to the Estonian history museum on the outskirts of Tallinn. Confusion greeted us here as well: Liz spotted abandoned busts and statues of Stalin, Lenin and others lying in a heap outside the back door. Inside, there was a mural depicting Stalin doling out awards to a group of 'happy' workers. The whole museum had a desperate air about it, as though nobody knew exactly what it should be showing.

Scarlett was confused, and back in the taxi she tried to explain why. 'I'm used to museums and art galleries getting history "right", but here in Tallinn nobody seems to know quite what "right" is. People have differing views.'

The taxi-driver, a very friendly man called Constantin, joined our conversation. He told Scarlett that with a Russian father and a German mother he was undecided what was 'right' for him. He had trained as a textile engineer in Leningrad under the Soviets but now, since Estonian independence, the country's textile industry had foundered and he had lost his job. His sympathies were Russian, but he was wary of articulating them as most Estonians were fiercely against their previous rulers.

From the museum he took us up the coast to a restaurant in the shape of an upturned boat on the edge of a rocky shore. Liz ate a huge smoked fish washed down with copious amounts of vodka while Scarlett and I settled for an insipid soup. To take our minds off the food, Liz regaled us with her delight in the tsars, the virtues of communism and the failures of capitalism. As usual, she was untroubled by the apparent contradictions in her viewpoints.

'Well, as far as I'm concerned communism has something to answer for if, twenty years after its demise, Estonia still can't produce a decent meal for a tourist beside the sea,' I pronounced.

That evening we did have a decent French-inspired meal at Bonaparte's restaurant. Through the branches of leafy trees an early evening Chekhovian sunlight dappled the room through wide windows. We all relaxed; tucked into duck confit, and rhubarb stacked up like a woodpile.

While we were waiting for the second course, Scarlett asked me quite unexpectedly why I had divorced her grandfather. She was close to him; he was a regular visitor to her family's house and shared her musical interests. I found it difficult to answer her question. 'I suppose I wanted the freedom to lead a full life in every way, even if it proved to be painful at times. I didn't want any restrictions, even if the restrictions were partly the product of my imagination. I was very immature when I got married and started exploring life late in my twenties. I could see our marriage reaching a fork in the road.' I sensed that my answer wasn't adequate for Scarlett, but I wasn't prepared to go into it further. The complexities of relationships would be for her to find out for herself, later in life.

The next day we took the coach to St Petersburg. There was an interminable delay at the Russian border which Scarlett found impossible to understand. The coach would creep along a small piece of road for an hour and then we would all have to get out and wait for a further hour before walking through an office in single file to have our passports scrutinised closely by several bored officials. Nobody spoke and there appeared to be no obstruction in the road or obvious passport problem. All the oxygen seemed to have been sucked out of the bus and the three of us were becoming gloomier by the moment. We submitted to the pointless idiocy of this process by imagining that we were in a Russian spy thriller and had better toe the line or we might never see our families again.

Even Liz had been temporarily reduced to silence—then I realised that she was quaffing a bottle of Argentinean malbec which I had been given by the hotel in Tallinn as an apology for forgetting my wake-up call. She had roughly covered it with a paper bag and I prayed that the officials wouldn't spot her. I had visions of her being spirited away. Bored to the point of distraction, Liz decided to step up Scarlett's and my Russian education and started talking loudly about gulags within the horrified hearing of members of the queue. 'Shoosh, for heaven's sake,' I hissed, elbowing her in the ribs.

As soon as the bus started off again Liz's exuberance bubbled over once more. She loved being in Russia and stared out of the window, enchanted by the cosy wooden *dachas* she saw at the side of the road. I was less sanguine, having reached a high level of anxiety when I saw our driver apparently dozing off at the wheel, woken only when our coach crunched into the frequent pot holes.

I finally managed to doze off myself and dreamt that our driver had lost control of the bus and careered into a farmyard. Bursting through a barn and flattening a gaggle of geese and a pig, he ploughed on, reducing a tractor to pulp before coming to a halt at the edge of a dam, poised precariously, as if about to topple in. I saw Scarlett, thrown from the bus, lying unconscious on the grass as the wheels spun around. I screamed for Liz, but there was no reply. I woke abruptly from the nightmare and looked out of the window to find we were surrounded by grim high-rise flats. We were on the outskirts of St Petersburg.

'I'd commit suicide if I lived here. I've just had the most hideous dream and the sight of all these grey, cold buildings makes me think I'm still living in a nightmare.'

'You're going to give Scarlett a very dreary picture of Russia if you go on like that,' said Liz.

At last we arrived in the centre of the huge capital and eased ourselves off the coach into the bus station. I had totally forgotten that I had arranged for someone to meet us. Julia, a brisk, efficient young Russian woman, took us immediately to our hotel, which Liz was quick to tell us was miles from the centre but fortunately only yards from the upper end of Nevsky Prospekt, the central avenue of St Petersburg, built by Peter the Great.

We quickly stowed our luggage and set out to find some dinner. Everywhere there was bustle and activity. It was impossible to imagine that wolves had once roamed up and down Nevsky Prospekt and that the river had flooded so deeply in the 1700s that it was navigable. There were not many cars now, but the streets were jammed with crowded buses and people scurrying home.

The choice of nearby eateries was uninspiring and we were all tired, so we were forced to settle for a restaurant that served pizza and borscht. Scarlett and I ordered borscht.

'It isn't as good as your mum's, is it, Scar?'

'No way,' agreed Scarlett.

Though the borscht was edible, the chef had used beef stock, and Scarlett and I concluded that was probably the difference. Juliette's recipe gives the full flavour of the beetroot and tomato without the strong meaty taste.

* * * * *

Jules's Borscht

Serves 6

Ingredients

4 cups chicken stock (use stock cubes)

6 large beets, peeled, chopped

3 large potatoes, peeled, cut into cubes

4 cups vegetable stock (use stock cubes)

2 carrots, peeled, chopped

1 stick celery, chopped

½ cup chopped red capsicum

2 fresh tomatoes, finely chopped

1 tbsp extra-virgin olive oil

2 onions, peeled, quartered

2 cloves garlic, finely chopped

2 g caraway seeds (optional)

2 cups thinly sliced red cabbage

¾ cup chopped fresh dill

1 tin tomato pieces

salt and pepper, to taste

3 tbsp red wine vinegar

1 cup sour cream

fresh parsley, to serve

Preparation

1. Bring pot of chicken stock to the boil and add the beetroots and potatoes. Make sure the vegetables are covered.

2. Reduce heat and simmer 20 minutes, until the vegetables are tender.

3. Remove the beetroot and potatoes with a slotted spoon and reserve the stock.

4. Blend the beetroot and potatoes in half the stock. Reserve the remaining stock.

5. In another stockpot, bring 6 cups of chicken and vegetable stock to the boil in a large stockpot.

6. Add the carrots, celery, capsicum and fresh tomatoes and bring back to the boil. Reduce the heat and simmer about 15 minutes, until the vegetables are tender. Blend half the vegetables and add to the blended beetroot and potato. Reserve remaining vegetables.

7. Heat 1 tablespoon of oil in a skillet. Stir in the onion, garlic and caraway seeds and sauté until the onion becomes soft and translucent.

8. Stir in the red cabbage, ½ cup dill and the tomato pieces.

9. Cook about 15 minutes, until the cabbage is tender. Do not overcook.

10. Combine the contents of the skillet with the beetroot, potato and vegetables.

11. Season to taste with salt and pepper. Stir in the vinegar.

12. Ladle the soup into bowls. Top with sour cream, parsley and the remaining ¼ cup dill.

* * * * *

The service in the restaurant was slow and people smoked inside. I decided that bed was the best course of action: we all needed a good night's sleep. Hopefully St Petersburg would reveal its charm when we woke to a smiling new day.

And so it came to pass. After a leisurely breakfast we took a bus down Nevsky Prospekt and through rose-tinted spectacles saw our fellow Russian commuters in glowing friendly colours.

'The Prospekt is one of the great streets of the world,' Liz said, cheerfully pointing out the Literaturnaya Café at number 18. She consulted her guidebook and added, 'Alexander Pushkin, the poet, used to visit the confectionery company and Dostoyevsky and other literary giants drank coffee and ate blinis there while composing the plots of their masterpieces.'

'Personally, I prefer the Champs-Élysées,' I replied.

'Wait for it, on the right. Look!' shrilled Liz, as we came to the end of Nevsky Prospekt and lurched past Palace Square. And there it was—our first glimpse of the Winter Palace, dubbed by Liz 'the Christmas Cake'. The bus sped across Dvortsovy Bridge and we got off to gaze across at the Hermitage.

'It's *huge*, and I really like the green colour,' said Scarlett delightedly.

But then she and I spotted six Russian wedding parties having their formal photographic session with the iconic view of the Winter Palace behind them, and went over to have a look. The bridesmaids were primping and fussing with their bouquets and floral headdresses while the brides were far more interested in whether their dresses were being photographed from the best possible angle than they were in their grooms, who were longing to be photographed in a passionate clinch. 'You'll ruin my make-up,' I imagined I would hear the brides saying, had I a translator! After all, weddings have certain universal similarities. I snapped away happily and had to be dragged off by Liz, who was intent upon getting us to the Peter and Paul Fortress.

When we got there, I suggested to Liz that she and Scarlett forge ahead while I sat in the sun on the sand looking at the dreamy Neva River. A missionary from the Jehovah's Witnesses plonked herself down next to me, ruining my quiet time. There was only one thing to do, other than be rude, and that was to leave quietly before she got further into her narrative. I made my excuses and found Liz and Scarlett outside the church where the tsars are buried. They'd been inside and seen the many huge, plain tombs.

We decided to take a boat trip around the canals. There was a queue so I sat on the only chair in the shade, close to the ticket office. A man approached me. He had a thick neck, low, broad forehead and an aggressive expression.

'What you doing?' he said.

'I'm sitting down,' I said, rather obviously. (What did he think I was doing?)

'This not for you. You cannot stay here.' He was shouting now.

'I have bad legs and have to sit down. There is nowhere to sit and your boat does not come.'

At this point, not used to explaining himself to women, he growled in fury, 'Get out now.' His voice was ugly.

We were all shaken, but moved rapidly, fearing a public fracas if we continued arguing. I was not warming to Russian officialdom.

The boat ride around the canals showed us the elegance of St Petersburg. Liz was calling out all the sights as she chatted and laughed with the other tourists on the boat. What they made of her, goodness knows—they were largely Russian and didn't understand a word she said. The boat's commentary was in Russian too; we foreigners were unimportant.

Irina, whom the travel company had hired to take us around the Hermitage the next day, was charming and thoroughly professional, fluent in English and with a detailed knowledge of art and architectural history. She had fully embraced capitalism and everything it had to offer. I enjoyed her friendly manner and

Scarlett admired her chic clothes, but I could see that Liz was not happy that capitalism was well on the way to winning the soul of this young person. The Hermitage was vast and stunningly decorated. Scarlett and I were blown away by the size of the palace, the number of rooms, the endless ornate arched corridors, the never-ending art objects—and the hundreds of French impressionists. The effect of the French collection alone was mind-boggling.

'Why would one family need to have so much?' Scarlett said.

'They were bent on competing for the title of "boss",' said Liz. Irina smiled with just a hint of condescension.

In the afternoon we were on our own, jostling with thousands of others to get to Peterhof Palace on the hydrofoil, which plied its way from a pier opposite the Hermitage across the Neva and up the Baltic. Nobody spoke English on the pier or in the ticket office and there wasn't a whiff of capitalism about the rude and abrasive staff. Eventually, somehow, we got the 'good oil' about which queue, which ticket and what time to get on.

Arriving at Peterhof wharf we paused in amazement. At the end of a long formal path the elegant, airy palace dominated, with its golden orbs and cascades of fountains arching towards the sky. It looked like a fairytale and made me dizzy with delight. We approached the palace, where *le tout* St Petersburg were perambulating on this sunny Sunday afternoon. There were young lovers and families with whingeing small children, sleeping babies, bored teenagers and grannies in wheelchairs. Exhausted mums and dads pushed their prams through the wooded gardens on paths bordered by ornamental bushes while the kids fed the red squirrels bread as they both bounded about fearlessly. I sat happily watching the passing parade while Liz and Scar went exploring. At one point I felt a tug at my jacket and looked around to see a red squirrel had jumped into my lap. I felt this was a lucky sign, but the squirrel thought better of his daring and scampered off.

When the others returned we moved towards the lakes beneath the fountains to listen to the music. An orchestra played a feast of mostly Russian music from the Romantic period, Tchaikovsky's *Nutcracker*, works by Rimsky-Korsakov, Mussorgsky, Borodin and Johann Strauss's 'Blue Danube' added in to keep the mood super-light. The ornamental fountains were synchronised with the music and then at 4 pm the fireworks erupted too. Bursts of pink and gold stars rose skywards as the fountains shot higher and higher and the music came to a crescendo followed by a further flurry of golden, green and blue sparklers bursting into the bright blue sky. It was the most intoxicating public event I had enjoyed for many years. It was quite possible to imagine Tsar Peter presiding over proceedings from his palace balcony.

The hydrofoils stopped operating at four o'clock so we joined the crowds of people walking away from the palace towards the car park and hoped to locate public transport. Eventually we came across a bustle of buses and tried asking people how to get back to the city. But nobody spoke English and they looked at us very strangely as we gabbled away. So we went with the flow and got on one of the many buses. We were dropped at a huge overblown station, a giant brick folly presumably specially built for the tsar's party when they took themselves to his palace. The trains back to St Petersburg were bursting with crowds of people returning from their Sunday excursions. We were the only tourists and the passengers stared at us, and especially at Scarlett. One of them asked how old she was—at least that's what we assumed he said. Scarlett felt uncomfortable at the attention she was getting. I was particularly struck by how tired and worn most people looked;

I felt that life must be a daily struggle and it seemed that Sunday provided no respite.

Our hotel might not have been centre stage for the main sights of St Petersburg but it was near a market where we bought wild strawberries, which we ate in a little square near the house where Dostoyevsky lived. His apartment was very comfortable and inviting—quite unlike his tortured novels. Nearby was Rimsky-Korsakov's flat, which was large, and more formal, with a beautiful grand piano in the corner of the music room and a picture of a growling tabby cat arched ready to pounce which I thought would not be a calm and tranquil presence in one's home. While walking between the two flats we found a basement shop selling CDs and books. The shop was piled high with 'alternative' books, magazines and tapes. We talked to the two young guys working there, one of whom could speak a few words of English and who was the first friendly Russian we had met. They seemed to be the Russian equivalent of greenies. They were so delighted when we bought something that they threw in an ethnic Russian disc with the CDs we had chosen.

I had seen on a poster that Diana Vishneva, a prima ballerina with the Mariinsky Ballet Company at the Mariinsky Theatre, was giving a one-off solo performance while we were in St Petersburg and decided that it would make the perfect highlight to our stay. I knew it would be hard to get tickets, so invoked Irina's aid and asked her if she would like to come with us. She came up trumps with excellent seats in the stalls. Scarlett used the occasion to dress up and appeared wearing a long, slim, powder-blue dress with a silver bolero over it, silver shoes and delicate drop earrings. She looked like a prima ballerina in the making. The program was a series of modern one-act ballets created to show Vishneva's gifts.

She was astonishing: liquid, luminous and emotionally intense, and technically of an extraordinarily high standard.

In the interval, drinks from a tiny kiosk took ages to be served. I said, 'This is taking a long time.' Whereat the man in front turned round and spat out in broken English, 'We will take OUR time.'

Scarlett and I were horrified yet again at Russian rudeness. Liz laughed. 'You two never learn. Listen, these guys have had seventy years of communism, when they rarely saw a blue jean, a hamburger, or ate a decent meal, and now they've had twenty years of pretend capitalism. It's going to take decades for them to learn polite bourgeois consumer behaviour—and quite frankly, I'd prefer that they didn't bother. *Vive la différence.*'

Luckily the interval bell went and we returned to our seats, drinkless and with a Liz rant echoing in our ears. Scarlett squeezed my hand as we sat down. 'I wouldn't have missed the palaces and buildings and this ballet despite all the rudeness,' she said.

'Nor me,' I replied. 'Russia's been quite a revelation.'

*

We took the best part of the next day travelling on three flights to get to Venice. I was absolutely determined that we would end Scarlett's trip on a high note with a long weekend there—time to get a sense of the place, and Liz would be happy because the Venice Biennale was on.

Scarlett was in danger of being blown away as she stood at the bow of the water taxi gazing in disbelief across the lagoon at the distant roofs and church spires of Venice. We had left the airport and stepped straight into a snazzy water taxi which whisked us across the bay and up a narrow canal to our hotel in the Cannaregio.

'Oh my god, Ga, this is the most beautiful place I have ever seen in the whole of my life.'

Liz and I had been to the hotel before and I'd specially chosen it again with Scarlett in mind—she and I had a room overlooking a canal so that we were lulled to sleep with the gentle lapping of water and woken with the shouts and noises of boats delivering food and goods. Scarlett was enchanted and hung out of the window gazing at the *gondolieri* manoeuvring their boats below, and peering at what was going on in the houses opposite. So close were they that if she had known Italian she would have heard and understood every word they spoke.

Liz and I were so happy to be in Venice again. We knew our way around and bickered about who knew the best route to the Rialto for the great Grand Canal view (Liz did) and then went on to St Mark's Square, where we bickered again over whether to sit in Quadri's or Florian's. In the end we had a Bellini in both. Scar and I were in heaven drinking in 'the finest drawing room in Europe', as Napoleon dubbed St Mark's Square, while the basilica itself watched over us, gold and oriental in the fading light.

Liz pointed out that this was capitalism at its worst: overpriced drinks with leering waiters, no local people, just tourists looking vacantly around at the somewhat down-at-heel archetypical view. 'Lay off,' I said, drawing her to one side. 'Remember how you felt the first time you saw the Grand Canal and St Mark's Square? Venice may have gone down the gurgler in your estimation but there's still nothing to beat it for beauty and romance, particularly if you're wide-eyed, innocent and about to turn fifteen.'

'Fair enough,' Liz grudgingly agreed.

We decided to keep up the fairytale and leapt onto a *vaporetto* which chugged up the Grand Canal as the sun set. 'I can't believe how beautiful it is—whichever way you turn, it's perfect,' sighed Scarlett, her whole face alight and joyful.

The next day I decided Scar and I needed a restful, relaxed day, with a picnic on Torcello and possibly a little retail therapy, while Liz was keen to plunge into the Biennale.

We got up early and went to the market, where we bought cheese, salami, rolls and water in a small deli, and fruit and tomatoes from a stall. We caught a vaporetto first to Murano, where Scarlett watched a glass-blower show off his expertise by putting the finishing touches to the most elaborate multicoloured chandelier she had ever seen. Then there was the inevitable search for the perfect memento. Scarlett quickly selected the finest pieces on display, only asking to see the things she was really interested in, but still glancing around to make sure she hadn't missed anything. She finally found the perfect glass pendant and says that she has the greatest pleasure now when her friends ask her, 'Where did you get that cool pendant?' in replying airily, 'Oh . . . Venice.' 'I just feel so spoilt,' she says.

We roamed around Murano, a small sibling of Venice. By midday the sun was blazing so we sat on the edge of the wharf dipping our feet in the cool water, taking in the view and watching the vaporettos come and go.

Torcello was next. We took a vaporetto for a short distance and then walked down a long, winding path to the small cathedral surrounded by a field of poplars. There we settled down to our picnic. As we munched happily Scarlett and I were aware that it was a precious time for us, both a summer holiday and a special moment of intimacy. We went into the cathedral later and marvelled at the mosaics, and I reminded Scar to light a candle so that she would be sure to come back. We ambled back to the wharf and returned to Venice, tired, sunburnt, but very relaxed, our heads and hearts swimming with delicious sensations and fond memories.

Scarlett's newly developed visual acumen and judgement stood her in good stead when we got to the Biennale and to François Pinault's brilliant new contemporary art centre at the Punta della Dogana, which he had converted from the old customs house at the mouth of the Grand Canal. Scarlett, I observed, looked carefully at most things but concentrated on the pieces that really intrigued her. She enjoyed discussing what she liked and questioned us about the ones we disliked.

The next day a visit to the Rialto market reminded us of the pathetic one in Riga.

'Remember to say *meraviglioso*, which means "marvellous", if you see something you really like,' I suggested to Scarlett. 'It never hurts. Everyone likes praise.'

The stalls in Venice were laden with glowing vegetables, fruit, meat and fish. '*Meraviglioso!*' beamed Scarlett, pointing at a bank of luscious peaches. An old *nonna* beamed back at her and gave her a peach. '*Grazie*,' said Scarlett, touched by the gesture. The *nonna* tried to chat with her, but Scarlett threw her hands up in the air in frustration, unable to continue.

'Next time I come, I'll have learnt to speak Italian,' she vowed.

On this, our last evening in Venice, we returned to the Rialto, this time to a warehouse which had been cunningly refurbished and turned into a bar overlooking the Grand Canal. The three of us ate squid and a strange fish dredged from the lagoon, followed by dessert. As Scarlett licked the spoon from her lemon cassata she said, 'This has been an amazing month for me; quite different from how I imagined it would be before we left.'

Liz and I held our collective breath.

'I imagined a holiday with you two would be different...' Scarlett paused. 'Exciting, sometimes confronting ... I didn't really know what to expect.' She smiled, but seemed unclear as to how to continue.

'And so . . .' said Liz, egging her on. I leant forward. Scarlett began to look uncomfortable.

'I think I've been a bit overwhelmed at times,' she said and stopped short. 'It's all been so unreal compared with back home . . . I didn't realise there was so much else in the world.' She looked close to tears.

'Time for a gondola,' I said, breaking the mood. We left the table hand in hand and made for the Canal. It took no time to hail a gondola—there were so many waiting for a fare.

'It's been great for me too, Scarlett,' I murmured as the gondolier helped us into the boat, 'seeing you embrace so much, so quickly.' She gave me one of her special smiles as we collapsed onto the cushions.

As the water lapped gently against the ancient stone walls and the gondolier propelled us through the tranquil back 'streets' of his city, Scarlett told us that she felt part of Venice now; it didn't seem like one big tourist playground at all. She later wrote in her journal:

> *I loved every minute of it and know that I will return, someday, somehow. I picture two lovers strolling along a canal late at night, the moon above, the warm air embracing them and Venice, their protector. One of those lovers will be me, in a flowing summer dress, with a red flower in my hair, and Venice will become part of what shapes our love.*

> *It is such a strange concept for a granddaughter, to think that my grandma has lived a whole life up until now, and was a child like me once. It takes*

a long time to get to really know that person, as they are made up of their past, some of which I have played no part in. It makes me wonder what I will be like when I am in my seventies?

What I do know is that this trip will be an ongoing adventure, something that I will take my grandchildren on, and so on . . . all in memory of Ga.

The next morning we left for London at 5 am so that Scarlett could catch the plane back to Sydney that same evening. She travelled light and only had to throw her dirty clothes into the bag. I thought it was much more important to make our Italian idyll last as long as possible.

I bid a fond but sad farewell to Scar and asked the flight attendant to make sure she looked after her well—anxious granny as usual, even though I knew Scarlett was more than capable of looking after herself. After all, the tables had already turned and she had spent a lot of the holiday looking after me!

*

A few days after Scarlett had gone, Liz and I went to Ireland. We went by train, a five-hour journey across England and Wales before a three-hour ferry ride. Plenty of time for chats about the Scarlett holiday. And much to my surprise Liz cracked open her emotional carapace.

'It was great fun showing Scarlett around. She's terrific. I liked the way she listened so carefully to all that ranting I go in for—and took it all with a pinch of salt.' Liz beamed.

'I'm so pleased you came. I could never have done it without you.'

'Now then, Hilly, none of that soppy stuff.'

*

The chapel was crammed with proud parents and family members. Duncan and I had gathered to listen to a piano concert put on by Scarlett's piano teacher, showing off the talents of her pupils. As we listened to Scarlett, composed and confident, playing her own composition, 'My Private World', we were moved to tears by the beauty of her music. I wondered: was it the cascading fountains of Peterhof washing over us or pink fireworks bursting into the blue summer sky? Was it the twinkling lights shimmering on inky black water as our gondola glided down the Venetian canals? Was it the fluidity of Diana Vishneva dancing in the Mariinsky Theatre in St Petersburg? Or was it the scent of red roses in Peter the Great's Kadriorg gardens in Tallinn? Had all these recent experiences filled Scarlett's heart to bursting point and inspired her composition? I hoped so.

Epilogue

Fifteen years on—what next?

'Do you remember that night in Turkey when you jumped, blind drunk, into the wine cupboard and I locked you in?' I giggled.

'. . . and when Joachim finally opened it, I fell into his arms and fainted,' Liz laughed uproariously.

Liz and I were going to the ballet, and then to an exhibition, then a concert, but first we were having a picnic brunch in the Botanical Gardens with Miranda, celebrating our fifteen years of travel—the same Miranda who had reintroduced us all those years ago. The reminiscences came tumbling out.

'Do you remember peeing on the chair in Fez?'

'Certainly do—it was mortifying!'

'And what about your gorgeous gaucho in Patagonia?'

'And your Himba incident in Namibia,' I added. We were off. Unstoppable. Poor Miranda—it must have been worse than looking at other people's holiday snaps. She tried to break into the babble.

'What I want to know is, how did you get on? Have you changed over the years?'

We paused for a minute.

'A lot has happened to us over all that time,' I said. 'I think we've changed as individuals. Not earth-shattering changes, but travelling together, often in close proximity, has produced some change—hopefully for the better!'

'The experience has been Huge,' said Liz, 'some would say disgraceful in its scope and intensity. We did exactly as we wanted to do within the limits of our imagination and, best of all, we had tremendous fun. We met scores and scores of people, which Hilly loved, and even though I'd never thought people were my bag I quickly began to enjoy them too.'

'Liz wrote sixty articles for the *Karachi Evening Star* before it ceased publication and I took at least 15,000 photos,' I said.

'Can you trace any of them in that computer jungle you've created?' Liz was needling me now.

Miranda refocused us. 'It's all very well going off, as you do, spending vast amounts of money. Anybody would enjoy themselves in those circumstances.'

'That's true,' I said. 'We're very lucky to be able to have "High End" holidays, as Lizzie calls them. But I think there's a lot more to it than that. We've taken risks, plunged in rather than held back.'

'And dare I say,' piped up Liz, 'I enjoy my Low End holliers staying in hostels and travelling by bus and train just as much as my travels with Hilly.'

I refused to allow Liz to make a virtue of discomfort. Her stories of rooms full of bunk beds and strangers, showers shared with sixteen others and sorting your own food in primitive communal kitchens didn't thrill me. I was glad that my thirty years of extremely hard work had given me the luxury of nicely plumped pillows, room service and good food after a strenuous day of sightseeing.

We got up to go.

'One last question before you leave,' said Miranda, who always loved a serious philosophical discussion. 'You've travelled enough in this life—what will you do for an encore? If there is a next life—if you believe in reincarnation—how will you come back?'

'Well,' said Liz, unwilling to be drawn into a serious debate, 'I want to come back as a member of the corps de ballet in a communist country ballet company. It would suit my civil service background. I need to be part of a finely tuned, cohesive group.'

'My reincarnation fantasies change weekly,' I said. 'I'd like to return as a director—it would suit my bossy nature—making films and theatre—comedy to cheer people up and drama and documentary to challenge and, with luck, change the audience's thinking, hopefully for the good. That's the serious week. Then, another week, I'll be a genius painter making pots of money. And another month I'll be the wife of a ruggedly handsome farmer, an earth mother with a vast brood of children—and a nanny, of course! I'll bottle gooseberries, gather duck eggs and cure my own beef grown on our large estate and sell my own organic produce. But my latest fantasy is that I'll return as a courtesan of massive intellect and sexual athleticism!' We all laughed.

I looked at my watch. 'We'd better move if we're going to the ballet.' We gave Miranda a farewell hug, and set off through the gardens.

It was Sydney Festival time, and a beautiful day, so we walked down to the Opera House, the water gently lapping beside us.

'Stunning,' said Liz, waving her arms around, startling some passers-by as she embarked on an incoherent rant about diamond-flashing harbour waters. As usual, she was walking too fast and talking too much.

'Slow down, Lizzie, for goodness sake,' I said. 'There's no need to rush. Let's grab a coffee before we go in.'

'Honestly, Hilly,' said Liz, as we waited in the foyer, 'you've been a saint putting up with me all these years. How did you manage it?'

'Well, funnily enough, when we started travelling I thought I would be able to change the worst of your idiosyncrasies. But little by little I came to the conclusion that you had as much right to your weirdnesses as I had to mine! There's no point trying to change people—apart from anything else, it doesn't work! Look at you in Latvia, when I thought you might drown. There was no point in giving you a row afterwards.'

'So what are you doing instead?' asked Liz.

'I try not to dwell on the negatives and I laugh a lot. And I suppose I've also learnt to live in the moment—just as well, given my rapidly departing memory!'

'I've certainly been lucky to have a well-developed imagination,' said Liz. 'I suppose living such a restricted life in government offices and without proper domestic responsibilities meant that I had to rely on conjuring up fantasies and fun as a substitute for living.'

'But, Lizzie, answer this question. Do you think you've changed in the fifteen years we've been travelling together?'

'Honestly, Hil, what an impossible question. If you'd asked me that when we were with Miranda I would have said I hadn't changed a jot. But now perhaps I might just admit that our travels and your influence have made me less wayward, more cautious, especially when I meet new people. But there again, people have become less tolerant of odd behaviour over the last decade or so. I may be responding to that.'

'I think you are far less judgemental, much less likely to dismiss people on first encounter. It's a relief,' I said.

'You surely remember you once described our travels as therapy on the move.'

'Yes, your therapy.'

Liz went on, 'But I really enjoy the way you want more, more and more all the time—more experiences, more fun, more food. You keep on trucking even when you're aching from neck to toe, your ankles are the size of melons and your jet lag's gone on for a week. I've learnt from you how to demand a little more from life than I did before. I'd like to think that I don't give in as easily as I used to. And I love that determination you have, especially when circumstances are at their worst. Remember the stolen wallet in Venice and your handbag in Lima?'

The stage manager announced over the tannoy that the show was about to begin so we hurried in.

*

'Great choreography, plenty of soul and the virtue of being short and sweet,' I said as we emerged afterwards.

'Good festival fodder,' added Liz. 'I especially liked the way the rhythm and pace changed so cleverly throughout the ballet. Not unlike our travels,' she said thoughtfully. 'We do all that darting around, covering a lot of ground and garnering great experiences, but we enjoy ourselves most, and get the most out of it, when we add a bit of pace and rhythm.'

We settled down for a drink by the side of the Opera House. *Le tout* Sydney was out and about. We sat companionably silent, staring at the activity on the harbour—tiny sailing boats scudding about, ferries busying their way to Manly, water police standing erect in their motor launches looking self-important as they accelerated past boat traffic at full speed, and a huge cruise ship tied up at the overseas terminal, disgorging ancient Americans on their world tours.

'Isn't this view extraordinary—I don't think Sydneysiders appreciate how lucky we are to have this magnificent harbour—free—on our doorstep.'

'Sydney at its hedonistic best.'

'Do you think we've reached another hinge moment in our travels?' I asked Liz.

'Funnily enough, yes,' she answered, 'on two counts.'

I already knew what the first would be. 'I know you feel strongly about the environment—we'll have to stop scooting around, treating planes like skateboards and leaving our carbon footprints on the fragile planet. What's the second?'

'Well, at the end of the Scarlett trip I felt strongly that it was even more fun doing something for somebody else than simply enjoying oneself.'

'That's so true,' I said. 'But I've got a third reason why it's a hinge moment in my travelling life: I'm going to have to get fit if I'm to continue travelling into my eighties!'

'Gosh, Hilly, what on earth are you advocating? Don't tell me—a period of Abstinence and Responsible Travel.'

'Well, perhaps not just yet.' I hesitated, but not for long. 'I'm raring to go, but maybe at a more leisurely pace. I know you like to return to familiar places but there's still a lot of world we should see. I want to take a mail boat through the Scandinavian fjords; see Lapland's northern lights and then spend Christmas in a little snow-covered Swiss village in the mountains; then there's the blossoms in springtime Japan; I want to cheer the encores of all New York's latest musicals and I'm also determined to track down the best of Cuban music in the cafés and bars of Havana. And what about the orangutans in Borneo? Do you fancy treating them to an afternoon banana and tea?

'By the time we've seen that lot, I might have the courage to try India and China again with you this time. My introduction to those countries wasn't good. I have vivid memories of drinking Indian beer in Delhi in temperatures of 50 degrees and getting a screaming migraine; then in a field in the Chinese countryside I was violently ill in the scrub, while the rest of my party were being shown over a model village. They had to find the nearest town and leave me behind in a darkened room. When I recovered sufficiently, I rejoined the party and plunged into teeming markets, coming face to face with a dog, cowed and frightened, sitting in a cage and, hung up beside him, the carcass of another dog—probably his mother. I felt sick, and became acutely aware of the hordes of people trying to survive and overwhelmed when I thought about the population numbers in both countries.'

'Hold on, Hilly—even your gargantuan appetite is in overdrive. Back to the present. We need to find your car in that nightmare Opera House car park.'

We jostled our way past the bars, past young girls perched on bar stools with miniskirts up to their navels, drinks poised, lots of cleavage, on the razzle, eyes scanning the scene, like the gulls below fearlessly picking their way round the tables, snapping up the crumbs from the left-over crisp packets. The search for the pick-up was on. And the boys were up for it, hugging the perimeter and earmarking the cream of the crop before moving in for the conquest.

Liz and I moved on and made our way to the lifts, descending to the car in the airless underground parking bay.

'Did you know that it costs almost as much to park as it does to buy a ticket for a show?' I told Liz.

'If we're going to go to that National Trust exhibition, we'll need to conserve our energies; we've got a spare hour, but remember we've still got the open-air concert this evening in the Domain,' said Liz firmly.

I normally drive straight to the entrance to the National Trust Centre near the Harbour Bridge by turning left illegally and continuing through a gate, which is usually open. This way I avoid being swept onto six lanes of Harbour Bridge traffic. But when we arrived this time, it had all changed. The gate had been replaced by two metal posts and a shiny, well-oiled metal beam which slid across the opening.

'Shit! I'll have to drive over the bridge and double back. Maddening.'

But, no, I hadn't bargained for Ms Fixit. Liz bounced out of the car, crawled under the bar and pressed a green button she had spied on a box on the other side of the metal beam.

'Security,' said a hollow voice from the box.

'Could you raise the beam, please?' requested Liz in muted English public school tone.

'Who are you?' enquired the Box.

'Clover Moore, the Mayor.'

Without a pause the beam slid sideways, allowing us to speed through. We burst into peals of laughter.

'What a triumph,' I hooted.

'It's a sort of metaphor for life and, indeed, our travels together,' said Liz, as we sauntered into the exhibition.

'Find a button to press, use your imagination and, hey presto! The impossible happens.'

THE END

Acknowledgements

Our thanks go to:

Jane Palfreyman and Elizabeth Cowell from Allen & Unwin, and to Tricia Dearborn, for all their help and support during the writing of this book.

To Scarlett Stemler for her contribution to the book.

To Claire Scobie for her mentoring and to Pam Brewster and Jan Cornall for their support and feedback.

To Sandra Levy, Miranda Worsley, Jodi Shields, Patrick Barlow, Jean Mostyn, Candy Baker, Rob Drewe, Trish Booth, Kate Richter, Wendy Harmer, Helen Scott, Iain Maitland, Robyn Love, Ron Cobb, Judy Gregan, John Gregan, Elisabeth Wynhausen, Louis Klaassen, Jenny Coopes, Mark Lucas, Louis Nowra, Mandy Sayer, Susie Carleton and Aviva Ziegler for their encouragement.

To Ed, a huge thank you for being such a support throughout the writing of this book, and in life.

*

Hilary: To my family, Duncan, Juliette, Scarlett, Paris and Django, for living with this book for four years and supporting me.

Liz: A big thank you to Asif Noorani, editor of the *Karachi Evening Star*, for starting me on a travel writing career late in life.

〳

Ingram Content Group Australia Pty Ltd
Printed in Australia
AUHW021334120423
376882AU00001B/135

9 781743 314692